The Fundamentals of Municipal Bonds

The Fundamentals of Municipal Bonds

Securities Industry and
Financial Markets Association

Sixth Edition

Written by

NEIL O'HARA

WILEY

John Wiley & Sons, Inc.

Published by John Wiley & Sons, Inc., Hoboken, New Jersey.
Published simultaneously in Canada.

For general information on our other products and services or for technical support, please contact our Customer Care Department within the United States at (800) 762-2974, outside the United States at (317) 572-3993 or fax (317) 572-4002.

Wiley also publishes its books in a variety of electronic formats. Some content that appears in print may not be available in electronic books. For more information about Wiley products, visit our web site at www.wiley.com.

Library of Congress Cataloging-in-Publication Data:

O'Hara, Neil.
   The fundamentals of municipal bonds / SIFMA; written by Neil O'Hara. –
6th ed.
      p. cm.—(Wiley finance series)
   Includes bibliographical references and index.
   Previous ed. entered under: Wesalo Temel, Judy.
   ISBN 978-0-470-90338-4 (cloth); ISBN 978-1-118-16682-6 (ebk);
   ISBN 978-1-118-16683-3 (ebk); ISBN 978-1-118-16684-0 (ebk)
   1. Municipal bonds–United States.   I. Wesalo Temel, Judy. Fundamentals of municipal bonds.   II. Securities Industry and Financial Markets Association.   III. Title.
   HG4952.F86 2012
   332.63'2330973—dc23   2011029935

Printed in the United States of America.

10 9 8 7 6 5 4 3 2 1

Contents

Preface   ix

Writer's Acknowledgments   xi

CHAPTER 1
Overview of the Municipal Bond Market   1
   Introduction   1
   The Issuers   4
   Municipal Bond Dealers   7
   The Lawyers   10
   Financial Advisors, Specialists, and Other Consultants   11
   The Rating Agencies   12
   Bond Brokers   13
   The Credit Enhancers   13
   The Trustees and Paying Agents   17
   The Investors   17
   Information and Technology   18
   The Regulators   19
   Other Participants   21

CHAPTER 2
The Basics of Municipal Securities   23
   Description of Municipal Securities   23
   Yield and Price   26
   Types of Yields   28
   Tax Exemption of Municipal Bonds   29
   Types of Municipal Bonds   35
   Short-Term Securities   36
   Other Characteristics of Municipal Bonds   45

CHAPTER 3
The Issuers   **55**
Introduction   55
Authorities and Special Districts   56
The Theory of Municipal Debt: Pay-As-You-Use versus
  Pay-As-You-Go   57
The Uses of Municipal Debt   59
The Security for Municipal Bonds   61
The Financing Process   68
The Financing Documents   71
Structuring the Debt   81
State and Local Government Accounting   87

CHAPTER 4
The Primary Market   **93**
Issuance Trends in the Primary Market   93
The Basics of Underwriting   96
Negotiated Underwriting   101
Competitive Underwriting   105
Orders and Procedures   111

CHAPTER 5
The Secondary Market   **117**
Introduction   117
The Over-the-Counter Market   117
E-Commerce, Information, and Technology   119
Selling Municipal Bonds   121
The Basics of Municipal Bond Trading   123
Municipal Bond Trading   124
How a Trade Is Done   128
Municipal Futures   130
Providers of Data in the Municipal Market   131
Market Statistics and Indexes   132
MSRB Record-Keeping Rules   136

CHAPTER 6
Investing in Bonds   **139**
Introduction   139
The Basic Principles of Investing in Bonds   139
Measures of Yield and Return   143
Yield to Maturity and Price   145

Investment Objectives   147
Risk Factors   148
Investor Strategies   150
Taxation of Municipal Bonds   152
Other Investment Factors   161
Investor Categories   163

CHAPTER 7
Credit Analysis   **173**
Introduction   173
The Rating Agencies   175
The Rating Process   176
General Obligation Bonds   179
Revenue Bonds   197
Other Factors Affecting Credit   207

CHAPTER 8
Understanding Interest Rates   **211**
Introduction   211
Determinants of the Overall Level of Interest Rates   212
Term Structure of Interest Rates   216
Municipal Bond Rates   221

CHAPTER 9
Regulatory and Disclosure Requirements   **225**
Introduction   225
The Basis of Federal Tax Exemption   226
History of Federal Tax Legislation Affecting
    Municipal Securities   228
The Current Statutory Exemption   230
Application of Federal Securities Laws to
    Municipal Securities   233
The Municipal Securities Rulemaking Board   239

CHAPTER 10
Financial Products   **247**
Introduction   247
Interest Rate Swaps   247
Interest Rate Caps, Floors, and Collars   252
Other Swap Products   253
Managing the Asset Side   253
Credit Default Swaps   254

APPENDIX
  Municipal Securities Rulemaking Board Rule G-33   **257**

Glossary   **265**

Bibliography   **283**
  Web Sites   283
  Books and Publications   284

About the Writer   **285**

Index   **287**

G. K. Chesterton, reflecting on his tour of the United States in 1921 in his book *What I Saw in America*, wrote "The only purely popular government is local, and founded on local knowledge. The citizens can rule the city because they know the city." The British writer, philosopher and poet recognized that under the American federal system of government, states and localities are responsible for providing numerous public services. Political decision-making—weighing competing priorities and determining how to allocate public resources—takes place to a great extent at the state and local level.

Policy and public service objectives often involve capital investment in hard assets. Roads, transit systems, schools, water and sewer systems, police and fire stations, parks and numerous other projects are vital components of transportation, education, public safety, and environmental policy. Because these projects often have useful lives measured in decades, it would be unfair and impractical to expect current citizens to bear the entire cost of these often very expensive investments. Instead, most states and communities choose to borrow to finance public capital investment and to retire that borrowing over time. This is the nexus of the municipal bond market.

The U.S. municipal bond market is large and complex with $2.9 trillion outstanding by official estimates. It is also the most diverse and eclectic sector of the U.S. capital markets. The more than 50,000 issuers range from large states that sometimes borrow $1 billion or more at a time to small, rural communities that may borrow less than $1 million every few years. Credits range from full-faith-and-credit pledges backed by governments' full taxing powers to private corporations whose borrowing is backed solely by commercial revenues. The market is unique in that the interest on the vast majority of borrowing is free from federal and often state and local income tax. While this provides for attractive after-tax returns for investors, the tax-exempt nature of the market causes some of the biggest and most active institutional investors like pension funds to stay away from.

Since The Bond Market Association, one of SIFMA's predecessor organizations, published the last edition of *The Fundamentals of Municipal Bonds* in 2001, the world and the municipal bond market have changed dramatically. The last ten years have witnessed the growth of municipal derivatives and long-term, variable-rate financing, the entrance of new market participants such as hedge funds, and the painful uncertainties of the financial crisis of 2008. At its core, however, the municipal market serves the same purpose it has since before the founding of the republic, bringing together borrowers and investors to provide financing for public investment essential to the nation's economic success. Today, the market is bigger, more transparent, more diverse, and more sophisticated than ever.

The Fundamentals of Municipal Bonds has long been regarded as an important primary source for those beginning to explore the municipal market. The origins of Fundamentals date back to the 1960s, when early editions were published by the Investment Bankers Association of America. This sixth edition thoroughly covers both recent developments and trends as well as the enduring foundations of the market. The book outlines the key participants and describes the factors which make financing and trading possible.

SIFMA is deeply grateful to the author, Neil O'Hara, for his work on the book and for the expertise and knowledge he brought to the task. We also thank the SIFMA members and other market participants who made vital contributions to the content of the book by answering questions, providing feedback and perspective, and reviewing the manuscript. Without the cooperation and enthusiasm of SIFMA's members and other contributors, this book would not have been possible.

The majority of the nation's roads, schools, and other public infrastructure we all use every day was financed using municipal bonds. The energy and competitive spirit among SIFMA's members fuel the innovation that drives the market and help make it possible for states and localities to finance their investments as efficiently as possible.

Writer's Acknowledgments

I would like to thank the Securities Industry and Financial Markets Association for asking me to write *The Fundamentals of Municipal Bonds*, now in its sixth edition. It is a singular honor to update a book that has already introduced so many industry professionals, government officials, students, and other interested parties to the municipal bond business.

In the 10 years since the previous edition was published, the Internet and electronic commerce have revolutionized the financial services industry. I have revised the text and added new passages where necessary to describe how the municipal bond market functions today. In addition, any book about a dynamic business that has been through multiple editions under different authorship tends to accumulate inaccuracies in passages that were correct when first written but no longer reflect current practice. To the best of my ability, I have tried to weed out these flaws, too.

None of this would have been possible without assistance from the numerous industry professionals who so generously shared their invaluable expertise. In particular, I would like to thank Alan Anders, David Brownstein, George Friedlander, Kenneth Gibbs, Robert Mackintosh, Hugh McGuirk, John Miller, Hector Negroni, Tony Pusateri, Mitch Rapaport, Walter St. Onge, Kevin Schwartz, and James Wangsness whose detailed explanations of market practices pervade the entire book. I must also thank Leon Bijou, who not only steered this project through its early stages but also provided feedback on two chapters, and Richard Shapiro, who brought his encyclopedic knowledge of tax law to bear in helping me revise certain passages. I am equally grateful to those who, at SIFMA's behest, reviewed other parts of the book, including Joseph Geraci, Andrew Goodwin, Michael Marz, Paige Pierce, Mark Ryan, Doug Vissicchio, and Dan Wisniewski.

At SIFMA, I would like to thank Sharon Sung for her patience in responding to my repeated requests for help in gathering information for the numerous data tables and figures that appear throughout the book. Michael Decker, Leslie Norwood, Randy Snook, and David Cohen also provided support, including introductions to many of the industry professionals named above, as well as an extensive review of the manuscript.

Finally, I want to thank my wife, Katherine, who allowed me to regale her with tales of the municipal bond book project for so many months without complaint. Her grace and tolerance for my foibles make her the lynchpin of my life, and it is to her I dedicate this book.

N.O.

The Fundamentals of Municipal Bonds

CHAPTER 1

Overview of the Municipal Bond Market

INTRODUCTION

Municipal bonds, or municipal securities, represent a promise by state or local governmental units (called the *issuers*) or other qualified issuers to repay to lenders (*investors*) an amount of money borrowed, called *principal*, along with *interest* according to a fixed schedule. Municipal bonds generally are repaid, or *mature*, anywhere from 1 to 40 years from the date they are issued. At the end of 2010, there were $2.9 trillion in municipal bonds outstanding, representing the cumulative issuance of bonds over many years. These bonds have been used to finance a vast array of projects; a small sample includes:

- Elementary and secondary school buildings.
- Streets and roads.
- Government office buildings.
- Higher-education buildings, research laboratories, and dormitories.
- Transportation facilities, including bridges, highways, roads, airports, ports, and surface transit.
- Electric power-generating and -transmission facilities.
- Water tunnels and sewage treatment plants.
- Resource recovery plants.
- Hospitals, health-care and assisted living facilities, and nursing homes.
- Housing for low- and moderate-income families.

The municipal bond market is composed of thousands of dedicated professionals throughout the United States who have the diverse skills needed to raise money in the capital markets for state and local governments. Distinct roles are played by state and local government officials, public finance investment bankers, underwriters, salespeople, traders, analysts,

1

lawyers, financial advisors, rating agencies, insurers, commercial bankers, investors, brokers, technology developers and vendors, the media, and regulators; yet all are working together toward the common goal of providing funds to state and local government units to build needed public projects and infrastructure.

Municipal securities are also commonly called *tax-exempt bonds,* because the interest paid to the investor is subject neither to federal income taxes nor (often) to state or local taxation. With regard to tax exemption, it must be noted that each household and organization's tax status is unique and different. Although this book delineates the general principles of municipal bonds, investors should consult with their own financial advisors when considering the purchase or sale of municipal securities.

The American Recovery and Reinvestment Act of 2009 created Build America Bonds and other categories of municipal bonds where the interest is taxable to investors. The issuing municipalities received a grant from the federal government equal to 35 percent of the interest payments, which meant that the effective cost to the issuer was comparable to, or sometimes better than, the rate they would pay on a conventional tax-exempt municipal bond. The Build America Bonds program expired on December 31, 2010, and at the time of this writing had not been renewed.

In addition, a small market exists for taxable municipal bonds typically issued for purposes that are not eligible for either tax exemption under the U.S. tax code or a federal interest subsidy. Throughout this book, references to municipal bonds are to tax-exempt securities or Build America Bonds, except where it is expressly stated that they are taxable bonds that do not qualify for the federal interest subsidy.

One statistic that is key to understanding the municipal bond market is the dollar volume of new bond issues that are sold each year. Fluctuations in volume can reflect national economic trends as well as events that are unique and specific to the municipal bond market. The causes and effects of volume changes in the municipal market will be examined in detail throughout this book, which also includes a general discussion of the overall level of interest rates. Table 1.1 tracks 25 years of new-issue volume.

The municipal bond market consists of the primary market, which deals in the new securities of issuers, and the secondary market, where securities are bought, sold, and traded after they have been issued. Figure 1.1 presents the flow of funds through the primary market.

The process begins when an issuer sees a need for money to pay for capital improvements or to fill gaps in its cash flow. The issuer then takes a series of steps that lead to the primary market. There, the municipal bond dealer, usually a securities firm or a bank, purchases the issuer's bonds through a process called *underwriting.* The bonds are resold to institutional

TABLE 1.1 Total Long-Term and Short-Term Municipal Issuance 1986 to 2010 ($ billions)

Year	Long-Term Issuance	Short-Term Issuance	Total Municipal Issuance
1986	147.6	22.0	169.7
1987	101.6	20.5	122.1
1988	117.1	23.6	140.8
1989	122.3	29.6	151.9
1990	125.9	34.8	160.7
1991	169.8	44.4	214.2
1992	232.3	43.0	275.3
1993	290.3	47.5	337.8
1994	162.2	40.4	202.6
1995	155.8	38.4	194.2
1996	181.1	41.7	222.8
1997	214.0	46.4	260.4
1998	280.4	34.7	315.2
1999	219.4	36.7	256.0
2000	194.1	41.2	235.4
2001	284.2	56.9	341.1
2002	355.2	72.4	427.6
2003	378.5	69.8	448.4
2004	355.9	56.9	412.8
2005	406.4	50.5	456.9
2006	382.1	44.0	426.1
2007	424.2	57.9	482.1
2008	386.5	60.8	447.3
2009	406.8	64.7	471.6
2010	433.3	65.3	498.6

Source: Thomson Reuters.

and individual investors, who pay the dealer directly for the debt they have purchased. The dealer uses these funds to reimburse itself for its capital that was used to purchase the bonds from the issuer. If an issue is under-written and there are not enough buyers for all the bonds being issued, the underwriter assumes the risk of holding the bonds in inventory until they are eventually sold. Both principal and interest are paid to the investors by the issuer, usually through a bank acting as paying agent, on a fixed schedule.

The secondary market consists of the trading and other activity in se-curities after they have been sold as new issues. This market also supports the primary market by providing liquidity to investors who are more likely

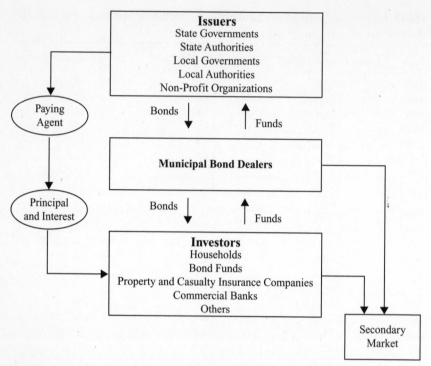

FIGURE 1.1   Flow of Funds in the Primary Market
Source: Securities Industry and Financial Markets Association.

to buy a security if they know they can sell that security at a fair market price prior to its stated maturity. Most municipal bond dealers have trading departments that make secondary markets in outstanding bond issues.

THE ISSUERS

According to the 2007 U.S. Economic Census, there were more than 89,500 units of state and local governments. The Census categorizes governmental units as states, counties, municipalities, towns and townships, school districts, and special districts. Municipal bonds are issued by state and local governmental units, either directly under their own names or through a special authority. An *authority* is a separate state or local governmental issuer expressly created to issue bonds or to run an enterprise, or both. Authorities such as those for transportation or power can issue bonds on their own behalf. Other authorities can issue bonds for the benefit of other, qualified, nongovernmental parties, such as not-for-profit hospitals, private colleges, and certain private companies.

Municipal bonds are authorized and issued pursuant to express state and local laws, which impose restrictions on the size and financial structure of the debt. Moreover, each new issue usually requires the approval of the governing body of the issuer, sometimes through an ordinance or resolution. Bonds are generally sold to provide funds for capital improvement projects—for the bricks and mortar that make up the public infrastructure. With few exceptions, bonds are not sold to finance the normal, everyday operating expenses of government, such as employees' salaries and benefits. States and local governmental units—such as counties, municipalities (which include cities), and school districts—issue bonds for roads, parks, courthouses, and schools. These securities are usually general obligation bonds (GOs) for which the full faith, credit, and taxing power of the issuer is pledged to and obliged to be used for the repayment of the bonds. Depending on the governmental issuer, approval by voter referendum is frequently required for the issuance of GOs. The public purpose projects funded by GOs provide benefits for the common good and so are repaid by taxes on everyone who is subject to taxes in that governmental unit. There are times when it is not feasible or possible to provide a general obligation pledge, so other forms of *tax-backed* or *tax-supported bonds* have been developed to provide a financing structure. Tax-backed bonds are discussed in greater depth throughout the book.

State and local governments also sell securities for which specific revenues, not governments' full faith, credit, and taxing power, are the source of repayment. These obligations are known as *revenue bonds*. The issuer can be the government itself or a separate authority. Revenue bonds are issued for the construction of facilities and plants that provide electric power, water, wastewater treatment, and resource recovery and transportation, among others. Revenues and user fees that can be pledged to the bonds include electric rates and charges, water and sewage usage fees, waste disposal and tipping fees, and tolls and landing fees.

Table 1.2 shows the average issuance in each of eight broad categories of state and local governmental issuers in the 10-year period from 2000 through 2009 as a percentage of the total new-issue market by dollar volume. State authorities, including housing, economic development, transportation, and other state-level authorities, were the largest category of issuers, followed by similar bodies created at the local or regional level. Cities, towns, and villages were the largest government issuers, followed by states and counties or parishes.

Although municipal bonds are issued for thousands of unique projects, they can be classified in a few broad categories, which may change over

TABLE 1.2 Issuers of Long-Term Municipal
Bonds, 2000 to 2009

Issuers	Issuance (%)
State authority	31.8
Local authority	18.3
District	16.0
City, town, or village	13.3
State governments	10.3
County/parish	6.3
College or university	2.5
Direct issuer	1.1
Total	100.0

Note: Average annual issuance as a percent of
dollar volume.
Source: Thomson Reuters.

time. Table 1.3 lists the purposes for which bonds were issued in 1989
compared to 2009. In 1989, the top two categories, "general purpose/public
improvement" and "education," accounted for 40 percent of debt issuance.
By 2009, the share of debt sold to support projects in these two categories
had increased to 54 percent. The snapshots of issuance over 20 years clearly
show that general governmental purposes and education have continued
to dominate the market. These bonds have not always been issued with
traditional general obligation security, however. Many novel tax-backed

TABLE 1.3 Major Uses of Municipal Debt, 1989 and 2009

Use of Proceeds	1989 (%)	2009 (%)
General purpose/public improvement	24.5	31.4
Education	15.6	22.3
Transportation	8.8	12.0
Health care	12.5	11.2
Water, sewer, and gas	12.6	10.2
Other	8.2	4.9
Public power	6.7	3.9
Housing	9.2	2.5
Pollution control	1.9	1.5
Total	100.0	100.0

Source: Thomson Reuters.

security structures have evolved that permit issuers to raise money for general governmental purposes without a general obligation pledge.

MUNICIPAL BOND DEALERS

In order to raise money in the market, the issuer works with a municipal bond dealer. The *municipal bond dealer* is most often found in a department of a securities firm or bank that provides other financial services. Public finance investment banking, underwriting, marketing, and trading municipal securities are jobs undertaken by the municipal bond departments of securities firms and banks. Some municipal bond departments are fully integrated as one department, with all the functional areas organized as one business unit. In other firms, those areas are divided between a firm's fixed income division and the investment-banking division. Any number of other organizational combinations are possible, too. Because of the broad range and regional nature of the business, some dealers operate solely in the municipal bond market, and may even concentrate on a single market sector. Others do mostly retail business, working with individual or household investors.

Public Finance

Public finance is the investment-banking arm of the municipal bond business. The investment bankers work with existing clients and develop new business with other issuers. Public finance specialists, with support from underwriters and traders, respond to the issuers' needs and the needs of investors with traditional and innovative financing structures. Investment bankers are responsible for coordinating and responding to the many written and oral Requests for Proposals (RFPs) that are sent to them by issuers. These RFPs, which include detailed plans and financial analyses of the issuer, form the basis of the issuer's selection of a municipal bond dealer in a negotiated underwriting (discussed in greater detail below in the underwriting section). This selection of underwriters for a negotiated sale is highly competitive, as many firms vie for an issuer's business.

Public finance departments can be organized along geographic, market-sector, or product lines. Sometimes they also perform financial advisory work.

Underwriting

The underwriters set prices and yields on new issues. The two main ways that an underwriter can purchase bonds from an issuer are through a competitive sale or a negotiated sale. A *competitive sale* is a type of auction where sealed bids for the bonds are submitted to the issuer at a specific time on a specific date. Normally, more than one underwriter will submit a bid to the issuer. The bonds are awarded to the underwriter who offers the issuer the lowest interest cost. Underwriters will often bid on bonds as part of a *syndicate,* a group of two or more firms who agree to make a bid together to an issuer in order to share underwriting risk. Competitive sales are also called *advertised sales* or *sealed bid sales.*

In a *negotiated sale,* the issuer, prior to the public sale date, selects the *lead underwriter* or *senior manager,* whose job is to coordinate and manage the financing through all its many stages. The selection process (sometimes for one transaction and sometimes for a series of transactions), which usually includes presenting a written response to the RFP, often also entails an oral interview at which the public finance investment bankers, underwriters, and other key members of the firm present and defend their proposed financing strategies. The issuer often selects other managers from competing firms to act as comanagers. The managers, acting together or with more firms through a syndicate, make an offer to purchase the bonds from the issuer at a price that will produce the lowest possible interest cost to the issuer while still enabling the underwriter to sell the bonds to investors. There is greater flexibility in structuring the bonds and in reacting to the most current market conditions in a negotiated sale. As in a competitive sale, the underwriters work closely with traders and salespeople to determine the right price for a new issue.

Trading

Traders maintain the secondary market for securities by actively buying bonds from, and selling bonds to, other dealers and investors. A good trader is familiar at all times with the bonds available in the municipal market and factors affecting their prices as well as overall conditions in the other fixed income markets. Typically, traders specialize in one sector of the market, such as hospital bonds; in certain bond maturities, such as 1 to 10 years; or in *dollar bonds* (bonds that are quoted and traded in dollar prices rather than in terms of yield). Retail orders are sometimes executed on electronic trading platforms, but large institutional orders are typically handled in person by a conventional trading desk.

Sales

The salespeople develop and maintain direct contact with institutional investors. They sit in the trading room close to the underwriters and traders. In addition to selling new issues that the firm has underwritten, the salesperson is familiar with investors' portfolios and looks for opportunities to serve investors in the secondary market. The sales force can be organized in various ways: geographically, by client relationships, by the maturity of the bond, or by a combination of any of these.

Sales Liaison

Securities firms that have a client base with many individual investors often have a retail sales liaison force. The *sales liaison* staff is normally located in the trading room and works with the account executives (variously known as stockbrokers, registered representatives, financial advisors, account executives, or private client service representatives) in the firm's main and branch offices. The account executive calls the sales liaison with inquiries and orders, and the liaison works with the underwriter or trader to fill the investor's needs. Several securities firms also have regional trading departments similar to their main office trading operations on a smaller scale. The salespeople and liaison staffs in these regional offices work in much the same way as they do in the main office.

Research and Credit Analysis

The complexity of the municipal market, the financial challenges of some state and local governments, and the post-2008 reduction in the use of third-party credit enhancement have led municipal bond dealers to place greater emphasis on the creditworthiness of municipal issuers. Dealers have *research and credit analysts* who are responsible for reviewing and monitoring issuers in the primary and secondary market. Research analysts may prepare a short opinion that can be distributed internally (within the firm) or externally to investors on competitive or negotiated issues coming to market, or they may write comprehensive reports on specific market sectors or on market strategy. In some firms, research and credit analysts work with the public finance investment bankers on responding to RFPs and, once the firm is awarded the negotiated business, on credit and rating issues as well. Research and credit analysts are responsible for reviewing official statements under the disclosure rules at many firms.

Rating agencies, bond insurers, and institutional investors also employ research and credit professionals.

Capital Markets

Capital markets blend investment banking and market expertise. They are responsible for creating financial and investment products such as derivatives, swaps, and synthetic products that are used by both municipal issuers and investors. These products are created with information from the users and with the firm's own risk management team. They may also create financial products for the firm's own proprietary trading. A firm will often have a special, more highly rated subsidiary that enters into derivative transactions to offer the issuer the most secure counterparty structure.

Operations

Operations involves the complex processing associated with the buying and selling of municipal securities. The adoption of industry-wide requirements for orders, record keeping, and confirmations has largely automated and standardized the functions of the operations group. Its duties include processing orders and payments, verifying and delivering securities, issuing confirmations, and maintaining customer accounts and other required documentation. The operations rules of the Municipal Securities Rulemaking Board (MSRB, a self-regulatory organization) are discussed in detail throughout this book.

THE LAWYERS

Lawyers of various specialties play important roles in the financing process.

Bond Counsel

Virtually every municipal security is accompanied by an opinion of *bond counsel*, who represents the legal interests of the bondholders. That opinion addresses the main legal issues: that the bonds constitute legal, valid, and binding obligations of the issuer, and that interest on the bonds is exempt from federal income taxation under applicable tax laws (or, in the case of a Build America Bond, that the issue qualifies for the federal interest rate subsidy). In rendering the opinion, a bond counsel (1) undertakes a review and examination of all applicable laws authorizing the issuance of securities, (2) ascertains that all required procedural steps have been completed to assure proper authorization and issuance of the securities, and (3) determines that all federal tax laws governing the issuance of the bonds have been complied with. In connection with a review of laws and procedure, bond counsel assembles all relevant documentation into a *transcript of proceedings*. The transcript serves as a permanent record and reference of the steps taken to issue the bonds and of the underlying payment and security arrangements.

Underwriter's Counsel

Underwriter's counsel represents the underwriters in a negotiated issue. The underwriter's counsel conducts a thorough due diligence analysis of the issuer. *Due diligence* involves questioning the issuer and any important related parties about their financial condition, plans, reports, and other factors that are important for a purchaser to know in order to make an investment decision. At the closing, underwriter's counsel provides a 10-b-5 certificate to the underwriter stating that nothing material to the transaction has been omitted from the disclosure process and that everything material to making an investment decision has been included. Underwriter's counsel also prepares the *bond purchase agreement* or *contract*, pursuant to which the debt is sold to the underwriter.

Other Counsel

Because of the diverse and complex nature of the municipal market, some issues may require opinions in addition to those normally provided by bond counsel and underwriter's counsel. These opinions may include those of special tax counsel, bank counsel, disclosure counsel, outside bond counsel, and/or borrower's counsel. Chapter 4 discusses in detail the roles of the counsels.

FINANCIAL ADVISORS, SPECIALISTS, AND OTHER CONSULTANTS

State and local governments often seek the advice of a financial advisor and other professional experts. Financial advisors perform a variety of tasks, including (1) analyzing the financing needs of the issuer, (2) helping to choose an underwriter or organize a competitive sale, (3) structuring the issue, (4) working with the rating agencies and credit enhancers, (5) helping negotiate a purchase price on a negotiated financing, and (6) advising on other matters related to the issuer's debt and capital plans. Bond issuers sometimes retain dealers to serve as financial advisors.

Capital improvement projects often require the advice of specialists in addition to that given the financial advisors. Some consultants, for example, advise solely on the feasibility of health-care projects; others take on the financial, engineering, and architectural aspects of airports; still other specialists evaluate toll roads or public utilities. The issuer's accountants also play a part in the financing process. The opinions of consultants are important not only for establishing the merits of a particular project but also for attracting voter approval and promoting investor acceptance and confidence in the bonds.

Municipal derivatives specialists, or *swap advisors,* are financial advisors who specialize in advising on transactions involving derivatives. They provide advice on a wide range of services, including structuring transactions involving interest rate swaps and pricing swaps and other derivatives, among others. *Arbitrage rebate specialists* also may be part of a larger organization or stand alone; they advise on compliance with arbitrage regulations and offer reporting services. They work with issuers on bond rebate calculations, bond verifications, allocations of commingled funds, cash flow models, yield computations, and reporting systems.

A broker, dealer, or municipal securities dealer may also engage consultants on its behalf subject to MSRB Rule G-38. A written consultant agreement must be entered into before the consultant engages in any direct or indirect communication with an issuer on behalf of the broker, dealer, or municipal securities dealer. The use of a consultant must also be disclosed to the issuer and to the MSRB.

THE RATING AGENCIES

There are tens of thousands of municipal issuers. Because of the large number of issuers and the variety of security structures in the market, bond or debt ratings play a prominent role in the municipal market. A *rating* is an alphabetic and/or numeric symbol used to give relative indications of credit quality. A rating is generally considered obligatory for the sale of any major issue. Some issues may be marketed on a nonrated basis if, for example, they are privately placed, their credit standing is well known to the investors buying the bonds, or they cannot achieve an investment-grade rating.

Underwriters or financial advisors are sometimes involved in preparing or making presentations to rating agencies on behalf of issuers prior to a bond sale. In addition to providing an initial rating, rating agencies review their ratings periodically and analyze issuers' ongoing financial and operational information. In addition, the agencies provide a review process for municipalities seeking an *upgrade* or improvement to their ratings; lists of bonds with potential rating changes; analyses of credit trends; and other rating services.

The three dominant rating agencies for municipal securities are Moody's Investors Service, Standard & Poor's, and Fitch Ratings. All three are headquartered in New York City. Moody's has been rating municipal bonds since 1909, Standard & Poor's since 1940, and Fitch since 1913. All three rate long-term issues, short-term notes, commercial paper, and obligations

TABLE 1.4 Credit Ratings

Credit Risk	Moody's	Standard & Poor's	Fitch Ratings
Investment Grade	Aaa	AAA	AAA
Strongest	Aa	AA	AA
	A	A	A
	Baa	BBB	BBB
Noninvestment Grade	Ba	BB	BB
	B, Caa, Ca, C	B, CCC, CC, C	B, CCC, CC, C
Weakest	C	D	D

Source: Securities Industry and Financial Markets Association.

secured by insurance, bank, and other credit enhancements. Although each agency has unique features in its own rating scale, triple-A is the highest rating for each one, and each scale descends down the alphabet as the opinion of creditworthiness declines. Moody's ratings within certain categories are modified by numbers (1, 2, and 3), whereas those of Standard & Poor's and Fitch are modified by "+" and "–" symbols. The lowest investment grade rating for Moody's is Baa3, and for Standard & Poor's and Fitch it is BBB–.

Ratings can be classified in the general categories listed in Table 1.4.

BOND BROKERS

Municipal bond brokers, or *brokers' brokers,* trade only for municipal bond dealers and dealer banks; they do not work directly with either institutional or individual investors. Brokers are sometimes able to facilitate trades in a more efficient way than if the dealers did the trades themselves. For example, dealers often try to sell bonds in their inventories through brokers by asking a broker to seek bids from other dealers. This is known as the *bid-wanted* process. In other cases, a dealer who is looking for particular bonds for a customer may tell the bond broker the specified yield or price at which he or she would be willing to buy the securities. In this instance, the broker will seek these bonds from other dealers.

THE CREDIT ENHANCERS

Credit enhancement is a term denoting the credit of a stronger, more highly rated entity that is used to strengthen or enhance the credit of a lower-rated entity. Credit enhancement grew substantially in the 1990s and early 2000s for many reasons, including (1) investor concerns about the credit quality of underlying issuers, (2) increasingly complex security features, (3) increased issuance in the short-term market, and (4) cost efficiency in the pricing of insurance. Its use has plummeted since 2008, when many bond insurers encountered financial difficulties that undermined the value of their credit enhancement. The major forms of credit enhancement are private bond insurance, bank letters of credit and lines of credit, which are discussed in this section. Public forms of credit enhancement are discussed in Chapters 3 and 7. A bond is said to be *unenhanced* if it carries only its own rating and not that of a third-party enhanced provider.

Bond Insurers

Bond insurance is a legal commitment by an insurance company to make payments of principal and interest on debt in the event that the issuer fails to make those payments on time. Generally, such payments will be made as originally scheduled, and the principal will not be accelerated (paid earlier than its scheduled date). Bond insurance typically covers the full maturity range of the bonds.

Although bond insurance provides significant additional security to the investor, the issuers are the first source for payment of principal and interest on their bonds. For that reason (and for other technical and tax-related considerations), not all insured bonds carry identical prices and yields. The perceived strength of the insurer by the market is a major determinant of that insurer's trading value. The relative quality of insurers is evaluated by their financial strengths and by the portfolios of bonds that they have previously insured.

The role of municipal bond insurance in the market is threefold: (1) to reduce interest costs to issuers, (2) to provide a high level of security to investors, and (3) to furnish improved secondary-market liquidity and price support. From 1985 through 2005, there was tremendous growth in the use of bond insurance, as shown in Table 1.5. Bond insurance grew from 16.2 percent of the $147.6 billion new-issue, long-term market in 1986 to more than 57.3 percent of the $406.4 billion new-issue, long-term market in 2005.

Beginning in late 2007, most of the major bond insurers encountered severe financial difficulties due to losses on structured debt and other instruments not related to municipal bonds. The rating agencies downgraded the major bond insurers, which they considered less capable of making investors whole in the event of issuer default. Investors refocused on the credit quality of underlying issuers and were no longer willing to pay a significant premium for most insured bonds. Issuers saw no reason to pay for insurance

TABLE 1.5 Bond Insurance as a Percentage of the Long-Term New-Issue Market, 1986 to 2010

Year	Long-Term Issuance with Bond Insurance	Percentage of Long-Term Issuance Insured	Long-Term Issuance ($ billions)
1986	23.9	16.2	147.6
1987	19.3	19.0	101.6
1988	27.0	23.1	117.1
1989	31.0	25.3	122.3
1990	33.7	26.7	125.9
1991	51.9	30.6	169.8
1992	80.5	34.7	232.3
1993	107.5	37.1	290.3
1994	61.4	37.8	162.2
1995	68.4	43.9	155.8
1996	85.6	47.3	181.1
1997	107.0	50.0	214.0
1998	144.5	51.5	280.4
1999	104.8	47.8	219.4
2000	78.8	40.6	194.1
2001	134.0	47.2	284.2
2002	178.2	50.2	355.2
2003	190.2	50.2	378.5
2004	194.4	54.6	355.9
2005	232.8	57.3	406.4
2006	190.3	49.8	382.1
2007	200.3	47.2	424.2
2008	72.2	18.7	386.5
2009	35.4	8.7	406.8
2010	26.9	6.2	433.3

Source: Thomson Reuters.

if the lower interest rate it achieved did not offset the cost. The use of bond insurance plummeted as a result; in 2010, insured bond issues accounted for just 6.2 percent of the new-issue long-term market.

Banks

Bank letters and bank lines of credit are other forms of credit enhancement. *Bank letters of credit* are typically written for a much shorter term (anywhere from 1 to 10 years) than bond insurance. A letter of credit pays the investor principal and accrued interest if an event of default has occurred. It is stronger than a *line of credit,* which has many more conditions that must be satisfied before the issuer can draw money to pay principal or interest to investors. Issues with bank letters of credit receive the rating of the bank. This may be the short-term rating, the long-term rating, or both. Issues with lines of credit do not necessarily get the bank rating. Analysts look at the conditions under which the line will pay in addition to the financial condition of the issuer.

The use of letters of credit has fluctuated greatly over the years, as shown in Table 1.6. Usage typically increases at times of stress in the overall credit markets, such as 1994, 2000, and 2008. Usage decreases when credit

TABLE 1.6 Letters of Credit as Percentage of the Long-Term New-Issue Market, 1986 to 2010

Year	Long-Term Issuance with Letters of Credit	Percentage of Long-Term Issuance with Letters of Credit	Long-Term Issuance ($ billions)
1986	12.2	8.3	147.6
1987	12.4	12.2	101.6
1988	15.2	13.0	117.1
1989	10.0	8.2	122.3
1990	11.2	8.9	125.9
1991	8.3	4.9	169.8
1992	7.4	3.2	232.3
1993	8.8	3.0	290.3
1994	15.1	9.3	162.2
1995	9.9	6.4	155.8
1996	10.4	5.7	181.1
1997	12.2	5.7	214.0
1998	10.3	3.7	280.4
1999	10.0	4.6	219.4
2000	13.6	7.0	194.1
2001	13.1	4.6	284.2
2002	15.5	4.4	355.2
2003	14.6	3.9	378.5
2004	23.3	6.5	355.9
2005	26.9	6.6	406.4
2006	21.1	5.5	382.1
2007	20.5	4.8	424.2
2008	71.2	18.4	386.5
2009	20.4	5.0	406.8
2010	11.8	2.7	433.3

Source: Thomson Reuters.

is more readily available in the market, hitting cyclical lows in 1993, 1998, 2003, and 2007. High interest rates prompt issuers to rely on shorter-term financing such as variable rate demand notes, which require a letter of credit to assure investors that cash will be available if an event triggers their right to *put* the notes (sell the notes back to the issuer at 100 percent of par). The variability in bank credit enhancement is related to many factors, including (1) the credit quality of banks, making the credit substitution less cost efficient when credit quality declines; (2) cost of the letter of credit; and (3) availability of alternative forms of credit enhancement.

In late 2008, a severe credit crisis effectively shut down the new issue market for long-term municipal bonds for several weeks. The only way issuers could access the market was through short-term debt or variable rate demand notes. In addition, many issuers converted auction rate securities to variable rate bonds that required letters of credit. The proportion of issues backed by letters of credit soared, but quickly fell back to historical levels in 2009 when the fixed rate municipal bond market reopened. Financial pressure on the banks made letters of credit more difficult to obtain and more expensive, too.

THE TRUSTEES AND PAYING AGENTS

The *trustee* is responsible for carrying out the administrative functions that are required under the bond documents. These functions include establishing the accounts and holding the funds relating to the debt issue, authenticating the bonds, maintaining a list of holders of the bonds, passing through principal and interest payments on the debt, and representing the interests of the bondholders in the event of default. There are times when a paying or fiscal agent carries out some of these functions.

The Depository Trust & Clearing Corporation (DTCC) is a securities depository and a national clearinghouse for the clearance and settlement of trades in corporate and municipal securities. DTCC is owned by banks and securities firms that use its services. Trustees and paying agents make a single interest and principal payment per maturity to DTCC, and DTCC distributes those payments to participating firms for the benefit of their clients.

THE INVESTORS

Three classes of investors dominate the municipal marketplace: (1) households, consisting of individuals acting directly or through investment advisors; (2) household proxies, that is, bond funds such as open-end mutual

TABLE 1.7 Holdings of Municipal Bonds by Category of Investor, 1990 to 2010 (percent)

Category	1990	2000	2010
Households	55.0	35.9	37.1
Open-End Funds	9.6	15.6	18.7
Money Market Funds	7.1	16.4	11.6
Closed-End Funds	1.2	4.6	2.9
Commercial Banks	10.0	7.7	8.0
Property and Casualty Insurance	11.6	12.4	13.0
Other	5.6	7.5	8.8

Note: Includes mutual funds, money market funds, and closed-end funds.
Source: Federal Reserve System.

funds, managed closed-end funds, and money market funds; and (3) institutions, particularly commercial banks and property and casualty insurance companies. The principal characteristic of all buyers of traditional municipal bonds is that they are subject to federal income tax so that they can benefit from the tax exemption.

Build America Bonds and similiar taxable securities attract different investors because the interest on these bonds is taxable. They appeal to pension funds, foundations, and endowments that are exempt from tax as well as life insurance companies and some foreign investors. Mutual funds buy these bonds, too, but not in traditional municipal bond funds; instead, BABs are bought by funds that hold taxable bonds, including federal government bonds and investment grade corporate bonds.

In 1990, there were $1.2 trillion in bonds outstanding; by the end of 2010, that figure had grown to $2.8 trillion. Table 1.7 illustrates the key trends in the holdings of municipal securities from 1990 to 2010. Two changes over this time are particularly striking. First, in 1990, households represented 55.0 percent of all municipal holdings, but by 2009, they had fallen to 37.1 percent of all holdings. Meanwhile, holdings of household proxies rose from 17.9 percent in 1990 to 33.2 percent in 2010. Taken together, the overall share of households and household proxies changed relatively little, declining from 72.9 percent in 1990 to 70.3 percent in 2010.

INFORMATION AND TECHNOLOGY

Like other markets, the municipal market has been transformed by the Internet and the growing use of electronic trading systems, which have improved both transparency and price discovery. The Municipal Securities Rulemaking Board has created the Electronic Municipal Market Access (EMMA) system, a comprehensive source for official statements, continuing disclosure documents, advance refunding documents, and real-time trade price information on municipal securities (http://emma.msrb.org). In addition, dealers and other market professionals have created web sites that offer extensive information and trading capabilities to investors. Both the primary and secondary markets make extensive use of technology and information, and a discussion of technology is included in Chapter 5.

THE REGULATORS

The municipal bond market is heavily regulated by a number of regulatory agencies.

The Securities and Exchange Commission

The Securities and Exchange Commission (SEC, or the "Commission") is an independent, nonpartisan, quasi-judicial regulatory agency with responsibility for administering the federal securities laws. It was created by Congress under the Securities Exchange Act of 1934. There are five commissioners, all of whom are appointed by the President of the United States, with advice and consent of the Senate, for fixed five-year terms. The terms are staggered, with one expiring in June of each year. Not more than three members may be of the same political party. The president also designates the Commission's Chair.

The SEC enforces federal securities laws to provide protection for investors, to ensure that they have access to disclosure of material information, and to see that the securities markets operate fairly and honestly. The laws that are under the SEC's jurisdiction are the:

- Securities Act of 1933
- Securities Exchange Act of 1934
- Public Utility Holding Company Act of 1935
- Trust Indenture Act of 1939
- Investment Company Act of 1940
- Investment Advisors Act of 1940

The Commission also serves as advisor to federal courts in corporate reorganization proceedings under Chapter 11 of the bankruptcy statute. There are 11 regional and district offices of the SEC, staffed by lawyers, accountants, financial analysts, economists, and other professionals.

The Municipal Securities Rulemaking Board

The Municipal Securities Rulemaking Board (MSRB) was established in 1975 by Congress to develop rules and set standards regulating securities firms and banks involved in underwriting, trading, and selling municipal securities. The MSRB is a self-regulatory organization that is subject to oversight by the SEC.

The board, which was composed of 21 members as of 2011, includes ten representatives from regulated entities—bank dealers, securities firms, and municipal advisors—and 11 representatives from the public. At least one public member must be representative of issuers and one of investors to ensure that all perspectives of the municipal securities market are represented. The MSRB has authority to make rules regulating the municipal securities activities of banks, securities firms, and municipal advisors only; it does not have authority over either issuers of municipal securities or investors.

The MSRB's rule-making authority includes the areas of professional qualification standards; fair practice; record keeping; confirmation, clearance, and settlement of transactions; the scope and frequency of compliance examinations; the nature of securities quotations; arbitration of disputes involving municipal securities transactions; and the dissemination by dealers of information supplied by issuers of municipal securities. The MSRB also provides support for the enforcement functions of The Financial Industry Regulatory Authority (FINRA) and other enforcement agencies. The MSRB's missions also include promoting market transparency, investor education and market research.

One of the first rules the MSRB adopted requires that all persons involved with "any transaction" in municipal securities must pass a qualifying examination.

The Financial Industry Regulatory Authority

The Financial Industry Regulatory Authority (FINRA) is an independent regulator for securities firms doing business in the United States. It was formed in July 2007 from the merger of NASD Regulation, a subsidiary of the National Association of Securities Dealers, and the member regulation, enforcement and arbitration functions of the New York Stock Exchange. FINRA has a broad remit, including education, registration, and testing of securities professionals; field examinations of securities firms to determine their compliance with federal securities laws, the rules of the MSRB, and FINRA rules and regulations; surveillance of the Nasdaq Stock Market, the

American Stock Exchange, the International Securities Exchange, and the Chicago Climate Exchange; and other services.

Continuing Education

In 1995, the SEC approved Rule 1120 of the NASD Membership and Registration Rules, which at the time set the requirements for the Securities Industry Continuing Education Program. NASD, the MSRB, the American Stock Exchange, the Chicago Board Options Exchange, the New York Stock Exchange, and the Philadelphia Stock Exchange developed a two-part continuing education program that is a uniform requirement across the securities industry. FINRA, the successor to NASD Regulation, administers the first part, the Regulatory Element, for municipal professionals. The rules were revised in 2005 to eliminate grandfather provisions that exempted certain individuals with long experience from the continuing education program. The Regulatory Element is a computer-based training program now required for all persons within 120 days of the second anniversary of their initial securities registration and every three years thereafter. This training relates to compliance, regulatory, ethical, and sales practice standards. The second part of the program is the Firm Element, which consists of annual, firm-developed and administered training programs designed to keep specified registered employees current regarding job- and product-related subjects.

OTHER PARTICIPANTS

A number of other organizations and entities also play roles in the municipal bond market.

Information Repositories

Prior to July 2009, four companies acted as nationally recognized municipal securities information repositories (NRMSIRs): DPC Data Inc.; Securities Evaluation Inc.; Interactive Data Pricing and Reference Data Inc.; and Bloomberg Municipal Repository. On July 1, 2009, the SEC withdrew its recognition of these four entities and designated EMMA as the sole repository for information about municipal securities. EMMA displays information provided by issuers but does not verify its accuracy. In addition, state information depositories (SIDs) may collect and disseminate data about local issuers. Disclosure requirements are more fully discussed in Chapter 9.

CUSIP

The Committee on Uniform Security Identification Procedures (CUSIP) Service Bureau was established in 1964 and is operated by Standard & Poor's for the American Bankers Association. The CUSIP Service Bureau assigns unique numbers and standardized descriptions to practically every sector of the financial markets, including the municipal market. A CUSIP number has a combination of nine numbers and letters.

CHAPTER 2

The Basics of Municipal Securities

DESCRIPTION OF MUNICIPAL SECURITIES

The municipal market includes different types of municipal securities. Traditional *municipal bonds* are interest-bearing securities issued by state and local governments on their own behalf or on behalf of qualified entities to finance capital projects and certain cash flow needs. Because interest on most of these securities is exempt from taxation at the federal level and sometimes at state and local levels, they are also called *tax-exempt bonds*. Build America Bonds, and certain other categories of bonds created by the American Recovery and Reinvestment Act of 2009, are subject to federal, state, and local taxes, however; they are *taxable bonds*.

The *par* value, *face* value, or *principal* amount is what is paid to investors when the security comes due or matures, with *interest* having been paid throughout the life of the security. Generally, when a security matures in one year or more, it is a *long-term* financial instrument and is called a *bond*. Municipal bonds usually have maturities ranging from 1 to 30 years, although some bonds have been issued with maturities ranging from 40 to 100 years. Generally, when a security has a term of less than 13 months, it is a *short-term* instrument. Municipal short-term instruments include notes and commercial paper. *Variable-rate demand obligations* (VRDOs) usually have short-term interest rate resets—and so are often treated by the market as short-term securities—but the final maturity of the security is usually long term. *Zero coupon bonds* do not pay interest periodically; instead, the interest accrues at the stated yield until maturity.

Municipal bonds are typically issued in denominations of $5,000 or integral multiples of $5,000, but some market terminology is based on a $1,000 bond. For example, a dealer who says "one bond" is typically referring to $1,000 par value. "Twenty-five bonds" are $25,000 par value, although there may be only five units in denominations of $5,000 each. Some municipalities have experimented with denominations as small as $100 to try to attract smaller investors, but the practice has not become widespread.

A bond or note is identified by six pieces of information:

1. *Name of issuer.* Identification of the issuing body is the first essential piece of information. When the issuer is an authority or agency issuing on behalf of another party, the name of the obligated party is also included.

2. *Coupon.* The interest rate stated on the bond and payable to the bondholder. Municipal bonds can pay either a fixed rate of interest throughout the life of the bond, a variable rate of interest, or, in the case of accrual bonds, no current interest at all. The rate is referred to as the *coupon* as a throw-back to when bonds actually had interest coupons physically attached. (Today, only so-called *bearer bonds* issued before 1982 have these coupons attached.) With a fixed-rate bond, the amount of interest paid semiannually (the *convention*) over the life of the bond is the same every six months and is a percentage of the face value. For example, a $1,000 bond with a coupon rate of 5 percent will pay $50 a year to the bondholder, $25 on each semiannual payment date. In a variable-rate bond, the interest paid changes on a regular basis (daily, weekly, monthly, semiannually, etc.) based on an index or a formula in order to keep the yield in line with market conditions.

3. *Maturity date.* The day, month, and year on which investors receive payment of principal, or par amount, of the bond and the final interest payment.

4. *Dated date.* The day, month, and year from which bondholders are entitled to receive interest, even though the bonds may actually be sold and delivered at some other date.

5. *Yield and price.* Municipal bonds are generally quoted in terms of *yield* because of the enormous range of issues with different maturities. There are many different yields, including *current yield, yield to maturity,* and *yield to call.* Municipal bonds are generally quoted in terms of yield to maturity. Bond prices are stated as a percentage of the par value. *Par value* equals 100; a discount bond trades at a price below 100—at 99.5, for instance, which is $995 for a bond with a par value of $1,000; a premium bond trades at a price above 100—at 102, for instance, or $1,020 for a bond with a $1,000 par value.

6. *CUSIP number.* The CUSIP number is a unique identifier of a bond or commercial paper. It consists of nine characters: a base number of six digits known as the *issuer number* (the fourth, fifth, and/or sixth digit of which may be a letter or a number) and a two-character suffix. This suffix is alphanumeric, and is the *issue number.* The ninth digit is a check number.

Applying these six pieces of information, a typical municipal bond quotation, as indicated in Figure 2.1 (which is from a Bloomberg screen) would be as follows: "State of California, G.O. Bonds, dated 12/02/2010, 5.25 percent due November 1, 2040, at 5.500 percent." The quotation reflects that the bonds were originally priced at 96.346, making them discount bonds, with a yield to maturity of 5.500 percent. The bond description also shows that the coupons are paid on a semiannual basis, and that the bonds are exempt from federal and state taxes and are in book-entry form. The Moody's, Standard & Poor's, and Fitch ratings are listed, as is trading information.

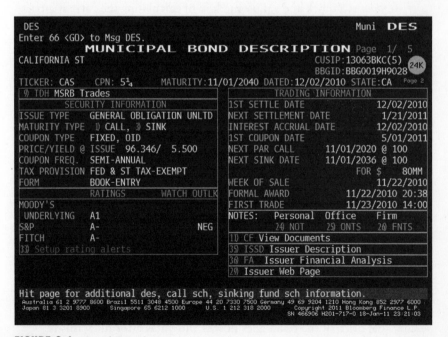

FIGURE 2.1   Bond Description
Source: Bloomberg LP.

YIELD AND PRICE

There is a direct, inverse relationship between yield and price in all fixed-income securities, including municipal bonds. Municipal bonds fluctuate in yield for the same economic reasons that other bonds do (see Chapter 8). General shifts in interest rates due to Federal Reserve monetary policy or to changing expectations about inflation, for example, affect municipal interest rates as well as other interest rates. Many other factors can also cause fluctuations in yield: short-term swings in the demand for municipal bonds on the part of investors, the perceived creditworthiness of a particular bond issuer, and the total volume of municipal bonds issued, for example. When the coupon interest payment is fixed, the price of the bond itself must change in order to keep the yield in line with the yields of bonds issued in the primary market as well as other bonds trading in the secondary market.

Current Yield

Current yield is a quick and simple method of calculating the current income on a bond. The current yield is equal to the coupon interest payment divided by the current *price* of the bond. Current yield is of limited use because it does not take into account the time value of money and the accrual of interest-on-interest, which yield to maturity does. Municipal bonds are not sold on the basis of current yield. However, current yield may be a useful metric due to its ease of calculation.

Assume that a bond is issued with a 5 percent coupon at par. The formula for current yield would be

$$CY = \frac{C}{P}$$

where CY is current yield, C is coupon, and P is price.

The current yield is

$$CY = \frac{50}{1,000}$$

or 5 percent. Then, if the current yield goes up, from 5 percent to 5.05 percent, the price of the bond goes down. Shown as a formula, this is

$$5.05\% = \frac{50}{P}$$

where 50 is the annual coupon payment, P is the price of the bond, and 5.05 percent is the new current yield. Solving for P, the new bond price is 990.

Conversely, when the yield goes down from 5 percent to 4.95 percent, the price of the bond goes up. Shown as a formula, this is

$$4.95\% = \frac{50}{P}$$

where 50 is the annual coupon payment, P is the price of the bond, and 4.95 percent is the new current yield. Solving for P, the new bond price is \$1,010. When the interest rate is variable, the yield also adjusts to the current market, and the price hovers around par.

Therefore, investors who pay less than par for a bond with a 5 percent coupon receive more than 5 percent in yield because they receive \$50 of interest each year on an investment of less than \$1,000. Investors who pay more than par for the same bond would receive a yield of less than 5 percent.

Consider another example of how the price and yield of older issues must adjust in order to be competitive with new issues. Assume a bond was issued early in 2000 with a coupon of 6 percent and a 16-year maturity. Six years later, a new bond of similar creditworthiness with a 10-year maturity is issued carrying a coupon of 7 percent. Both bonds are due to mature in 2016. Therefore, the bond with the 6 percent coupon must fall in price so that its yield will approximate the yield on the new 7 percent bond. Ignoring the effects of taxes on pricing, sellers would not find a buyer for the older bond until its price fell to \$92.89, the point where the yield would be competitive with the yield of the new bond.

Yield to Maturity

Current yield does not take into account the time value of money. Yield to maturity does take into account the time value of money in a way similar to the concept of the internal rate of return. The formula for yield to maturity for a bond paying interest once per year is as follows:

$$P = \sum_{t=1}^{n} \frac{C_t}{(1 + \text{YTM})^t} + \frac{M}{(1 + \text{YTM})^n}$$

where P = price, C = coupon, n = years to maturity, t = index of period, M = maturity value of the bond, and YTM = yield to maturity.

Years to maturity and the index of the period in this formula are yearly measurements. Most coupon payments are semiannual and interest is compounded semiannually, so the actual calculation would reflect that. An initial estimate of YTM must be made, and through a series of trial and error calculations, or iterations, the value of YTM is found. This is a very difficult and time-consuming formula to solve by hand. Yield to maturity, which years ago was calculated by using a basis book, is now easily calculated on computers and financial calculators.

Another important concept involves calculating the value of the .05 or, even more specifically, the .01. Yields on municipal bonds are usually quoted in terms of basis points, with one basis point equal to one one-hundredth of 1 percent. The value of a .05 is the amount that the dollar price changes with each move of five basis points in the market. The value of the .01 is the amount the dollar price changes with each move of one basis point in the market. The values of both the .05 and the .01 change the longer the bond's duration.

Look at an example of the change in the .01. Assume a new bond is issued at 5 percent on December 1, 2010, due December 1, 2017, at par. If interest rates go up in the secondary market to 5.01 percent, the dollar price of that bond would fall to $99.925, because as rates go up, dollar prices fall. The value of the .01 in this case, where the market moved one basis point up, is 7.5 cents. If that 5 percent bond had a maturity of December 1, 2047, 30 years longer, and the market moved up one basis point, the bonds would fall in price to $99.844, a drop of 15.6 cents. The value of the .01 is more volatile farther out on the yield curve.

Conversely, if that same 5 percent bond due on December 1, 2017, dropped in yield by one basis point to 4.99 percent, the bonds would rise in price to $100.075, an increase of 7.5 cents. The .01 of a 5 percent bond due on December 1, 2047, would be 15.6 cents, making the dollar price $100.156. The ability to measure and manage the value of the .01 is key in trading.

TYPES OF YIELDS

Yield to maturity is used to describe bonds trading in the market because it takes into account the time value of money. Municipal bonds are bought and sold in the market on the basis of yield to maturity. In simplest terms, yield to maturity is the internal rate of return, compounded semiannually, that an investor would earn from all interest and principal payments over the life of the bond. One important assumption in yield to maturity calculations is that all interest payments are reinvested at the same rate as the bond yield. If an investor knows that this will not be the case, adjustments can and should be made to the calculations to get a true internal rate of return.

The yield to maturity of a bond with a 5 percent coupon bought at par is 5 percent. If the bond is bought at a discount or a premium, however, the calculation gets more complicated. For example, in the case of bonds that are priced at 99.5 (an original issue discount), the yield to maturity of 5.05 percent takes into account the value of that discount.

Yield to call is the annual return, compounded semiannually, that an investor would earn from payments of principal and interest, assuming the bonds are redeemed at the first call date. If the bonds are redeemed at a premium, the premium price is reflected in the yield.

Yield to worst is the lowest possible yield that the bond can have, given all of its parameters. If a bond can be called before maturity, the yield to call and yield to maturity will be calculated. The lower of the two, the yield to worst, will reflect the more conservative price of possible outcomes. This yield must be quoted to customers under current MSRB rules. Some extraordinary cases are unpredictable and cannot be accurately priced into the bond's yield. In the event of an extraordinary call the broker must inform the client of this under MSRB rules.

Appendix A includes MSRB Rule G-33, which details standard bond calculations.

Under current federal tax laws, any capital gains earned by selling tax-exempt bonds at a price higher than the purchase price, or by redeeming bonds at par that were bought at a discount, are subject to federal income taxes, as is market discount, or a price discount attributable to a bond selling in the secondary market at a price lower than the price at which it was originally offered. This affects both the yield to maturity after taxes and the way the bonds are priced in the market.

TAX EXEMPTION OF MUNICIPAL BONDS

The interest on most municipal bonds, except for Build America Bonds and certain others, is exempt from federal income taxation. Municipal bonds issued by entities domiciled in a particular state are typically exempt from taxation by that state, too.

Federal Tax Exemption

The significance of this characteristic is reflected by the fact that municipal securities are also commonly referred to simply as *tax-exempt bonds*. And, as discussed in this and later chapters, the federal tax status of interest and related tax consequences on municipal securities greatly influences the nature, type, and level of investor interest.

As discussed in detail in Chapter 9, the historical basis of the federal income tax exemption for municipal securities was originally premised upon Supreme Court decisions predating the ratification of the Sixteenth Amendment to the U.S. Constitution in 1913, which authorized Congress to impose a federal income tax. Since that ratification, all such tax laws, including the current Internal Revenue Code of 1986, have provided for municipal securities' tax exemption. However, federal tax laws have increasingly imposed significant restrictions and limitations on the types and amounts of tax-exempt municipal securities that can be issued. In addition, such tax laws as the alternative minimum tax (AMT) provisions of the 1986 Tax Code and amendments to the Social Security Act enacted in 1983 reduced the tax exemption applicable to certain types of bonds and to certain taxpayers. The taxable municipal securities market that developed, in part, because of such federal tax limitations and restrictions is described later in this chapter, along with Build America Bonds, which are not exempt from federal income tax either.

The savings that the tax exemption affords to state and local issuers became obvious soon after the first federal income tax was initiated. Before 1913, interest rates on municipal securities were about the same as rates on corporate bonds, because neither was subject to federal income taxation. After 1913, the rates on tax-exempt municipal securities fell sharply relative to taxable corporate bond rates.

The Tax-Exempt/Taxable Yield Equivalent Formula

Investors in municipal bonds are willing to accept lower yields because they gain advantages from the tax exemption; the higher the investor's tax bracket, the greater the advantage. The standard way of demonstrating the relative advantages of tax-exempt bonds is represented by the tax-exempt versus taxable yield equivalent formula. The essential variable in computing equivalent yields is an investor's federal marginal tax rate. (Since federal income tax rates increase with additional dollars earned, the marginal tax rate is the rate that would be applied to any additional income earned.)

Marginal tax rates for 2010 are listed in Figure 2.2. For example, a married couple filing a joint return on a taxable income of $140,000 for the 2011 tax year would pay taxes at an effective rate of 28 percent on any additional income. For every additional $1,000 of taxable income they would have to pay an additional $280 in tax. Thus, this couple would have to earn only $720 in interest on a tax-exempt bond to do as well as they

Tax-Exempt/Taxable Yield Equivalents
2010 Tax Year

HOW TO USE THIS CHART
1. Find the appropriate return (single or joint).
2. Determine your tax bracket by locating the taxable income category that you fall into. Taxable income is income after appropriate exemptions and deductions are taken. (The table does not account for special provisions affecting federal tax rates, such as the Alternative Minimum Tax.)
3. The numbers in the column under your tax bracket give you the approximate taxable yield equivalent for each of the tax-exempt yields in the near left column. Example: If you are single and have a taxable income of $85,000 ($140,000 if married), you would fall into the 28% tax bracket. According to the table, you would need to earn 6.94% on a taxable security to match a 5% yield from a tax-exempt security.

		Taxable Income*				
Single return	$0–8,375	$8,376–34,000	$34,001–82,400	$82,401–171,850	$171,851–373,650	$373,651 & over
Joint return	0–$16,750	$16,751–68,000	$68,001–137,300	$137,301–209,250	$209,251–373,650	$373,651 & over
Tax Bracket	10%	15%	25%	28%	33%	35%
Tax-Exempt Yields	Taxable Yield Equivalents (%)					
1.0%	1.11	1.18	1.33	1.39	1.49	1.54
1.5%	1.67	1.76	2.00	2.08	2.24	2.31
2.0%	2.22	2.35	2.67	2.78	2.99	3.08
2.5%	2.78	2.94	3.33	3.47	3.73	3.85
3.0%	3.33	3.53	4.00	4.17	4.48	4.62
3.5%	3.89	4.12	4.67	4.86	5.22	5.38
4.0%	4.44	4.71	5.33	5.56	5.97	6.15
4.5%	5.00	5.29	6.00	6.25	6.72	6.92
5.0%	5.56	5.88	6.67	6.94	7.46	7.69
5.5%	6.11	6.47	7.33	7.64	8.21	8.46
6.0%	6.67	7.06	8.00	8.33	8.96	9.23
6.5%	7.22	7.65	8.67	9.03	9.70	10.00
7.0%	7.78	8.24	9.33	9.72	10.45	10.77
7.5%	8.33	8.82	10.00	10.42	11.19	11.54

FIGURE 2.2 Tax-Exempt/Taxable Equivalent Yield Rate (2010 tax year) *The income brackets to which the tax rates apply are adjusted annually for inflation. Those listed above are for 2010.
Source: Securities Industry and Financial Markets Association.

would if they earned $1,000 in interest on a taxable bond. The formula below calculates exactly what a taxable bond would have to yield in order to equal the yield earned on a tax-free municipal bond:

$$\frac{\text{Tax-free yield}}{100\%-\text{Marginal tax rate}} = \text{Taxable equivalent yield}$$

For the couple who earned $140,000 and bought a tax-exempt bond yielding 5 percent, the taxable yield equivalent was 6.94 percent, as follows:

$$\frac{5\%}{1-.28} = \frac{5\%}{.72} = 6.94\%$$

At the same time, an investor in the 35 percent marginal tax bracket would have had to earn 7.69 percent on a taxable bond to earn the net equivalent of earnings on a 5 percent municipal bond.

The Securities Industry and Financial Markets Association maintains a taxable equivalent yield calculator on its web site, www.investinginbonds .com. This calculator allows an investor to find the taxable equivalent yield of a tax-exempt bond by inputting his or her state, income, and tax filing status into a series of drop-down menus.

State Taxation of Municipal Bonds

The relative advantage of tax-exempt bonds can be even greater for an investor living in a state that imposes state and local income taxes, because, frequently, municipal bonds are exempt from these taxes as well. Many states exempt interest income only on bonds issued within their own boundaries. Other states do not exempt interest income on bonds issued in their own state. For example, in 2010, a married couple residing in New Jersey with a combined taxable income of $140,000 would be in the 28 percent federal tax bracket and would be subject to a state income tax of 6.37 percent. That is a total of 34.37 percent. Note, however, that state (and, if applicable, local) income tax payments are generally deductible on the federal tax return under current law. If this couple itemizes deductions, the effect of the state and local taxes must therefore be offset by the amount gained back from the deduction on the federal return. Thus, the total effective income tax rate for that individual is not 34.37 percent, but $28 + 6.37 \times (1 - 0.28)$, or 32.59 percent.

A 5 percent return on a municipal bond issued within the state for that couple, therefore, has the same after-tax benefit as a 7.42 percent taxable bond, since $7.42 = 5/(1 - .3259)$. Table 2.1 shows each state's taxation of municipal bonds for individuals.

Restrictions on Tax-Exempt Bond Issuance

The types of municipal securities, the purposes for which they may be issued, the taxes and other sources that may be pledged to their payment, and the manner in which such securities may be issued and sold are all subject to state and local law. Consequently, applicable state and local statutes must be carefully examined in connection with structuring and issuing municipal securities. In addition, as covered in Chapter 9, federal tax legislation significantly affects the manner in which, and the purposes for which, tax-exempt municipal securities may be issued. For example, the Tax Reform Act of 1984 and the Tax Reform Act of 1986 both curbed the issuance of

TABLE 2.1 State Taxation of Municipal Bonds for Individuals (2010)

State	State's Own Bonds	Other States' Bonds	U.S. Bonds
Alabama	Exempt	Taxable	Exempt
Alaska	Exempt	Exempt	Exempt
Arizona	Exempt	Taxable	Exempt
Arkansas	Exempt	Taxable	Exempt
California	Exempt	Taxable	Exempt
Colorado	Exempt	Taxable	Exempt
Connecticut	Taxable	Taxable	Taxable
Delaware	Exempt	Taxable	Exempt
District of Columbia	Exempt	Taxable	Exempt
Florida	Taxable	Taxable	Taxable
	(No personal or corporate income tax)		
Georgia	Exempt	Taxable	Exempt
Hawaii	Exempt	Taxable	Exempt
Idaho	Exempt	Taxable	Exempt
Illinois[1]	Taxable	Taxable	Exempt[1]
Indiana	Exempt	Exempt (prior to 2012)	Exempt
		Taxable (after 2011)	
Iowa[1]	Taxable	Taxable	Exempt
Kansas	Exempt	Taxable	Exempt
Kentucky	Exempt	Taxable	Exempt
Louisiana[2]	Exempt	Exempt (after 2005)	Exempt
Maine[2]	Exempt	Taxable	Exempt
Maryland	Exempt	Taxable	Exempt
Massachusetts	Exempt	Taxable	Taxable
Michigan	Exempt	Taxable	Exempt
Minnesota	Taxable	Taxable	Taxable
Mississippi	Exempt	Taxable	Exempt
Missouri	Exempt	Taxable	Exempt
Montana[1]	Taxable	Taxable	Taxable
Nebraska	Exempt	Taxable	Exempt
Nevada	(No personal or corporate income tax)		
New Hampshire	Exempt	Exempt	Exempt
New Jersey	Taxable	Taxable	Taxable
New Mexico	Exempt	Taxable	Exempt
New York	Taxable	Taxable	Taxable
North Carolina	Exempt	Taxable	Exempt
North Dakota	Exempt	Taxable	Exempt
Ohio[3]	Exempt	Exempt	Exempt
Oklahoma[1]	Taxable	Taxable	Exempt
Oregon	Exempt	Taxable	Exempt
Pennsylvania	Exempt	Exempt	Exempt

(continued)

TABLE 2.1 (*Continued*)

State	State's Own Bonds	Other States' Bonds	U.S. Bonds
Rhode Island	Exempt	Taxable	Exempt
South Carolina	Exempt	Taxable	Exempt
South Dakota	(No personal income tax)		
Tennessee	Taxable	Taxable	Taxable
Texas	Exempt	Exempt	Exempt
Utah	Taxable	Taxable	Taxable
Vermont	Exempt	Taxable	Exempt
Virginia[2]	Exempt	Taxable	Exempt
Washington	(No personal or corporate income tax)		
West Virginia[1,2]	Taxable	Taxable	Exempt
Wisconsin[1]	Taxable	Taxable	Exempt
Wyoming	(No personal or corporate income tax)		

[1]Income from certain specified obligations is exempt. Interest from all other obligations is taxable.

[2]Interest on obligations of federal authorities, commissions, or instrumentalities that is exempt for federal tax but not from state tax is taxable.

[3]Exempt, for both Ohio commercial activity tax and franchise tax purposes.

Source: © CCH INCORPORATED, a Wolters Kluwer Business. All Rights Reserved. Reprinted with permission.

bonds characterized as "private activity bonds." There are different limits, including volume caps by state, for certain housing and other private activity bonds. The 1986 Act also limited the number of times that an issuer can undertake certain refinancings of debt; for bonds issued after 1985, only one advance refunding transaction is permitted per specific issue.

Taxable Bonds and Alternative Minimum Tax Bonds

Certain types of municipal bonds are taxable, including Build America Bonds. Issuance of traditional, fully tax-exempt bonds in 2010 was only 63.6 percent of all municipal issuance as municipalities and investors embraced BABs and similar bonds, resulting in the further development of an already existing modest market for taxable municipal bonds that do not receive a federal subsidy on interest payments. Certain types of traditional municipal bonds are subject only to the *alternative minimum tax* (AMT). Table 2.2 shows that AMT bond issuance has fluctuated greatly, ranging from a low of 0.4 percent of total sales in 2009 to a high of 12.3 percent in 2000. The

TABLE 2.2 Issuance of Long-Term, Tax-Exempt, Taxable, and AMT Securities, 1996 to 2010

Year	Long-Term Issuance ($ billions)	Tax-Exempt Percentage of Long-Term	Taxable Percentage of Long-Term	AMT Percentage of Long-Term
1996	181.5	84.0	5.2	10.8
1997	214.1	83.6	5.7	10.7
1998	280.5	86.5	5.1	8.3
1999	219.5	83.6	6.3	10.1
2000	194.6	81.6	6.1	12.3
2001	284.5	85.1	5.2	9.7
2002	355.5	86.6	5.3	8.1
2003	378.5	83.3	10.6	6.1
2004	356.9	86.9	6.7	6.5
2005	406.4	86.4	6.2	7.4
2006	382.5	83.4	7.4	9.2
2007	424.5	84.5	6.7	8.8
2008	386.5	87.7	6.1	6.2
2009	406.8	78.9	20.7	0.4
2010	433.3	63.6	35.1	1.3

Note: AMT is alternative minimum tax.
Source: Thomson Reuters.

percentage of taxable municipal bonds ranged from 5.1 percent to 10.6 percent through 2008, but the advent of BABs pushed the taxable percentage up to 35.1 percent in 2010.

TYPES OF MUNICIPAL BONDS

The municipal market is recognized for the diverse purposes that the bonds finance and for the different security features that are offered to investors. Municipal bonds and municipal short-term securities are generally broken down into two major categories: general obligation bonds and revenue bonds.

The security for the *general obligation bonds* (GOs) is the general credit and the taxing power of the state or local government issuing the bonds. Most municipal governments depend largely on *ad valorem* (Latin meaning "to the value added"), or value-based, property taxes for their revenues. State governments, on the other hand, usually do not levy real estate taxes but rely mostly on sales and income taxes. The full faith and credit backing of a GO bond implies that all sources of revenue, unless specifically dedicated to other purposes, will be used to pay debt service on the bonds.

Revenue bonds are those that are generally issued to finance a specific revenue-generating project and, unless backed by a third-party guarantee, are usually secured solely by the revenues from that project. Revenue bonds have enabled state and local governments to finance a wide range of capital improvements. Income-generating bridges, airports, water and sewage treatment facilities, health-care facilities, and state and local housing projects, among others, have generally been financed by revenue bonds.

There are times when specific revenues of an enterprise are additionally backed by a general obligation pledge. These hybrid obligations are called *double-barreled bonds* because of the two pledges.

Other types of municipal securities that do not fall exactly into the general obligation or revenue bond categories are special tax bonds and moral obligation bonds. General obligation bonds, revenue bonds, and other types of municipal securities are discussed in greater detail in Chapter 3.

SHORT-TERM SECURITIES

State and local governments sometimes use short-term financing to bridge the gap between the time when expenses occur and when revenues become available from incoming tax revenues, grants, other revenue sources or new issues of bonds. Municipal short-term securities—often called *anticipation notes*—usually represent maturities of 13 months or less. Interest on notes is usually paid when they mature. Some municipalities, however, issue notes at a discount to their value at maturity, much like Treasury bills.

Notes

The issuance of short-term securities by state and local governments and the issuance of housing project notes represented a high percentage of all new issues in the early 1970s. After New York City's fiscal crisis in the 1970s, the use by state and local governments of short-term debt declined. Beginning in 1979, as interest rates rose and the issuance of *project notes* (short-term, tax-exempt securities issued to fund housing and urban renewal projects and secured by the project's revenue and the U.S. government) accelerated, short-term debt increased again. With the elimination of project notes by Congress in 1984, together with a decline in intermediate- and long-term interest rates, the rapid rise of overall long-term financing, and increased use of alternative forms of financing such as variable-rate demand bonds, there

TABLE 2.3 Short-Term Issuance as Percentage of
All-New Municipal Issuance, 1990 to 2010

Year	Short-Term Issuance ($ billions)	Percentage Short-Term of Total Issuance (%)
1990	34.8	21.6
1991	44.4	20.7
1992	43.0	15.6
1993	47.5	14.1
1994	40.4	19.9
1995	38.4	19.8
1996	41.7	18.7
1997	46.4	17.8
1998	34.7	11.0
1999	36.7	14.3
2000	41.2	17.5
2001	56.9	16.7
2002	72.4	16.9
2003	69.8	15.6
2004	56.9	13.8
2005	50.5	11.0
2006	44.0	10.3
2007	57.9	12.0
2008	60.8	13.6
2009	64.7	13.7
2010	65.3	13.1

Source: Thomson Reuters.

was a reduction in the percentage of short-term municipal securities. The issuance of short-term securities now tends to fluctuate with the economic cycle. In 2010, short-term securities accounted for 13.1 percent of all new issues. Table 2.3 shows note issuance as a percentage of the total new issuance market from 1990 to 2010.

State and local governments frequently issue the following types of notes:

- *Tax anticipation notes.* Known in the market as TANs, they are issued in anticipation of tax receipts (usually property taxes) and are payable from those receipts.
- *Revenue anticipation notes.* RANs are issued in anticipation of other sources of future revenue, typically either from state or federal sources.

Notes issued in anticipation of both tax receipts and other revenues are known as TRANs.

■ *Bond anticipation notes.* BANs provide a means of interim financing in anticipation of a future bond offering. Unless they are otherwise secured, they are dependent on the local government's ability to issue those bonds and are viewed as the least secure type of note.

■ *Grant anticipation notes.* GANs are issued in anticipation of grants and are payable when those grants are received. Most grants come from the federal government, such as federal highway grants.

■ *General obligation notes.* Some state and local governments issue notes for a variety of purposes, backed by the full credit of the issuer.

Tax-Exempt Commercial Paper

Commercial paper is a short-term promissory note issued for periods up to 270 days, with maturities commonly at 30, 60, and 90 days. It is often used for the same purposes as BANs, TANs, RANs, and general obligation notes. Its advantage is that it offers greater flexibility in both setting maturities and determining rates. Bank lines or letters of credit are often used to provide backup liquidity for maturing commercial paper. The strongest issuers of commercial paper, such as universities with large endowments, have financial assets substantial enough to enable them to provide their own backup liquidity without having to use an outside source.

Variable-Rate Demand Obligations

Before 1980, the phrase *short-term municipal* referred only to notes and short-term municipal bonds. However, the highly dynamic interest rate movements of the late 1970s and early 1980s and the emergence and growth of tax-exempt money market funds fostered one of the most significant developments in the tax-exempt market during that period: a much broader class of short-term municipal securities. These short-term municipal securities were investment vehicles that evolved to meet issuer and investor concerns about the effect of interest rates. Investors were concerned about fluctuations in the value of their portfolios while issuers were concerned about the high cost of borrowing.

These short-term municipals, generically known as demand obligations or *variable-rate demand obligations* (VRDOs), are bonds with traditional, long-dated nominal maturities that also have short-term demand features. VRDOs offer investors the assurance of preservation of principal and offer issuers a means of borrowing at a significantly lower rate, at least in theory.

TABLE 2.4 Variable-Rate Demand Obligations (VRDO) Issuance as a Percentage of the Long-Term Market, 1990 to 2010

Year	VRDO Issuance ($ billions)	VRDO as Percentage of Total Issuance (%)
1990	12.6	10.0
1991	12.0	7.1
1992	15.1	6.5
1993	17.8	6.1
1994	15.8	9.8
1995	18.4	11.8
1996	18.1	10.0
1997	25.7	12.0
1998	23.8	8.5
1999	23.2	10.6
2000	35.9	18.5
2001	37.5	13.2
2002	47.5	13.4
2003	45.6	12.0
2004	47.0	13.2
2005	61.0	15.0
2006	54.5	14.3
2007	49.3	11.6
2008	115.7	29.9
2009	31.4	7.7
2010	24.8	5.7

Source: Thomson Reuters.

VRDO issuance plummeted after the 2008 financial crisis, when banks came under pressure to boost their regulatory capital and became less willing or able to provide low margin standby liquidity facilities. Table 2.4 shows the volume of VRDO issuance over the past 21 years. VRDOs' market share is calculated as a percentage only of the long-term market because they have a nominal long-term maturity.

When issuing VRDOs, municipal issuers sell long-term bonds that have yields determined as if they were short-term notes. The reason that the yields are like those of short-term notes is that the holders of the bonds are entitled to demand repurchase of their bonds at par, plus accrued interest, on a regular basis. From a bondholder's point of view, a bond subject to such repurchase is similar to a bond that matures on the date the bondholder is entitled to demand purchase. Therefore, a bond entitling the holder to demand payment every seven days carries a yield close to if it matured in a week. From the issuers' point of view, this structure offers flexibility by enabling them to take advantage of rates at the short end of the yield curve without constantly having to reissue and reauthorize the debt.

For most of these issues, the coupon rate may change only at a point when the holder can demand payment. Since this market evolved over several years, various names, such as "floaters," "lower floaters," or "put" bonds, may all refer to the same security structure. As the market in these securities emerged, certain structures have become more common than others. Nevertheless, the structure of these transactions typically has four primary components, as follows.

1. *Demand feature.* The demand feature of the VRDO is the key element that allows for the short-term interest rate. Although bonds with daily, weekly, or monthly demand periods are the most common, some bonds have quarterly, semiannual, or annual demand periods. To exercise the demand feature, the VRDO holder must give notice to a tender agent in the transaction a specified number of days prior to the date that the bond will be tendered for purchase at a price of par plus accrued interest. The tender agent then notifies the *remarketing agent* (generally a municipal bond dealer), which will use its best efforts to sell the tendered bonds to another purchaser. Since most VRDOs are usually sold through a negotiated sale, the remarketing agent is most often one of the municipal bond dealers that managed the financing.

2. *Variable interest rate.* VRDOs reset the interest rate periodically. VRDO holders can exercise the demand right at any time and will receive their money back after the demand interval. As a general rule, each time the interest rate is reset, holders are allowed to tender their bonds for par purchase. The opposite, however, is not true; that is, the interest rate reset may be less frequent than the demand for payment. The remarketing agent typically determines the new interest rate based upon prevailing short-term market conditions and a determination of what yield is necessary to place all the VRDOs tendered by existing bondholders.

3. *Liquidity and/or credit support.* Because VRDOs allow the holder to demand purchase upon specified notice, the issuer must have some form of liquidity or credit support in order to meet a demand. The most common forms of liquidity support are letters of credit (LOCs), lines of credit, or standby purchase agreements provided by financial institutions. There are conditions under which the bank will not be obliged to advance funds in lines of credit and in standby purchase agreements. Letters of credit, which are generally irrevocable, fully support the bond and there are usually no conditions under which the bank will not honor draws for liquidity or credit needs. As a practical matter, in normal market

conditions, offers by VRDO holders demanding payment are satisfied from the remarketing of the security to new buyers through the efforts of the remarketing agent. However, if a holder demands payment and no new purchasers can be arranged by the remarketing agent, then the liquidity support is available to meet the demand. The terms of LOCs are usually shorter than the maturities of VRDOs, necessitating that issuers renew their LOCS periodically over the life of the bonds. Issuers with particularly strong credit may use their own financial resources to provide liquidity. This is called *self-liquidity*.

4. *Conversion to a fixed rate.* Most VRDOs allow the issuer to convert the security to a fixed interest rate structure under specified conditions and procedures. If, for example, long-term interest rates decline significantly, then the issuer may want to lock in a fixed rate of interest while rates are favorable. In order to convert a VRDO to a fixed-rate structure, the trustee notifies all holders of the issuer's intent. The notice generally requires that the holders tender their VRDOs as of the specified fixed-rate date. This mandatory tender requirement serves to protect the bondholder against a change in the security of the issue since, commonly, the liquidity or credit support expires at conversion.

Issuers often prefer the certainty of a fixed interest rate to floating rate financing, so many VRDO issuers choose to enter into interest rate swap agreements under which they agree to pay a fixed interest rate to a major bank or securities dealer that effectively assumed their floating rate payment obligation. Through much of the 2000s, the net cost to an issuer of a VRDO and an interest rate swap was often much lower than the issuer could have achieved if it had issued long-term fixed rate bonds at the outset.

In late 2008, a severe financial crisis caused some investors to lose confidence in certain banks that backed VRDOs under LOC and similar facilities. At the same time, many bond insurers who provided credit enhancement on VRDOs were downgraded by credit rating agencies. This hampered remarketing efforts and resulted in many VRDOs being put to banks. This often triggered automatic conversion of VRDOs into fixed rate bonds at punitive interest rates or began a process leading to acceleration of the bonds' maturity dates. In practice, many issuers whose bonds remained with banks chose to refinance by issuing fixed rate bonds at market rates and using the proceeds to pay off the VRDOs. Either way, some of those issuers whose bonds were not successfully remarketed still had to honor their obligations under interest rate swaps they no longer needed at a time when short-term interest rates—the payments they received from the swap counterparty—had fallen to historic lows. The combination imposed higher than expected costs on some issuers just as revenues came under pressure from a weak economy and a decline in house prices. In some cases, downgrades of LOC banks led to rates on VRDOs that diverged from the index-based payments received on swap contracts. Some issuers faced an unpalatable choice: They could either incur a relatively high interest cost over the remaining life of the swap, or make a one-time cash payment to terminate the swap contract at its market value.

Since the financial crisis of 2008 abated, VRDO issuers with related outstanding swaps have managed through their circumstances in various ways. For some, their VRDOs and related swaps are performing as designed. Others refinanced out of their existing transactions into fixed-rate or other bonds. Still others have replaced their outstanding VRDOs with bank loans or similar structures while in many cases maintaining their swaps against the new financing.

Dutch Auction Securities (Auction Rate Securities)

Dutch auction securities, or auction-rate securities (ARS), are another form of a variable rate bond. The major difference between a traditional VRDO and a Dutch auction security is that a VRDO generally requires a liquidity facility, while a Dutch auction security does not. The liquidity for the ARS is created through the Dutch auction procedure.

At a Dutch auction, the rate is set at the lowest interest rate at which buyers are willing to purchase all of the securities of potential sellers. The current holder of the security can submit one of several orders to an auction agent. A "hold at any" bid indicates the ARS holder will hold the existing position regardless of the new interest rate. A "hold at rate" bid signals the investor will hold their securities at a specified minimum rate. If the clearing rate is lower than the specified rate, the holder is obligated to sell the securities they hold. If the investor wishes to "sell" securities, they request to sell the existing position regardless of the interest rate set at the auction.

Investors wishing to "buy" bonds specify the volume, typically in denominations of $25,000, they wish to purchase at the bid rate, or the interest rate payable on the securities which they are willing to accept. The auction agent, typically a third-party bank selected by the ARS issuer, collects all bids and ranks them from the lowest to the highest minimum bid rate. If there are any sell orders, the auction agent then matches bids to purchase with the minimum bid rate and successively higher rates until all sell orders are filled. The lowest bid rate at which all securities can be sold at par establishes the interest rate, or the clearing rate. The clearing rate is the interest rate paid on the entire issue until the next auction, often 35 days. If not enough bids are received (a failed auction), the rate is set by a formula disclosed in the official statement that determines the penalty rate.

ARS issuers do not pay for a credit facility in the same way as VRDOs. In addition, there is no risk that the liquidity facility will be downgraded, because there is no external liquidity facility. There is also no renewal of and repricing risk of any external bank line or letter of credit.

The market for ARS collapsed in 2008 after a series of failed auctions, sparked by downgrades of bond insurers, which left some issuers burdened with high penalty interest rates. Like VRDO issuers, some also faced the issue of unwinding interest rate swaps associated with their outstanding ARS. Although no new ARS have been issued since the 2008 financial crisis, some remain outstanding. Some auctions continue to function as designed, but many have failed perpetually since the crisis. For most issuers with failed ARS outstanding, the "penalty" rate is very low, usually linked to a short-term interest rate index.

Tender Option Bonds

Tender option bonds (TOBs) are considered a secondary derivative product, meaning that they are not issued directly by a governmental issuer. The TOB structure evolved in the early 1990s as a way for sophisticated investors (primarily closed-end funds at first, then later banks and hedge funds as well) to finance municipal bond portfolios while preserving the tax exemption on the interest received. They also satisfied demand from municipal money market mutual funds for short-term variable rate securities.

In its simplest form, a trust, usually sponsored by a dealer, hedge fund or other investor, acquires fixed rate, long-term municipal bonds. The trust finances the purchase by issuing two variable rate bonds backed by cash flow from the underlying portfolio, a floating rate certificate and an inverse floating rate certificate. The floater certificates pay a variable rate of interest based on short-term money market rates, while the inverse floaters (or residual certificates) pay a variable rate equal to the fixed coupon (derived from the underlying bond portfolio) minus the payments on the floater certificates.

For example, if the trust acquires $100 million worth of bonds with an average coupon of 5.0 percent, the trust may issue $75 million of floater certificates and $25 million of inverse floaters.

If the municipal money market interest rate is 1 percent, the annual interest of $5 million would be divided as follows:

$750,000 to the floater certificates (1 percent of $75 million)

$4,250,000 to the inverse floaters (an effective rate of 17 percent on $25 million, calculated as $[100 \div 25] = 4 \times$ the fixed coupon rate minus $[75 \div 25] = 3 \times$ the floater certificate rate]

Municipal money market funds typically buy the floater certificates, while the transaction sponsor may retain the inverse floaters or sell them to hedge funds, closed-end funds, and dealers interested in leveraged exposure to municipal bonds. The amount of leverage in the structure varies according to the proportion of floaters and inverse floaters issued.

From a tax perspective, the trust is a pass-through conduit that has no effect on the cash flows. The tax-exempt interest on the underlying bond portfolio remains the same, it is merely apportioned between the floater and inverse floaters.

The tender option provides the holder of the floating rate certificate a put option at par—typically on any day upon seven days' notice. The tender option shortens the duration of the certificate and allows it to qualify as an eligible security under the SEC's Rule 2a-7—the regulatory framework that governs money market funds. The put option is supported by a liquidity facility provided by a commercial bank (similar to the facilities behind a VRDO). The holder's right to tender is not irrevocable, but is conditioned on several factors, including the bond ratings, tax status, bankruptcy of the issuer, and payment performance of the bond, in order to preserve the tax exemption on interest payments coming from the trust. The interest rate is typically reset every seven days.

The use of TOBs expanded dramatically between 2000 and 2007. Market participants estimate that up to $500 billion of municipal bonds were in these vehicles at the peak of the market. In effect, the structure brought new capital into the market from sources that were not otherwise buyers of municipal bonds.

Most of underlying bonds in TOBs were insured, and the banks that provided standby liquidity facilities had the right to terminate their credit lines if the bond credit ratings fell below a threshold level. When most monoline insurance companies were downgraded to below investment grade in the wake of the 2008 crisis, the liquidity support for TOBs evaporated and the trusts had to sell the underlying bonds into an already weak market. Holders of the inverse floaters suffered losses as a result.

Inverse floater holders often hedged their interest rate exposure using LIBOR-related instruments, which had historically exhibited a relatively high correlation to long-term municipal bond rates. During the credit crisis of 2008, that relationship broke down: Long-term municipal interest rates rose while LIBOR fell sharply, compounding the pain for investors, who suffered losses on both sides of their purportedly hedged positions. The volume of TOBs outstanding dropped precipitously in late 2008 through early 2009 and stabilized at a fraction of the peak level.

OTHER CHARACTERISTICS OF MUNICIPAL BONDS

Other important features and practices distinguish municipal securities from other kinds of securities. A summary of the most important of them follows.

Size of the Primary and Secondary Markets

The municipal securities primary market differs from other fixed income markets in that it has many smaller issues. Table 2.5 shows the number of bond issues in 2010 with par amounts less than and more than $10 million. There were 6,871 issues with par amounts less than $10 million, but this accounted for only $24.7 billion, or 6 percent of the total new issue volume for the year.

The municipal secondary market, or after market, is distinct from other secondary markets in several important ways. The vast majority of trading in municipal securities is done over the counter, and many trades are still made on a so-called dealer basis. That is, the dealers who trade municipal securities for investors own, if only temporarily, the securities they buy from one investor and sell to another or keep for their own inventory. The difference between the price for which they can sell the securities and the price at which they bought them is known as the spread.

The traditional method of trading securities is changing as the market takes advantage of technology, particularly for retail investors. Online electronic trading systems operate as centralized trading platforms, which helps to reduce costs and improve price transparency. Investors still rely on dealers to handle most of their orders, however.

TABLE 2.5 Long-Term Issue Size, 2010

Par Amount	Total Dollar Amount ($ billions)	Percentage of New-Issue Volume (%)	Number of Issues	Percentage of New Issues (%)
Less than $10,000,000	30	7	8,200	60
$10,000,000 and over	401	93	5,389	40
Total	431	100	13,589	100

Note: Total principal amount and number of issues may differ from their actual sums due to database allocation of data.
Source: Thomson Reuters.

The municipal secondary market is also different from other markets because of the sheer number and variety of issues. Trading is most active in the period shortly after issuance, but after a few weeks the bonds become seasoned and trading tapers off. Thereafter, activity in any individual municipal issue may be infrequent, particularly among the smaller serial bond maturities.

Legal Opinion

In order to be marketable, municipal bonds must be accompanied by a legal opinion, which addresses two principal areas: first, that the bonds are legal and binding obligations of the issuer under applicable state and local laws; and second, that the interest on the bonds is exempt under applicable federal and state income tax laws, or, in the case of Build America Bonds, that the bonds qualify for the 35 percent federal subsidy on interest payments.

The opinion requirement grew out of widespread defaults in the late nineteenth century on municipal bonds that had been issued to finance railroad construction. When such defaults occurred, some issuers successfully avoided their payment obligation on the basis that the bonds had not been duly authorized or properly issued under applicable laws. In order to restore marketplace confidence, issuers and underwriters began the practice of obtaining bond counsel opinions at the time bonds were initially issued. The increased complexity of financial structures and of federal tax restrictions has further resulted in a broadening of the traditional bond counsel role.

Official Statement

Although municipal securities are exempt from SEC registration requirements, an offering document, known as an official statement, is almost always prepared in connection with the initial (or primary) offering of municipal securities. This is the municipal market counterpart of a corporate prospectus, but with significant differences. Underwriters are required by MSRB Rule G-32 to make official statements, if prepared for a new issue of municipal securities, available to each investor in those securities. Moreover, as discussed in Chapter 9, SEC Rule 15c2-12 requires underwriters of a municipal securities offering $1 million or more in aggregate principal amount to obtain and review an official statement before bidding on or purchasing the offering, unless the offering is exempt from the requirements of the Rule. Although the Rule applies directly to underwriters, its effect is to require issuers seeking access to the public securities market to provide official statements in connection with the primary offering of municipal securities. Without such statements, underwriters would not be able to comply with the Rule. In addition, MSRB Rule G-36 requires underwriters to send copies of official statements to the MSRB.

Continuing Disclosure

The SEC-approved amendments to Rule 15c2-12 adopted in November 1994 (effective generally for issues sold after July 3, 1995) require an underwriter to determine, as a condition to underwriting a new issue of municipal securities subject to the Rule, that the issuer or one or more persons obligated with respect to payment of debt service on the issue has executed a Continuing Disclosure Agreement (CDA), a contractual commitment to provide ongoing disclosure with respect to the issue. The underwriter must also have a reasonable basis to believe that the issuer will comply with the CDA. Establishing a reasonable basis involves, among other issues, determining whether the issuer is in compliance with its previous CDAs, if any, over the last five years. The requirements have been updated from time to time, but in general, obligated persons with more than $10,000,000 of nonexempt securities outstanding must commit to the annual updating of financial information and operating data of the type included in the official statement for the primary offering and to provide notice of 14 specified events. More limited requirements apply if no obligated person with respect to an issue has more than $10,000,000 of nonexempt securities outstanding or if the new issue has a maturity that does not exceed nine months. The continuing disclosure requirement is the municipal securities market counterpart of the reporting requirement imposed on corporations subject to the Securities Exchange Act of 1934. Continuing disclosure requirements are discussed in greater detail in Chapter 9.

Serial and Term Bonds

Unlike most other types of fixed-income securities, municipal bond issues traditionally include serial bonds, which typically include as many as 20 or more different maturities. This structure helps the issuer to spread out debt service and stay within the legal restrictions of those states that require a bond issue to contain substantially equal annual debt service payments or maturities. Typically, a certain number of bonds fall due each year from, say, 1 to 20 years from their date of issue. Generally, the longer the maturity, the higher will be the interest rate offered. A representative maturity service schedule for $1,250,000,000 State of California Various Purpose General Obligation Bonds is shown in Figure 3.1.

In this example, serial bonds and term bonds are included in the issue. The serial bonds mature from November 1, 2011, to November 1, 2030.

The three term bonds are as follows: $55,000,000 bonds with a 5.375 percent coupon due November 1, 2035; $80,000,000 bonds with a 5.5 percent coupon due November 1, 2035; and $400,000,000 bonds with a 5.75 percent coupon due November 1, 2040. Unlike serial bonds, term bonds are due at only one maturity. They usually carry a sinking fund requirement with reserves set aside by the issuer to redeem term bonds to provide for their retirement. Except for being tax exempt, term bonds are very similar to traditional corporate debt. Municipal issues can include one or several term bonds.

Zero-Coupon Bonds

Term bonds that pay no periodic interest and have a coupon rate of zero interest are known as *zero-coupon bonds*. They are sold and purchased at a deep discount, and no interest is paid to the investor on a semiannual basis. Instead, at maturity, an amount equal to the principal invested plus the interest earned, compounded semiannually at the stated yield, is paid. This amount is usually the stated par value of the bonds. For example, a bond with a face amount of $20,000, maturing in 20 years, may be purchased for roughly $6,757 to yield 5.5 percent. At the end of the 20 years, the investor will receive $20,000. The difference between $20,000 and $6,757 represents the interest accrued over the life of the bond. The interest compounds at 5.5 percent until the bond matures as shown in Table 2.6.

Convertible-coupon bonds are a variation of zero-coupon bonds. They start out as zeros (albeit not with as deep a discount) and accrete interest for a number of years. Then they convert to traditional, semiannual, interest-bearing bonds until their final maturity. These bonds are aimed at investors who want both growth and income from their bonds at different times in their investment horizon (for example, parents saving for a child's college tuition).

TABLE 2.6   Estimated Future Value of a 20-Year, 5.5 Percent Zero-Coupon Municipal Bond Purchased for $6,757.04 on January 1, 2010

Year	Value ($)
2015	8,862.88
2020	11,625.01
2025	15,247.96
2030	20,000.00

Source: Securities Industry and Financial Markets Association.

Another variation of zero-coupon bonds is *stripped bonds*. Municipal bonds that pay interest semiannually can be stripped (that is, separated) into the corpus, or principal and the coupons, or interest. The coupons' cash flow, which is all the interest payments due over the life of the bond, is repackaged and sold to investors interested in current income while the stripped municipal bond is sold as a zero-coupon security with maturities ranging from six months to 30 years. Stripped municipals are also issued at a deep discount.

Call Provisions

A standard feature of many tax-exempt issues are call provisions, which give the issuer the option to retire all or a portion of the bonds before the stated maturity date and at a set price—usually at a premium to par (or to the accreted value of a zero coupon bond). The call option is a benefit to the issuer, which gains the flexibility to retire an outstanding bond issue prior to its stated maturity date and thus reduce debt costs. If interest rates have fallen since the original bond offering, the issuer can refund the older, high-interest issue and offer a new issue at lower rates. The call provisions are described in the bond resolution and official statement. Table 2.7 shows the redemption features of the State of California issue.

An *optional* call allows the issuer to redeem bonds, usually starting on a certain date after the date of issue. A series of call dates are specified for a period after this first call date. If the bonds are to be called on the first call date at a premium to par, bonds called on subsequent call dates will generally be redeemed at descending prices. For example, bonds might be callable 10 years from the date of issue at, say, 101 percent of par. In the 11th year, they would be callable at a lower price, and at later dates at prices declining to par. The first call date and the premium are determined by issuers to maximize their own flexibility and to maximize the bond's marketability. This applies to all types of calls.

A *mandatory* call requires the issuer to retire bonds before their stated maturity date. In the example of the State of California, each term bond has its own mandatory redemption schedule. Specific amounts, set out in the offering documents, are called, in this case, at par. Sinking funds can be used to help the issuer manage these mandatory call cash flows.

Sinking funds are reserves set aside yearly by the issuer to redeem term bonds over a specified period prior to the stated maturity date. Just as serial maturities help issuers spread their financial charges evenly, so do sinking funds help even out payments on term bonds. Instead of paying off the entire issue at maturity, the issuer pays a set amount annually into a sinking fund from which bonds are redeemed on a set schedule. Sinking funds, therefore, add a measure of security to the bonds.

TABLE 2.7 Sample Redemption Features

Redemption

Optional Redemption

The bonds maturing on or after November 1, 2021, are subject to optional redemption prior to their respective stated maturity dates, in whole or in part, in such order of maturity as may be designated by the State Treasurer and by lot within any maturity, on any date on or after November 1, 2020, at a redemption price equal to 100% of the principal amount thereof to be redeemed, plus accrued interest to the date fixed for redemption.

Sinking Fund Redemption

The bonds maturing on November 1, 2035, and bearing interest at 5.375% are subject to redemption prior to their stated maturity date, in part, by lot, from sinking fund payments made by the State, at a redemption price of 100% of the principal amount thereof plus accrued interest to the sinking fund payment date fixed for redemption, on November 1 of the years, and in the amounts, designated below:

Sinking Fund Payment Date (November 1)	Principal Amount Redeemed
2031	$11,000,000
2032	11,000,000
2033	11,000,000
2034	11,000,000
2035*	11,000,000

The bonds maturing on November 1, 2035, and bearing interest at 5.5% are subject to redemption prior to their stated maturity date, in part, by lot, from sinking fund payments made by the State, at a redemption price of 100% of the principal amount thereof plus accrued interest to the sinking fund payment date fixed for redemption, on November 1 of the years, and in the amounts, designated below:

Sinking Fund Payment Date (November 1)	Principal Amount Redeemed
2031	$16,000,000
2032	16,000,000
2033	16,000,000
2034	16,000,000
2035*	16,000,000

TABLE 2.7   (*Continued*)

The bonds maturing on November 1, 2040, are subject to redemption prior to their stated maturity date, in part, by lot, from sinking fund payments made by the State, at a redemption price of 100% of the principal amount thereof plus accrued interest to the sinking fund payment date fixed for redemption, on November 1 of the years, and in the amounts, designated below:

Sinking Fund Payment Date (November 1)	Principal Amount Redeemed
2036	$80,000,000
2037	80,000,000
2038	80,000,000
2039	80,000,000
2040*	80,000,000

If one or more maturities of the bonds subject to sinking fund redemption are called for optional redemption in part (see Optional Redemption above), the remaining sinking fund installments for the term bonds of such maturity or maturities shall be adjusted as determined by the State Treasurer.

---

*Maturity Date.
Source: $1,250,000,000 State of California General Obligation Bonds, Official Statement Dated December 1, 2010.

Sinking fund retirements can be optional or mandatory. A provision might require or permit the issuer to redeem a certain principal amount of bonds beginning in 10 years, or to buy bonds in that principal amount in the open market. If the bonds are redeemed, the price is always at par or higher, though sometimes the bonds can be bought below par in the open market. If interest rates have risen over the period, creating a downward pressure on bond prices, the possibility of early redemption by operations of the sinking fund will tend to keep the price of the bonds up. On the other hand, if falling interest rates tend to push prices above par, the sinking fund provisions can keep a lid on prices. The bonds to be retired are usually chosen at random, by lot. The procedure is spelled out clearly in the official statement.

A *super sinker* is a fund that functions much like a conventional sinking fund. Super sinkers are attached to single-family mortgage revenue bond issues. These bonds have a specifically identified maturity date, but all mortgage prepayments are applied to the fund so that bonds can be retired before maturity. Such bonds typically carry a long-term maturity date (20 to 30 years, for example) but have a much shorter actual life (usually between four and six years), depending on the issuer's prepayment expectations.

Changes have evolved in call features to accommodate the needs of particular types of bond issues. For example, single-family housing revenue bonds typically contain a provision allowing the issuer to call the bonds at par at any time, using funds from unexpended bond proceeds or prepayments. This provision clearly benefits the issuer. If all the mortgage money is not loaned to mortgagees (perhaps because the interest rate was not competitive with that of less restrictive, conventional financing or because there were fewer mortgage applicants than predicted), the bonds can be called at par in as little as one year from date of issue. Also, if considerable mortgage prepayments are made, owing to a fall in conventional mortgage rates, a par call can be made at any time. Healthcare issuers have provisions in their documents that allow a call at any time if there are changes in their ownership that make outstanding bond covenants onerous.

Even if an issue carries conventional call features such as the 10-year optional call protection, however, the potential for capital gains is limited. Further, if the bonds are called, the investor is usually left with the principal to be reinvested at a lower interest rate. A yield to call, therefore, is commonly computed for callable bonds, especially those selling at a premium. It is simply the yield to maturity calculated to the call price and first call date. When buying and selling these bonds, dealers will customarily tell investors both the yield to call and the yield to maturity. The MSRB has adopted a rule requiring in a transaction effected on a yield basis that the dollar price be calculated to the lower of price to call or price to maturity and be disclosed in confirmations of transactions to investors and other dealers.

Bearer Bonds versus Registered Bonds

Under federal tax laws enacted in 1982 and with limited exceptions, all municipal bonds issued on and after July 1, 1983, must be registered as to principal and interest. Investors who purchase a fully registered bond will receive the interest payments, as well as the principal when due, without having to clip paper coupons. Until 1982, it was traditional for most municipalities to issue physical bonds, which are negotiable by anyone who holds them and can prove ownership. Attached to bearer bonds are coupons representing interest due, which the bondholder must clip and deposit in a bank for collection from the issuer's paying agent. Only a handful of bearer bonds remain outstanding and available in the secondary market.

The use of registered bonds led to the development of *book-entry* securities for municipals patterned after the way the U.S. government securities market operate. With book-entry, issuers deposit a single global certificate for each maturity of an issue at a central clearinghouse, the Depository Trust & Clearing Corporation (DTCC). Ownership positions and transactions in each security, including purchases, sales, and interest or principal payments, are initially reflected in DTCC's records and thereafter in the records of thousands of participating banks and brokers nationwide. The investor does not receive a physical certificate representing bond ownership, as all records are kept electronically. New issues in 2004 and every year thereafter have been in book-entry form only.

Collecting the Interest

As stated previously, interest on fixed-rate municipal bonds is generally paid semiannually, usually on the 1st or 15th of the designated month. Holders of book-entry bonds and registered bonds receive their interest payments automatically. Holders of bearer bonds must clip each coupon, which is numbered and dated, and present it to the issuer (usually to a bank that serves as the paying agent) in order to receive the interest.

The bondholder is entitled to accrued interest, beginning at a specified date on the bonds, known as the *dated date*, although the bonds are often actually sold or delivered at a different date. A so-called short coupon results when the time between the dated date and the first coupon date is less than six months. A long coupon results when the first coupon date is more than six months away from the dated date.

Trading Plus Accrued Interest

Because most trading of municipal bonds takes place between interest payment dates, it is necessary to allocate interest between buyers and sellers. The investor who sells bonds is entitled to the interest due since the last interest payment date. The convention in the industry is that the buyer of the bonds must pay the seller any interest due when the bonds are purchased. If the settlement date for an investor's bond sale is March 1, for example, and the last coupon date was January 1, the seller is entitled to two months' interest from the buyer. Municipal bonds, then, trade *plus accrued interest*. That is, the interest due is added to the price of the bonds. The buyer, in turn, will collect and keep the full six months of interest due on the next interest payment date.

CHAPTER **3**

The Issuers

INTRODUCTION

The history of municipal debt predates that of corporate debt by several centuries: During the Renaissance, Italian city-states borrowed money from the major merchant banking families. Although borrowing by some American cities dates back to the seventeenth century, careful records of U.S. municipal bond issues were begun only in the early 1800s. The first officially recorded municipal bond was a general obligation bond issued by New York City for a canal in 1812. By the 1840s, many U.S. cities were in the debt market, and in 1843 cities had about $25 million in outstanding debt. The following two decades of rapid urban development saw a correspondingly explosive growth in municipal debt, which financed both urban improvements and a burgeoning system of free public education.

For a few years after the Civil War, a great deal of local debt was issued to build railroads. Because railroads were private corporations, these bond issues were similar to today's industrial revenue bonds. In 1873, excessive construction costs on one of the largest transcontinental railroads, the Northern Pacific, closed down its access to new capital. The country's largest bank, which was owned by the same investor as Northern Pacific, collapsed because of this, as did smaller firms and the stock market. The Panic of 1873 and the several years of depression that followed put an abrupt, if temporary, halt to the rapid growth of municipal debt. In response to the widespread defaults that jolted the municipal bond market of the day, new state statutes were passed that restricted the issuance of local debt. Some states even wrote these restrictions into their constitutions. The legality of the railroad bonds was widely challenged, giving rise to the market-wide demand that an opinion of qualified bond counsel accompany each new issue.

Once the U.S. economy started to move forward again, municipal debt resumed its momentum, which it maintained well into the twentieth century. The Great Depression of the 1930s halted its growth, although defaults were not as severe as in the 1870s. The amount of municipal debt outstanding then fell during World War II as resources were devoted to the war effort. After the war, municipal debt burst into a new period of rapid growth for an ever-increasing variety of uses. Just after World War II, state and local debt was $145 per capita ($1,568 in 2006 dollars). By 2006, the latest available U.S. Census data, state debt was $2,915 per capita and local debt was $4,451 per capita. Federal debt was $28,360 per capita at the end of 2006 and has increased substantially since then.

In addition to the 50 states and their local governments (including cities, counties, villages, and school districts), the District of Columbia and U.S. territories and possessions (American Samoa, the Commonwealth of Puerto Rico, Guam, the Northern Mariana Islands, and the U.S. Virgin Islands) can and do issue municipal bonds. Another important category of municipal bond issuers includes authorities and special districts, which continue to grow in number and variety.

AUTHORITIES AND SPECIAL DISTRICTS

In the early part of the twentieth century, state and local governments began to create debt-issuing entities called *authorities* and *special districts*. Sometimes they were formed to serve a geographic area that encompassed or crossed several political boundaries; sometimes they were formed in order to raise money for a single project whose purpose and use were not necessarily limited to one state, county, or city. Two prominent early authorities were the Port of New York Authority, formed in 1921 and renamed Port Authority of New York and New Jersey in 1972, and the Triborough Bridge Authority (now the Triborough Bridge and Tunnel Authority), formed in 1933.

Today, authorities and special districts of all kinds are found across the country. The majority of states, for example, have housing authorities, which issue bonds. In addition, special district bonds are commonly issued to finance water, sewer, and utility services where user charges are involved. Indeed, bond-issuing authorities have been created to finance and construct a wide variety of public projects: surface transportation facilities including toll and non-toll roads; airports, docking facilities, and mass-transit systems; government-owned sports arenas and convention centers; resource-recovery systems; educational facilities; and hospitals.

The U.S. Bureau of the Census categorizes the nation's governmental units into seven groups. According to census figures for 2007, there were 89,527 units of government. Table 3.1 shows the distribution of governmental units in five-year increments from 1987 through 2007.

The 89,476 local governments reported in 2007 were 1,951 more than in 2002, an overall increase of 2.2 percent. Most of the increase was in

TABLE 3.1 Type of Governmental Unit

	1987	1992	1997	2002	2007
U.S. government	1	1	1	1	1
State governments	50	50	50	50	50
County	3,042	3,043	3,043	3,034	3,033
Municipal	19,200	19,279	19,372	19,429	19,492
Township and town	16,691	16,656	16,629	16,504	16,519
School district	14,721	14,422	13,726	13,506	13,051
Special district	29,532	31,555	34,683	35,052	37,381
Local governments	83,186	84,955	87,453	87,525	89,476
Total government units	83,237	85,006	87,504	87,576	89,527

Source: U.S. Bureau of the Census.

special district governments, which increased 6.6 percent over the five-year period and by 15.9 percent over 20 years. This increase in special district governments reflects greater demand for services not performed directly by the existing state and local governments as well as efforts to circumvent restrictions on direct issuance of state and local government debt. The number of school districts has steadily decreased, indicating that there were consolidations among these units.

THE THEORY OF MUNICIPAL DEBT: PAY-AS-YOU-USE VERSUS PAY-AS-YOU-GO

Corporations borrow to build facilities or to make other investments that will improve their profits and returns on equity. The cash flow from their businesses and investments is used to repay the debt. Most state and local governments do not have the same profit motive as privately held corporations. They borrow for public purposes that better the lives of the people who live in the community or of those who use the services of municipal enterprises and certain not-for-profit organizations. The decisions as to what kind of debt to issue, along with who will repay the debt and in what way, tend to depend on the political and economic climate of the community.

Proponents of debt financing argue that new facilities should be paid for over time by all of the people who benefit from them—the *pay-as-you-use* approach. According to this argument, a community that pays for a new water system immediately assumes a burden that should be shared by future users, who will also benefit from the water system. Furthermore, it is argued, a growing city will be better able to afford the debt payments over time—and new projects today may be necessary for the municipality's growth tomorrow. With this in mind, policy makers often want the repayment schedule for municipal debt incurred to finance a project to coincide with the minimum useful life of that project.

The theory behind municipal revenue bonds is, in part, an extension of this pay-as-you-use philosophy. Revenue bonds are repaid with revenues generated by the particular project being financed. The beneficiaries of the project—the customers or users—pay off the debt, not the community as a whole.

At a time when debt financing has become the norm for corporations, municipalities, and consumers alike, theoretical justifications for borrowing may seem unnecessary. However, there may be political or economic circumstances under which governmental officials or the taxpayers or ratepayers may favor a pay-as-you-go approach. In *pay-as-you-go*, the capital projects are fully funded at the time of construction in cash from current revenues or accumulated cash. The advantages of pay-as-you-go include no interest costs, no issuance costs, no debt covenants, no overissuance of debt, and no burdening of future generations with debt.

Political pressure as well as economic circumstances can also affect the issuance of municipal debt. One way to limit tax increases and the issuance of debt is through changes to a state's constitution. In 1978, for example, California voters amended the state's constitution to limit the real estate tax to 1 percent of full value of the property tax base. This dramatically limited property tax increases and substantially slowed the issuance of general obligation debt in the state. By 2007, 24 states had caps on either property taxes or annual increases in taxes tied to a specific percentage or the inflation rate. The trend toward property tax caps has continued: In 2010, the New Jersey legislature passed a law limiting property tax increases, while voters in Indiana approved Public Question 1, a property tax cap that takes effect in 2012.

Another way to limit the issuance of debt is through voter rejection of general obligation bond issues. General obligation municipal bonds almost always require the approval of voters through referenda. It is interesting to examine the percentage of general obligation municipal bonds that are approved at elections. Table 3.2 shows the percentage of bonds approved at selected elections held in the years since 1947. The five years since 1947 with the highest approval rates and the five years with the lowest approval rates are presented.

The postwar years had the highest approval rates of municipal bond issues, driven by low interest rates and high economic confidence—a combination that recurred in 2004. The more politically turbulent times of the late 1960s and early 1970s had the lowest approval rates. It is safe to conclude that the willingness of voters to have their governments issue

TABLE 3.2 Municipal Bond Approval
Rates, All Elections

Year	Percentage Approved (%)
Highest five years	
1947	91.9
2004	90.7
1951	88.2
1956	87.5
1946	87.4
Lowest five years	
1973	52.1
1994	41.7
1969	39.6
1971	34.9
1975	29.3

Source: The Bond Buyer, Thomson Reuters
2009 Yearbook.

bonds and debt for capital improvements fluctuates with both the health of the national economy and the political climate of the times.

The effect of property-tax limitations and swings in the approval rates for general obligation bond issues can be seen in the changing composition of state and local governmental units shown in Table 3.1. Debt and tax limitations on traditional governments are stimulants for creating special districts for financing operating and capital expenditures. However, these transformations are concentrated in a relatively small number of states. For example, more than half of the special districts in the United States are in 10 states, with Illinois at 3,249 and California at 2,765 districts being the two largest.

THE USES OF MUNICIPAL DEBT

Municipal bonds are issued for many purposes. The basic infrastructure needs of state and local governmental units, together with many other uses that provide public benefits, have led to a diverse market. Municipal bonds generally finance capital projects, those that will be of long-term use. The day-to-day operating expenses of state and local governments are paid for out of taxes and other current revenues.

The major purposes for which municipal debt has been issued in selected years are shown in Table 3.3.

TABLE 3.3 Major Purposes of Short- and Long-Term Municipal Debt, 1989, 1999, and 2009

General Use of Proceeds	January 1, 2000 to December 31, 2009		January 1, 1999 to December 31, 1999		January 1, 1989 to December 31, 1989	
	Principal Amount ($ millions)	Market Share (%)	Principal Amount ($ millions)	Market Share (%)	Principal Amount ($ millions)	Market Share (%)
Airports	7,947.9	2.0	5,666.6	2.6	2,603.9	2.1
Combined utilities	1,526.9	0.4	1,056.5	0.5	2,243.1	1.8
Economic development	2,341.3	0.6	3,695.4	1.7	2,175.4	1.8
Education	89,530.1	22.0	47,528.4	21.7	17,551.3	14.3
Health care	43,664.9	10.7	21,686.6	9.9	13,775.1	11.3
Industrial development	2,204.2	0.5	2,896.9	1.3	2,651.5	2.2
Multifamily housing	3,959.3	1.0	5,942.7	2.7	3,110.2	2.5
Nursing homes	1,946.2	0.5	4,984.6	2.3	1,561.5	1.3
Other miscellaneous	143,687.9	35.3	60,072.6	27.4	35,091.9	28.7
Pollution control	6,205.0	1.5	6,757.6	3.1	2,352.9	1.9
Public power	15,984.3	3.9	4,796.2	2.2	8,161.2	6.7
Single-family housing	6,144.2	1.5	12,615.9	5.8	8,109.2	6.6
Solid waste	1,728.5	0.4	967.5	0.4	2,623.1	2.1
Student loans	2,354.0	0.6	5,280.5	2.4	1,766.4	1.4
Transportation	40,858.5	10.0	17,139.4	7.8	8,208.6	6.7
Water, sewer, and gas	36,727.4	9.0	18,269.0	8.3	10,351.9	8.5
Total	406,810.6	100.0	219,356.4	100.0	122,337.2	100.0

Source: Thomson Reuters.

TABLE 3.4 Largest Long-Term Municipal Issues, 1947 to 2009

Sale Date	Rank and Issuer		State	Par Amount ($ Millions)
06/12/2003	1	Illinois, general obligation	IL	10,000.0
04/01/2009	2	California, general obligation	CA	6,543.0
11/01/2002	3	California Department of Water Resources	CA	6,313.5
10/29/2007	4	Buckeye Tobacco Settlement Finance Authority	OH	5,531.6
04/28/2009	5	California, general obligation	CA	5,000.0
05/11/2004	6	California, economic recovery	CA	4,671.5
03/14/2007	7	Golden State Tobacco Sec Corporation	CA	4,446.8
04/01/2007	8	California, general obligation	CA	4,096.4
10/30/2002	9	California Department of Water Resources	CA	3,750.0
01/29/2007	10	NJ Tobacco Settlement Finance Corp.	NJ	3,622.2

Source: Thomson Reuters.

The biggest change in the decade through 1999 was in education, which rose from 14.3 percent of total debt issuance in 1989 to 21.7 percent in 1999. In the decade through 2009, the other miscellaneous category (primarily general government purposes and public improvements) grew fastest, from 27.4 percent to 35.3 percent of total debt issuance.

The largest municipal issues, all launched in the 10 years through 2009, have been for general governmental purposes, water projects, and to monetize anticipated revenues from a legal settlement with the tobacco industry. Six of the 10 largest issues originated in California, although the largest of all time was a $10 billion Illinois general obligation bond issue in 2003. Table 3.4 lists the 10 largest municipal issues ever sold through the end of 2009.

THE SECURITY FOR MUNICIPAL BONDS

With the increased diversification of governmental units and of the purposes for which bonds are issued, there has been increased diversification in the security structures provided to bondholders. In the most general terms, securities can be categorized as general obligation (GO) or revenue bonds. Table 3.5 shows the issuance of GOs and revenue bonds, each as a

TABLE 3.5 Long-Term General Obligation and Revenue Bond Issuance, 1986 to 2010

Year	General Obligation		Revenue		Total Volume ($ billions)
	Principal Amount ($ billions)	Percent of Total	Principal Amount ($ billions)	Percent of Total	
1986	44.9	30.4	102.7	69.6	147.6
1987	30.4	29.9	71.2	70.1	101.6
1988	31.1	26.6	86.0	73.4	117.1
1989	37.7	30.8	84.7	69.2	122.3
1990	40.2	31.9	85.7	68.1	125.9
1991	57.0	33.5	112.9	66.5	169.8
1992	80.9	34.8	151.4	65.2	232.3
1993	91.7	31.6	198.6	68.4	290.3
1994	55.3	34.1	106.9	65.9	162.2
1995	60.2	38.6	95.6	61.4	155.8
1996	64.4	35.6	116.7	64.4	181.1
1997	72.2	33.7	141.8	66.3	214.0
1998	93.5	33.4	186.9	66.6	280.4
1999	70.9	32.3	148.5	67.7	219.4
2000	66.4	34.2	127.8	65.8	194.1
2001	101.1	35.6	183.1	64.4	284.2
2002	125.2	35.3	230.0	64.7	355.2
2003	139.9	37.0	238.6	63.0	378.5
2004	131.6	37.0	224.3	63.0	355.9
2005	144.9	35.7	261.5	64.3	406.4
2006	115.5	30.2	266.6	69.8	382.1
2007	132.0	31.1	292.2	68.9	424.2
2008	110.2	28.5	276.3	71.5	386.5
2009	154.5	38.0	252.3	62.0	406.8
2010	147.6	34.1	285.7	65.9	433.3

Source: Thomson Reuters.

percentage of the total new-issue market, from 1986 to 2010. The composition of new issuance depends on conditions in the credit markets; when investors become more risk averse (in 1995 or 2009, for example), general obligation bonds, which are usually considered higher quality credits than revenue bonds, represent a larger proportion of the total. Within these two broad categories, there are dozens of variations of security features. This next section offers a brief discussion of the diverse security features of GO and revenue bonds.

Tax-Backed Bonds

General Obligation Bonds   The terms *tax-backed* and *tax-supported* bonds are used to encompass both some of the most traditional and some of the most innovative forms of municipal securities. The security for GO bonds is the general creditworthiness and the taxing power of the state or local government issuing the bonds. Most municipal governments depend largely on *ad valorem* (to the value added), or value-based, property taxes for their revenues. State governments, however, usually do not levy real estate taxes but rely mostly on sales and income taxes. The *full-faith-and-credit* backing of a GO bond implies that all sources of revenue, unless specifically limited, will be used to pay debt service on the bonds. There are exceptions to this, as some issuers sell GO bonds backed by the "faith and credit" as opposed to "full faith and credit."

Unlimited tax bonds are GO securities that are backed by the full faith and credit of the state or local government. This means that the taxing power of the issuer in support of the payment of the securities is not limited as to rate or amount.

Conversely, *limited tax bonds* are used when the taxing power of the governmental issuer in support of the municipal security is specifically limited by their constitution or by statutes. The tax rate on assessed property value, for example, or the assessment rate itself, may have a ceiling.

Other Tax-Backed Bonds   *Moral obligation bonds* are securities with a governmental guarantor who does not have a legal obligation to repay the debt. The pledge is used most often to enhance the credit of an agency that issues revenue bonds (e.g., housing agencies). When revenues are insufficient to cover debt service, the debt service reserve fund is used to make the necessary payments. Such a fund usually holds six months to one year in principal and interest payments. The moral obligation mechanism then calls for notification to the legislature or other governing body to replenish the reserve fund before the next interest payment date, if the legislature so desires.

Government credit-enhancement bonds encompass programs that range from partial to total credit substitution of a stronger governmental entity for a weaker one. An example of this security is state school bond credit-enhancement programs, the structures for which vary considerably from state to state. A common form of enhancement is the *state-aid intercept mechanism*, whereby a state withholds state-aid payments otherwise due a school district that has defaulted, or is expected to default, on a debt-service payment. The state then forwards the intercepted state-aid payments to the bond trustee to be used to pay debt service. The extent to which the state credit substitutes for that of the school district will depend on the specific rules and procedures of each program. Some states directly guarantee the bonds of the participating school districts; in these cases, the school bonds enjoy the same rating as the state. Other states use intercept mechanisms to enhance the credit of school district bonds; in these cases, the districts' ratings will be lower than those of the states. Other government credit-enhancement programs include annual appropriations by a state to the issuer of the bonds.

Leases and appropriation-backed obligations may be used if the issuer is constitutionally prohibited from using general obligation debt or if voter approval for general obligations is considered unlikely. Rental payments are made to the governmental entity (such as a town or a school district), to a lessor (this can be a not-for-profit financing corporation or other governmental unit) for a specific asset, such as an office building or a school. The rental payments are derived from taxes or other revenues, and most municipal leases require an annual appropriation for principal and interest. This inherently makes them less creditworthy than GO bonds. The certificates-of-participation structure is widely used by governments for lease-backed financing property and equipment.

A *certificate of participation* (COP) is an arrangement in which investors buy certificates that entitle them to receive a participation, or share, in the lease payments from a particular project. The lease payments are passed through the lessor to the certificate holders with the tax advantages intact. The lessor typically assigns the lease and lease payments to a trustee, who then distributes the lease payments to the certificate holders.

The government lessee commits to making future payments without incurring "debt" by using a lease that must either contain an acceptance or rent abatement clause or be renewable subject to appropriation risk. The abatement clause provides that if a property cannot be utilized (e.g., because of damage by earthquake or construction delays) the lessee cannot be compelled to make the lease payments. This clause makes the lease payments "fees for services" rather than debt, but the obligation to make payments remains a long-term obligation. Insurance provisions are generally included to protect against abatement risk. A non-appropriation clause allows the government to terminate the lease if its appropriating body does not allocate the necessary funds. Other important considerations in a COP financing are the sources of funds for repayment and the useful life of the item being financed.

Special-purpose district bonds and *special-assessment bonds* are among the most rapidly growing areas of tax-backed financings. This is because only those who directly benefit from the bond-financed improvements are obligated to pay special taxes or special assessments on property for the repayment of the bonds.

Special-tax bonds are hybrid securities that combine elements of general obligation and revenue bonds. For example, specific but broad-based taxes such as motor fuel taxes may be used as part of a security package for a transportation financing.

Tax-increment bonds or *tax-allocation bonds* are used to finance improvements in developing and redeveloping areas. A base year for property assessment is set by a redevelopment agency. Taxes that are levied on the incremental growth in assessed valuation in the redevelopment district are used for debt repayment.

Tax-based notes, including TANs, RANs, BANs, general obligation notes, and certain forms of commercial paper, are also tax-backed securities.

Revenue Bonds

Revenue bonds are payable from a specific stream or streams of revenues other than property taxes and are not backed by the full-faith-and-credit taxing power of the issuer. Revenue bonds offer an advantage to the issuer in that they do not usually require electoral approval or constitute debt within the meaning of applicable constitutional or statutory limitations. They are issued to finance specific enterprises or projects and are usually secured solely by the revenues from those projects. In addition, the issuers may offer related covenants to assure the adequacy of the pledged revenue sources. Sometimes there will be a mortgage on the facilities financed by the revenue bonds, although this security feature has been used less often in recent years. There are times when an issuer will pledge its taxing power to offer additional security for its revenue bonds; these hybrid obligations are called *double-barreled bonds*.

The revenue bond issuer may be the state or local government itself, or the issuer may be an authority, as explained above. Revenue bonds can be grouped in six general categories: utilities; health care, higher education, and other not-for-profits; housing; transportation; and industrial development. Of course, the types of revenues that can be used to back the bonds are related to the categories of the bonds. Chapter 7 delves more deeply into how to analyze the credit quality of different types of revenue bonds.

Utilities Revenue bonds are used to finance electric power, gas, water, wastewater, and solid waste systems. Utilities that provide electric power and are owned by a local governmental unit or authority are also called *public power*. These agencies may (1) generate their own electricity, (2) distribute electricity, (3) both generate and distribute electricity, or (4) engage in joint action, in which two or more governmental units or authorities combine to finance one of these three options. Independent power producers and rural electric cooperatives also issue revenue bonds. Examples of public power issuers are the Washington Public Power Supply System, the Puerto Rico Electric Power Authority, and the Omaha Public Power District.

Water systems, wastewater systems, and combined systems are steady issuers of revenue bonds. Among the issuers is the municipality itself, for which the water and wastewater systems are accounted in separate enterprise funds. An example of this type of issuer is the City of Detroit Sewer Disposal System. The issuer can also be a separate municipal authority, such as the New York City Municipal Water Finance Authority. Although these systems have traditionally been financed at the local level, special state issuers called *revolving funds* have been established to assist localities in building facilities that will enable them to comply with environmental regulations; the New York State Environmental Facilities Corporation is an example. Gas systems can be financed under a city's name or as part of a combined utility system, such as the City of San Antonio Electric and Gas Systems. Solid waste and resource-recovery plants are often financed with revenue bonds, such as those of the Palm Beach County Solid Waste Authority in Florida.

Health Care, Higher Education, and Other Not-for-Profit Revenue bonds are used to finance hospitals, other health-care providers, public and private colleges and universities, private elementary and secondary schools, museums, and other not-for-profit institutions. State legislatures have not only created health, educational, dormitory, and cultural authorities but they have also authorized units of local government to issue bonds on behalf of not-for-profit entities (which are not in themselves municipalities) and public colleges. Not-for-profit entities are also often referred to as 501(c)(3)s, based on the section of the Internal Revenue Service Code under which they derive their tax exemption.

Bonds can be issued for medical facilities such as stand-alone hospitals, multihospital systems, and academic medical centers. Nursing homes, assisted living facilities, continuing care retirement communities, rehabilitation centers, and other health-care-related facilities are also financed with revenue bonds. The issuer in these examples is a state or local authority, acting as a conduit for the obligated party, which is the organization that will actually benefit from the bonds (i.e., the hospital). Examples of hospitals financed with bonds include: the Johns Hopkins Hospital, the Cleveland Clinic, and the Sisters of Mercy Health System.

Private colleges and universities can also issue revenue bonds through an authority for construction of educational facilities. Examples of this are the Dormitory Authority of New York, issuing on behalf of Cornell University, and the Connecticut Health and Educational Facility Authority, acting for Yale University. Public universities such as the Regents of the

University of California also issue bonds. Private elementary and secondary schools that have investment-grade ratings or that have been able to arrange credit enhancement have become greater issuers of bonds. Museums, such as the Museum of Modern Art in New York, and cultural institutions, such as Carnegie Hall, have issued bonds for capital projects. Other kinds of not-for-profit organizations that have issued bonds include social service providers, membership organization headquarters, federations, and biomedical research institutes.

The revenues generated from these organizations are used to repay the bonds. These revenues include, but are certainly not limited to, inpatient and outpatient charges and managed care contracts for hospitals; tuition, student, dormitory, and other fees for universities; and entrance fees, ticket sales, membership dues, and charitable contributions for museums, cultural institutions, and other not-for-profits.

Housing   Revenue bonds are used to finance multifamily housing for low- or moderate-income families, single-family housing for first-time home-buyers, and housing for the aged and veterans. State or local housing finance agencies issue these bonds. Housing bonds are structured in a variety of ways, in part because they are subject to significant restriction and regulation under federal tax laws. State housing agencies often administer a wide range of programs designed to meet the needs of the people of the state. Most states have a housing finance authority; some agencies have multiple programs, including the California Housing Finance Agency and the Pennsylvania Housing Finance Agency. Local housing finance agencies also issue bonds for single family, multifamily, and other housing purposes.

Housing bonds are payable from rents, mortgage payments, and various subsidies received under federal programs. A more detailed discussion of these revenues can be found in Chapter 7.

Transportation   Revenue bonds are used to finance highways, turnpikes, airports, ports, bridges, tunnels, and mass-transportation facilities. The issuer can be a state or local authority or the governmental unit itself. A road or bridge that collects tolls from users is an example of an entity that uses a portion of its revenues to repay the debt incurred to construct the specific revenue-generating project.

Each transportation project can have its own unique security structure, depending on the scope of the project and its community and political support. Surface transportation facilities such as highways and turnpikes may use tolls or specific taxes to repay bonds. Bridges, airports, tunnels, mass-transportation facilities, and similar projects that are financed by revenue bonds raise funds through tolls, fares, concessions, and direct fees. For example, car rental companies pay concession fees for use of space at airports.

Industrial Development, Pollution Control, and Other Exempt Facility Bonds *Industrial development bonds* (IDBs) and municipal securities issued for other types of exempt facilities are revenue bonds where the credit and repayment source is the private entity for which the facilities are financed. The term *exempt facilities* refers to specific types of privately owned or privately used facilities for which bonds can be issued on a tax-exempt basis under the Internal Revenue Code. Principal categories of exempt facilities for which, subject to restrictions and in some cases volume limitations, bonds that can be issued under the 1986 code include governmentally owned airports; docks, wharves, and mass-commuting facilities; water-supply systems; sewage facilities; certain solid waste-disposal facilities; qualified hazardous waste facilities; qualified residential rental projects; and facilities for local furnishing of electric energy or gas and local district heating or cooling facilities. In addition, IDBs may be issued to finance qualified projects for manufacturing, certain farming purposes, and qualified student loans and qualified redevelopment projects.

Typically, these bonds are issued by a local governmental unit to finance facilities that are then leased to the private-entity user at a rent equal to debt service on the bonds and for a term equal to the maturity of the securities. Alternatively, in some jurisdictions, the issuer loans the proceeds of the IDBs directly to the private-entity user on repayment terms equal to the terms on the IDBs. The advantage to the private-entity user is to obtain financing at tax-exempt rates in return for making a capital investment that contributes to enumerated public purposes of the issuer, such as job creation, the enhancement of air or water quality, or increase of the tax base.

THE FINANCING PROCESS

Capital Improvement Plan

The first step in the financing process is for the issuer to assess its capital and operational needs, taking into account current needs and new policy mandates. Depending on the issuer, this may involve studying population growth, patterns of commutation, business growth, utility usage, or the health-care needs of a community. A 5- to 10-year *capital improvement plan* (CIP) is then developed, detailing the uses and sources of funds. The needs, such as additional schools, roads, housing or health-care facilities, or expanded power generation, are quantified into dollars. Bonds may also be used for debt repayment. The sources of funds, including current and additional taxes or revenue, grants, and notes or bonds, are estimated over the same time period. For revenue bond issuers, the capital improvement plan usually contains projections of their income and balance sheets.

Political Factors

In addition to developing a CIP, the issuer must also shepherd the prospective financing through public scrutiny and the political process. Bond issues needing voter approval must be included in elections. For bond issues to pass, the potential users of and payers for the project should be knowledgeable about the costs and benefits. Community support is also important in the location of controversial or sensitive projects, such as sewage treatment plants and solid waste facilities.

There may be instances in which enabling legislation must be passed to create a new authority. An example of this is the establishment of the *Transitional Finance Authority* (TFA) in New York City in 1997. The city has an extensive and ongoing capital improvement plan, funded from a variety of sources, including general obligation bonds. In the mid-1990s New York City was close to its general obligation debt limit, meaning that traditional new bonds could not be sold to continue the multiyear program. The New York State Legislature passed a law creating the Transitional Finance Authority, whose bonds, secured by a portion of the city income tax, would be used for the city's capital purposes. As TFA bonds are not general obligations of the city, they are exempt from the debt limits embodied in the state constitution.

Selecting the Financing Team

The issuer identifies the professional services that are required to structure and sell the bond issue, including bond counsel, financial advisor, and underwriter. Issuers also increasingly employ their own investor relations professionals, who are available to answer questions and provide information to investors during the sale of the bonds and afterward.

Bond Counsel   Bond counsel perform many functions and are often selected early in the process, because expert legal advice is needed in interpreting existing legislation and state and local finance laws. If new legislation is needed, bond counsel can be instrumental in its drafting. Because municipal bond issues are not marketable without an opinion from a nationally recognized bond counsel, the selection of such a counsel is a critical first decision in the financing process. Bond counsel has eight responsibilities:

1. Affirms the issuer's conformity with all legal requirements and authorization of the bond offering.
2. Prepares and supervises bond proceedings.
3. Obtains necessary approvals from governmental authorities.
4. Attests to the validity and enforceability of the bonds.
5. Confirms the tax-exempt status of offering, or, if it was a Build America Bond, that the issue qualified for the federal interest rate subsidy.
6. Discloses and examines litigation that may jeopardize the validity of the offering.
7. Interprets arbitrage regulations and tax law and provides guidance in structuring the issue.
8. Drafts key financing documents.

Financial Advisor   When the issuer has sufficient internal resources to handle the details of bond transactions, it is not necessary to hire a financial advisor. However, both large, sophisticated issuers and smaller, less knowledgeable issuers sometimes employ financial advisors to work with them during their financings. This work includes seven areas:

1. Determining financing needs and preparing analyses and plans.
2. Evaluating financing options (e.g., long-term versus short-term debt) and different types of securities under different scenarios.
3. Recommending negotiated or competitive sales.
4. Assisting in underwriter selection for negotiated sale.
5. Assisting in preparation of documents (official statement and notice of sale) for competitive bond sales.
6. Preparing for and participating in rating agency presentations.
7. Giving advice during pricing and sale of bonds.

The Underwriter: Negotiated versus Competitive Sales   An issuer's decision to sell bonds either by competitive or by negotiated sale is often governed by state law. Certain types of municipal securities, particularly GO bonds, may be required by law to be offered pursuant to advertised sale or competitive bidding. Even where there are no such requirements, issuers who benefit from competitive bids include frequent or well-known issuers with a simple bond structures and higher quality credit. The issuer usually receives at least two sealed bids, and that may assure local officials that the bonds have been correctly priced. For complicated offerings, lower quality credits or lesser-known issuers or when an issuer would benefit from an ongoing relationship with a banker, a negotiated sale often offers a better alternative. In a negotiated sale, the underwriter markets the bonds more extensively by providing investors with detailed information about the issue. In addition, there is flexibility in the timing of negotiated offerings, enabling the underwriter to take advantage of market conditions and steer through volatile market periods, as well as to develop a structure that suits current market conditions. Underwriters usually employ separate counsel to represent their interests.

The trend in the market over the past 35 years has been the increased use of negotiated sales. In 1975, 34 percent of the new-issue market was negotiated, while by 2009, it had grown to 85 percent. Chapter 4, The Primary Market, includes several charts on negotiated and competitive sales.

Private placements occur when the investment banker offers the securities directly to investors, without a public underwriting. Typically, the placement agent (the term for the underwriter in this type of transaction) contacts one or more institutional investors. The investor has the ability to negotiate favorable covenants with the issuer and to have greater influence over how the deal is structured. An issuer may want to do a private placement if its credit is new, of lower grade, or unrated. An advantage of a private placement is that information on the issuer would remain contained and controlled and would not be disseminated outside of the immediate circle of investors. Investors often sign *investor letters*, which attest to their sophistication and delineate the allowable secondary-market activity.

THE FINANCING DOCUMENTS

The issuer, together with the bond counsel, the financial advisor, and, if the issue is to be sold on a negotiated basis, the underwriter and its counsel, develop the financing documents that are the backbone of the deal. Working group meetings are held so that all the parties become conversant with the basic terms of the financings. Strategic decisions about security, size, and maturity of the issue are made, using market barometers, relevant legislation, and the issuer's own planning tools, such as the capital improvement plan. It is more common than not for the structure to evolve and change many times before the closing. The financing documents that are drafted may include many of those described in this section, again depending on the individual deal structure and state law.

Web sites for working groups on new issues have been created by private data vendors. The working groups can set up secure sites on the Internet, where all phases of the issue—from the initial draft of the preliminary official statement to the final draft of the bond purchase agreement—can be accessed and shared by all members of the group. Because access to the site can be tracked, all members of the group can always know the working status of any document in progress.

Authorizing Resolution

The governing board of the issuer authorizes the sale of debt through a resolution. The authorizing resolution will state the general terms of the financing, such as the maturity schedule, the size of debt (limited to a not-to-exceed amount), and the maximum interest cost allowable. The legal basis for the debt, be it a local ordinance or state legislation, is also cited.

Bond Resolution, Indenture, and Trust Agreement

The bond resolution, the indenture, and the trust agreement are the heart of the issue's legal structure. The key elements of the contract between the issuer and the bondholders are written into these documents. It is common for a general obligation bond issue or a note issue to be accompanied by a bond or note resolution. Revenue bond issues have either a bond resolution or an indenture. Leases or certificates of participation generally use a trust agreement. Master trust indentures or master resolutions, with supplemental or series resolutions, have been used for cases in which many series of bonds have been issued over a period of time for the same ultimate borrower.

All these documents cover the mechanics of the issue, including the principal and interest payment dates, method and place of payment, and for variable rate bonds, the terms of how the interest rate will be set. They also establish key bond funds such as the construction fund, the debt-service fund, and required reserves. Redemption provisions, if any, are delineated. Other key sections of the indenture include the pledge of revenues and the order in which those funds are applied (called the *flow of funds*); key financial, operating, and tax covenants; and a description of the investments that the issuer is permitted to make with the monies held in the various bond funds. The importance of this is discussed further in Chapter 7. The indenture describes what the events of default are and the remedies that bondholders have, along with methods of defeasance and the rights of the credit enhancer, if any.

Lease Agreement

A lease agreement is used when the financing includes lease revenue bonds or certificates of participation. The agreement spells out the terms between the lessee (the governmental unit that uses the facility) and the lessor (a municipal authority or corporation or a not-for-profit corporation created by the governmental unit to act as the financing unit). The lease agreement includes sections relating to the maintenance of the property and to lease payments, just as would be found in a nonfinancing lease. It will also include the length of the lease (most often corresponding to the maturity schedule of the bonds) and what happens with prepayments (provisions should correspond to the trust agreement or indenture). The basic security, be it an annual appropriation of the lessee or, in some states, a covenant to budget and appropriate, is stated. The rights of the bondholders, as assigned to the trustee, are stated, including the ability of the trustee to repossess the property for nonappropriation of rentals.

Official Statement

The *official statement* (OS) is the issuer's offering document for publicly sold securities. The *preliminary official statement* (POS), distributed either by the underwriter (in a negotiated issue) or by the issuer or financial advisor (in a competitive sale), is used to inform potential investors about the issuer and about the preliminary terms of the bonds being offered. The preliminary official statement is also called a *red herring* because along the side of the prospectus, printed in red ink, are statements that the information contained in the POS is subject to completion or amendment and that the POS is not an offer to sell the securities. A *deemed final official statement* is, for all practical purposes, the same as a preliminary official statement. A final official statement includes the final terms of the issue, including the total principal amount, a list of serial and term bonds with their corresponding interest rates and maturities, and the sources and uses of the bond proceeds.

There is no list of mandatory information that must be included in the official statement. The SEC has recognized the extensive voluntary guidelines issued by the Government Finance Officer's Association, including its 2001 handbook, *Making Good Disclosure,* and the industry-specific guidelines published by groups such as the National Federation of Municipal Analysts. The SEC encourages market participants to refer to those voluntary guidelines in preparing disclosure documents. In practice, the information typically includes, but is not limited to:

- An introduction to serve as a guide to the official statement.
- A description of the securities being offered, including complete information regarding the purposes of the offering, the plan of financing, the security and sources of repayment, and the priority of the securities, as well as structural characteristics such as call provisions, tender

options, original-issue or deep discount, variable rates, and lease-purchase agreements.

- Information regarding the nature and extent of any credit enhancement and financial and business information about the issuer of the enhancement.
- A description of the government issuer or enterprise, including information about the issuer's range or level of service, capacity, and demographic factors, and in the case of revenue-supported offerings, information on the enterprise's organization, management, revenue structure, results of operations, and operating plan.
- With respect to the obligations of private, profit-making, and non-profit conduit issuers, information regarding the business or other activity, including the enterprise's form of organization and management, rate-making or pricing policies, and historical operations and plan or operation.
- A description of the issuer's outstanding debt, including the authority to incur debt, limitations on debt, and the prospective debt burden and rate of its retirement.
- A description of the basic documentation, such as indentures, trust agreements, and resolutions authorizing the issuance and establishing the rights of the parties.
- Financial information, including summary information regarding the issuer's or obligor's financial practices and results of operations and financial statements, all prepared in conformity with generally accepted accounting principles and audited in accordance with generally accepted auditing standards.
- Discussion of legal matters, such as pending judicial, administrative, or regulatory proceedings that may significantly affect the securities offered, legal opinions, and tax considerations.
- Discussion of other matters, including ratings and their descriptions and meanings, underwriting arrangements, arrangements with financial advisors, interests of named experts, pending legislation, and the availability of additional information and documentation.
- Description of any continuing disclosure undertaking for the offering and disclosure of any failure to comply in all material respects with previous continuing disclosure obligations in the preceding five years.

The cover page of an official statement gives a summary of the terms and features of the securities. Below are the Securities Industry and Financial Markets Association's (SIFMA's) recommendations for the information that should be included on the front cover of an official statement. (If there is insufficient space available on the front cover, this information should be included in the summary statement.) A sample cover page is shown in Figure 3.1 with the items in the following list indicated by number.

1. Dollar amount and name of the bond issue.
2. Name of issuer (may be omitted if contained within the name of the issue), conduit transactions, and identification of the underlying obligor.
3. Interest rate or rates, together with the maturity date, the interest-payment date or dates, and the serial and term maturity amounts. Identification of variable-rate formula for determining the rate and frequency of rate changes, the date from which interest is paid, and identification of any special-interest payment features (e.g., zero coupon, limited interest, variable rate).
4. The dated date of the bonds and (if different) the date interest begins to accrue, together with the terms of interest and principal payments, including dates and manner of payment.
5. Summary of bond counsel's tax opinion.
6. Brief description of sources of payment for the bonds.
7. Identification of credit enhancement, if any.
8. Purpose and authority for the bond issue.
9. Name and location of trustee and/or paying agent.
10. Authorized denominations and registration provisions.
11. Whether bonds are subject to redemption.
12. Initial offering prices and/or yields.
13. Ratings, if desired.
14. Date and location of expected delivery of bonds.
15. Name of counsel providing opinions.
16. Any other special terms or provisions.
17. If competitive sale, any bidding specifications.
18. Names of managing underwriters if offering is a negotiated sale, or statement that it is a competitive issue.
19. Date of the offering document.

Opinion of Bond Counsel

Even though the bond counsel's opinion is addressed to the issuer, the bondholders rely on this opinion to provide comfort about the legality of the issue. Investors insist on an unqualified opinion from a nationally recognized bond counsel.

The legal opinion covers three major areas: (1) that the bonds are valid and binding obligations of the issuer; (2) information on the security and sources of payment for the bonds; and (3) exemption of the interest on the

RATINGS:	Moody's:	A1
	S&P:	A–
	Fitch:	A–

(See "Ratings" herein)

In the opinion of Bond Counsel to the State of California (the "State"), interest on the Bonds is excluded from gross income for federal income tax purposes under Section 103 of the Internal Revenue Code of 1986, as amended, and is exempt from State personal income taxes, all as further discussed in "TAX MATTERS" herein.

STATE OF CALIFORNIA
$1,250,000,000
VARIOUS PURPOSE GENERAL OBLIGATION BONDS

Dated: Date of Delivery	Due: November 1, as shown on next page

Interest on the Bonds is payable on May 1 and November 1 of each year, commencing May 1, 2011, at the respective rates per annum set forth on the page immediately following this cover page. The Bonds may be purchased in principal amounts of $5,000 or multiples thereof in book-entry form only. See "THE BONDS—General" and APPENDIX B—"THE BOOK-ENTRY ONLY SYSTEM."

On November 18, 2010, the State sold $10,000,000,000 aggregate principal amount of revenue anticipation notes, which will be delivered on November 23, 2010, pursuant to a separate official statement, and on November 19, 2010, the State sold $3,275,000,000 aggregate principal amount of taxable general obligation bonds, which are expected to be delivered on or about December 1, 2010, pursuant to a separate offering memorandum.

Certain of the Bonds are subject to redemption prior to their stated maturities, as described herein. See "THE BONDS—Redemption."

The Bonds are general obligations of the State of which the full faith and credit of the State are pledged. The principal of and interest on all State general obligation bonds, including the Bonds, are payable from any moneys in the General Fund of the State, subject only to the prior application of such moneys to the support of the public school system and public institutions of higher education. See "AUTHORIZATION OF AND SECURITY FOR THE BONDS."

This cover page contains certain information for general reference only. It is not a summary of the security or terms of this issue. Investors are advised to read the entire Official Statement to obtain information essential to the making of an informed investment decision.

MATURITIES, PRINCIPAL AMOUNTS,
INTEREST RATES, PRICES OR YIELDS AND CUSIPS
(See Next Page)

The Bonds are offered when, as and if issued and received by the Underwriters, subject to the approval of validity by the Honorable Edmund G. Brown Jr., Attorney General of the State of California and by Orrick, Herrington & Sutcliffe LLP, Bond Counsel to the State. Orrick, Herrington & Sutcliffe LLP and Alexis S. M. Chiu, Esq., are serving as Co-Disclosure Counsel to the State with respect to the Bonds, Orrick, Herrington & Sutcliffe LLP and Stradling Yocca Carlson & Rauth, a Professional Corporation, are serving as Co-Disclosure Counsel to the State regarding Appendix A. Certain matters will be passed upon for the Underwriters by their counsel, Sidley Austin LLP. Public Resources Advisory Group is serving as the Financial Advisor to the State with respect to the Bonds. The Bonds are expected to be available for delivery through the facilities of The Depository Trust Company on or about December 2, 2010.

HONORABLE BILL LOCKYER
Treasurer of the State of California

Citi	RBC Capital Markets	Siebert Brandford Shank & Co., L.L.C.
Backstrom McCarley Berry & Co., LLC	Barclays Capital	BMO Capital Markets GKST Inc.
BNY Mellon Capital Markets, LLC	BefA Merrill Lynch	Brandis Tallman LLC
Cabrera Capital Markets, LLC	City National Securities, Inc.	De La Rosa & Co.
Estrada Hinojosa and Company, Inc.	Fidelity Capital Markets	Goldman, Sachs & Co.
Great Pacific Securities	Greencoast Capital Partners LLC	Jefferies & Company
J.P. Morgan	MFR Securities, Inc.	Morgan Stanley
Prager, Sealy & Co., LLC	RH Investment Corporation	Seattle-Northwest Securities Corporation
Southwest Securities, Inc.	Stinson Securities, LLC	Stone & Youngberg
The Williams Capital Group, L.P.	Touissant Capital Partners, LLC	Wedbush Securities
Wells Fargo Securities	Westhoff, Cone & Holmstedt	Wulff, Hansen & Co.

Official Statement Dated: November 22, 2010

FIGURE 3.1 Sample Front Cover of Official Statement

MATURITIES, PRINCIPAL, AMOUNT, INTEREST RATES, PRICES OR YIELDS AND CUSIPS

$1,250,000,000
STATE OF CALIFORNIA
VARIOUS PURPOSE GENERAL OBLIGATION BONDS

Base CUSIP[†]: 13063B

Maturity Date (November 1)	Principal Amount	Interest Rate	Price or Yield	CUSIP[†] Suffix	Maturity Date (November 1)	Principal Amount	Interest Rate	Price or Yield	CUSIP[†] Suffix
2011	$25,000,000	3.000%	1.100%	JF0	2020	$12,620,000	4.200%	4.230%	JQ6
2013	13,700,000	3.000	1.870	JH6	2020	37,380,000	5.000	4.230	KL5
2013	17,300,000	4.000	1.870	JG8	2021	15,000,000	4.400	4.420	JR4
2014	18,085,000	3.000	2.290	JJ2	2021	38,000,000	5.000	4.420[C]	KM3
2014	14,915,000	4.000	2.290	KE1	2022	12,550,000	4.550	4.560	JS2
2015	16,290,000	3.000	2.660	JK9	2022	18,450,000	5.000	4.560[C]	KN1
2015	19,710,000	5.000	2.660	KF8	2023	50,000,000	5.000	4.750[C]	JT0
2016	15,000,000	4.000	2.970	JL7	2024	40,000,000	5.000	4.880[C]	JU7
2016	23,000,000	5.000	2.970	KG6	2025	95,000,000	5.000	100	JV5
2017	10,460,000	3.300	3.340	JM5	2026	25,000,000	5.000	5.050	JW3
2017	31,540,000	5.000	3.340	KH4	2027	10,000,000	5.100	100	JX1
2018	4,340,000	3.650	3.680	JN3	2028	10,000,000	5.200	100	JY9
2018	39,660,000	5.000	3.680	KJ0	2029	35,000,000	5.200	5.230	JZ6
2019	14,040,000	4.000	3.980	JP8	2030	20,000,000	5.250	5.280	KA9
2019	32,960,000	5.000	3.980	KK7					

$55,000,000 5.375% Term Bonds Due November 1, 2035 Price: 100; CUSIP[†]: 13063BKB7

$80,000,000 5.500% Term Bonds Due November 1, 2035 Priced to Yield 5.375%[C]; CUSIP[†]: 13063BKP6

$400,000,000 5.250% Term Bonds Due November 1, 2040 Priced to Yield 5.500%; CUSIP[†]: 13063BKC5

---

† Copyright 2010, American Bankers Association. CUSIP® is a registered trademark of the American Bankers Association. CUSIP data herein is provided by the CUSIP Service Bureau, Operated by Standard & Poor's, a division of The McGraw-Hill Companies, Inc. This data is not intended to create a database and does not serve in any way as a substitute for the CUSIP Services Bureau. CUSIP numbers have been assigned by a independent company not affiliated with the State and are included solely for the convenience of the registered owners of the applicable Bonds. Neither the State nor the Underwriters are responsible for the selection or uses of these CUSIP numbers, and no representation is made as to their correctness on the applicable Bonds or as included herein. The CUSIP number for a specific maturity is subject to being changed after the issuance of the Bonds as a result of various subsequent actions including, but not limited to, a refunding in whole or in part or as a result of the procurement of secondary market portfolio insurance or other similar enhancement by investors that is applicable to all or a portion of certain maturities of the Bonds.

C Priced to November 1, 2020, call date at par.

FIGURE 3.1 *(Continued)*

issue from federal, state, and local income taxes, or, if it is a Build America Bond, qualification for the federal interest rate subsidy.

Figure 3.2 is the National Association of Bond Lawyers' model bond opinion for general obligation bonds.

Other Legal Opinions

In addition to the opinion of bond counsel, other legal opinions are given as part of the financing documents in more complex financings. A tax opinion, given by bond counsel or a special tax counsel, gives comfort that the issuer has complied with the applicable arbitrage regulations. Counsel for credit enhancers, particularly for banks providing letters of credit, may be asked to provide opinions regarding preference in a bankruptcy. Underwriter's counsel provides the underwriter with an opinion that the disclosure is complete and complies with the applicable securities laws—this is called a *10(b)(5) opinion.*

Credit-Enhancement Documents

When the issue carries credit enhancement, additional financing documents must be drafted. Credit enhancers have input into the indenture, and they try to write the strongest (from their point of view) covenants. Credit enhancers are concerned with, among other things, their security lien positions, rate covenants, and additional debt tests.

With a letter-of-credit financing, key documents include the letter of credit itself and the reimbursement agreement, which spells out how the issuer will pay back the bank in the event the letter is drawn upon. When the issue uses a line of credit, the document will include the definitions of events of default and the remedies that the bank can use if any of the named defaults occur.

Bond Purchase Agreement/Purchase Contract

In a negotiated sale, the purchase contract between the issuer and the underwriter is called the *bond purchase agreement* (BPA). The BPA includes the purchase price of the bonds, the principal amount of each maturity, the interest rates, and other specifics of the deal. It also includes an estimate of the closing date, the representations and warranties that the issuer makes to the underwriter, and the conditions under which the underwriter would or would not have to pick up the bond. The underwriter's counsel prepares this document. For a competitive sale, the purchase contract is essentially

I. GENERAL OBLIGATION BONDS (A)
MODEL OPINION

[*Note*: Letters in parentheses refer to the Commentary immediately following this opinion.]

(*Letterhead of Bond Counsel*)
(*Date*) **(B)**

(*Addressee*) **(C)**
(*Salutation*) **(D)**

(*Caption*)

We have acted as bond counsel to _____**(E)** in connection with the issuance by (*Name of Issuer*) (the "Issuer") of $_____ (*Title of Bonds*) Bonds dated _____ (*the "Bonds"*). **(F)** In such capacity, we have examined such law and such certified proceedings, certifications, and other documents as we have deemed necessary to render this opinion. **(G)**

Regarding questions of fact material to our opinion, we have relied on the certified proceedings and other certifications of public officials and others furnished to us without undertaking to verify the same by independent investigation.

Based on the foregoing, we are of the opinion **(H)** that, under existing law:

1. The Bonds have been duly authorized and executed by the Issuer, and are valid and binding general obligations of the Issuer. **(I)**

2. All taxable property in the territory of the Issuer is subject to *ad valorem* taxation without limitation regarding rate or amount to pay the Bonds. **(J)** The Issuer is required by law to include in its annual tax levy the principal and interest coming due on the Bonds to the extent that necessary funds are not provided from other sources. **(K)**

3. Interest on the Bonds is excludable **(L)** from gross income for federal income tax purposes and is not an item of tax preference for purposes of the federal alternative minimum tax imposed on individuals and corporations; however, such interest is taken into account in determining adjusted current earnings for the purpose of computing the alternative minimum tax imposed on certain corporations. The opinion set forth in the preceding sentence is subject to the condition that the Issuer comply with all requirements of the Internal Revenue

FIGURE 3.2 Sample Bond Counsel Opinion
Source: National Association of Bond Lawyers. Reprinted with permission.

Code of 1986, as amended, **(M)** that must be satisfied subsequent to the issuance of the Bonds in order that the interest thereon be, and continue to be, excludable from gross income for federal income tax purposes. **(N)** The Issuer has covenanted to comply with all such requirements. **(O)** Failure to comply with certain of such requirements may cause interest on the Bonds to be included in gross income for federal income tax purposes retroactively to the date of issuance of the Bonds. **(P)**

4. [Opinion regarding state tax exemption, if any.] **(Q)**

The rights of the owners of the Bonds and the enforceability of the Bonds are limited by bankruptcy, insolvency, reorganization, moratorium, and other similar laws affecting creditors' rights generally, and by equitable principles, whether considered at law or in equity. **(R)**

We express no opinion [herein] regarding the accuracy, adequacy, or completeness of the [disclosure document] relating to the Bonds. **(S)** Further, we express no opinion regarding tax consequences arising with respect to the Bonds other than as expressly set forth herein.

[This opinion is given as of the date hereof, and we assume no obligation to revise or supplement this opinion to reflect any facts or circumstances that may hereafter come to our attention, or any changes in law that may hereafter occur.] **(B)**

Very truly yours,

FIGURE 3.2   (*Continued*)

made up of the notice of sale, the winning bid, and the issuer's acceptance of the bid.

Continuing Disclosure Agreement

The continuing disclosure agreement is between the underwriter and the issuer. See Chapter 9 for a more in-depth discussion.

Other Documents

The *closing documents* are coordinated and handled by the bond counsel. They include executed (signed) copies of the major documents, title searches, and opinions of other counsel. In a refunding issue, the escrow documents relating to the securities used to pay off the old bonds are also prepared.

STRUCTURING THE DEBT

An issuer makes many decisions relating to the financial structure of the debt in the course of the financing. These decisions include the way the debt service schedule is structured, the inclusion or exclusion of call provisions, the use of premium or discount bonds, the method of calculating the interest cost, the use of bond insurance or other credit enhancements, and the use of financial products such as derivatives. These decisions are made in the context of the issuer's legal constraints, its policies and political constraints, and the market demand for the issuer's bonds at the time of sale.

Debt Repayment Schedules

There are three kinds of debt service schedules. In a *level debt* service schedule, the total of principal and interest repaid each year is generally level, or the same, throughout the life of the bond issue, with the principal amount of the serial maturities increasing each year. In a *level principal* or *declining debt* service schedule, the dollar amount of the annual serial maturities is the same each year throughout the life of the bond, and thus the interest portion of the debt service declines each year. In an *ascending debt* service schedule, the greatest principal payments are in the future, with little or no amortization of principal in the early years of the debt. Term bonds are usually structured with sinking fund redemptions that mimic serial maturities.

The arrangement of serial bond schedules can provide great flexibility to financial officers concerned with meeting annual budgets. For example, serial maturities can be constructed to dovetail with expected revenues and expenditures in a given year. Another area where serial maturities are advantageous is in large revenue bond projects, where local officials may want to ease the burden of rapidly increasing water or power rates. An ascending debt service schedule may be used to push the debt payments further out into the future in the belief that natural growth may be expected to pay off the debt. This strategy could be a negative factor in the rating or the issuer's ability to obtain credit enhancement, so the issuer has to weigh the positives and negatives carefully. Term maturities with all principal payments coming due 15 to 30 years after issuance can provide a useful financing option.

Indeed, marketability is an important factor in the choice of maturities. For many issues, particularly large ones, a maturity schedule incorporating short serial bonds and term bonds will usually broaden the appeal of an issue, attracting a variety of investors. The level of interest rates will also influence decisions concerning maturities. For example, if short-term interest rates are considered unusually low or if demand for short-term issues is strong, an issue weighted more heavily toward shorter-maturity serial bonds can be constructed. The bonds may also be more marketable at a given time if the issue includes *premium bonds*, which are priced initially greater than par, or *discount bonds*, which are priced below par. *Original issue discount* (OID) bonds can be used by an underwriter to create interest and demand in a specific term maturity of an issue. (OIDs are discussed in greater detail in Chapter 6.)

Redemption Provisions

The cost to an issuer of having a *call privilege* or *protection* can be a higher interest rate on the issue. Investors will often demand a higher yield for a security with a call provision because the potential for price appreciation and capital gain on a callable bond is limited. Also, if the issuer calls the bonds before they mature, the investors may be left to reinvest the principal at a lower interest rate. The question the issuer must consider, therefore, is whether the advantages of the call privilege outweigh the higher interest rate that must be offered to investors. When interest rates in general are high and volatile, a call provision is clearly most desirable, as it enables the issuer to refund an issue when interest rates are lower. Both the call premium and the amount of time that the investor has call protection have been changing markedly. Investors are highly cognizant of the importance of the call option to their portfolios, and they look for issues for which the call protection is the longest and the call premiums are the highest. Issuers, also cognizant of the value of the call option, may look to reduce the call premium and shorten the number of years of call protection they give the investor, all in order to give themselves as much flexibility as possible.

The issuers of callable bonds usually notify investors 30 days before the bonds are due to be called through an actual notice to bondholders or an advertisement in a financial publication. The notice or advertisement will state which bonds are being redeemed and how the bondholder will receive payment. The call provision normally states in which order bonds will be called (which is described in the official statement).

Refundings

A considerable portion of the municipal market involves the issuance of new bonds to refund old bonds. Table 3.6 details the volume of refunding bonds from 1990 through 2010.

TABLE 3.6 Long-Term Refunding Bond Issuance, 1990 to 2010

Year	Principal Amount ($ billions)	Percent of Total Issuance	All Long-Term Issuance ($ billions)
1990	25.43	20.2	125.94
1991	53.59	31.6	169.84
1992	122.33	52.7	232.28
1993	194.59	67.0	290.26
1994	50.59	31.2	162.20
1995	47.97	30.8	155.80
1996	60.58	33.5	181.08
1997	82.01	38.3	213.98
1998	124.75	44.5	280.43
1999	68.94	31.4	219.36
2000	35.13	18.1	194.13
2001	89.88	31.6	284.17
2002	120.23	33.8	355.21
2003	121.15	32.0	378.55
2004	130.89	36.8	355.86
2005	187.24	46.1	406.44
2006	128.63	33.7	382.12
2007	155.07	36.6	424.16
2008	180.91	46.8	386.47
2009	148.00	36.4	406.81
2010	152.74	35.5	430.82

Source: Thomson Reuters.

In a refunding, the proceeds of the new bonds are used to pay the principal, interest, and any call premium of an outstanding bond issue, to either the maturity or the call date. Issuers, with the help of financial advisors and investment bankers, regularly evaluate the feasibility of refunding outstanding debt with new bonds. Reasons to consider refunding include the opportunity to achieve interest rate savings, the need to extinguish old debt and thus remove or change outdated or unwanted covenants, the ability to make a favorable change in the debt service schedule, and the potential to garner other economic benefits.

The issuer monitors rates in both the municipal market and in the Treasury securities market to see when the refunding is economical and if interest rate savings targets can be met. This is because the proceeds from the refunding bonds are used to purchase permitted securities under the bond indenture that are often special *state and local government securities* (SLGSs), which are issued by the U.S. Treasury, and open-market Treasuries. The interest on the SLGS is then used to service the old debt. There are many federal tax laws that govern the issuance of refunding bonds and the amount of arbitrage that can be earned. *Arbitrage* in the municipal market is the difference between the interest paid on tax-exempt bonds and the interest earned on normally higher-yielding taxable securities. Moreover, federal tax law restricts the yield that can be earned on the investment in taxable bonds (the arbitrage yield).

Three characteristics are common to refunding bonds—escrow, timing, and level of interest rates. When refunding bond proceeds are deposited in an escrow account, and those proceeds can be used solely to pay principal and interest on the original maturity dates of the old bonds, the old bonds are said to be *escrowed to maturity* (ETM). When the refunding and proceeds are escrowed and can be used to pay principal, interest, and the call premium up to the call date of the old bonds, the old bonds are said to be *prerefunded*. In either case, once the escrow has been established, the bonds being refunded are said to be defeased and the principal and interest payments on the bonds are paid exclusively from the income derived from the escrow securities. The rights of the old bondholders are usually terminated with a refunding when payment provisions have been made.

Market timing determines whether the bonds can be current or advance refunded. In a *current refunding*, the old bonds are called or mature within 90 days of the issuance of the new refunding bonds. If the old bonds are called or mature more than 90 days after the issuance of new bonds, the old bonds are said to be *advance refunded*. U.S. Treasury concerns regarding what was perceived as overissuance of tax-exempt bonds have led to restrictions on advance refundings.

The level of interest rates determines whether the refunding is *high to low* or *low to high*. With a high-to-low refunding, high-coupon bonds are refunded with low-coupon bonds; this is generally done for interest rate savings. When, less commonly, low-coupon bonds are refunded with high-coupon bonds (a low-to-high refunding), covenant changes, rather than interest rate savings, are generally at work.

In addition to the characteristics of refundings that have been described there are three major classifications of refundings—net cash, crossover, and full cash. In a *net cash* refunding, the principal, interest, and call premium of the old bonds are paid from the proceeds and investment earnings of the refunding bonds. Most advance refundings follow the net cash model. In a *crossover refunding*, the debt service on the old bond is paid by the original revenue stream until the call date, when the revenue stream crosses over and is used to pay the debt service on the new refunding bonds. The refunding escrow pays debt service on the new bonds until the crossover date, when the escrow pays the principal and call premium on the old bonds. In this instance, the old bonds are not extinguished at the time of the refunding. A third type of refunding is a *full cash* or *gross refunding*. Here, the refunding issue itself is large enough to pay principal and interest on the old bonds. There are two series of full cash securities: refunding bonds, which pay debt service on the old bonds, and special obligation securities, which pay a portion of the debt service on the refunding bonds without reliance on investment earnings or escrowed securities. There have not been many full cash refundings in recent years.

True Interest Cost and Net Interest Cost

In a competitive sale, the issuer must decide on what basis competing syndicates will calculate their bids for the bonds. In most sales, the issuer looks to the true interest cost (TIC), which is also sometimes called the Canadian interest cost. TIC is the rate that will discount all future cash payments so the sum of the present value of all cash flows will equal the bond proceeds. This calculation takes into account the time value of money, producing a more accurate indication of the true interest cost of an issue, particularly ones that contain serial bonds. The formula for the TIC is

$$B = \sum_{n=e}^{f} \left(\sum_{t=1}^{n} \frac{C_t}{(1 + \text{TIC})^t} + \frac{M}{(1 + \text{TIC})^n} \right)$$

where B = price of the issue, e = number of periods to earliest bond maturity, f = number of periods to last bond maturity, n = years to maturity, t = index of period, C = Coupon, M = maturity value of the bond, and TIC = True Interest Cost.

An older, simpler arithmetic calculation used before the widespread use of computers is the net interest cost (NIC). The formula for the NIC is

$$\text{NIC} = \frac{\text{Total interest payments plus discount (or minus premium)}}{\text{Bond year dollars}}$$

Although NIC is rarely used anymore, the formula contains the important concept of *bond years*. Bond years alone are the number of bonds outstanding (in $1,000 denominations) multiplied by the number of years outstanding. For example, one bond year is one $1,000 bond outstanding for one year. A $25,000 bond due in one year would have 25 bond years. Bond-year dollars are the number of bond years multiplied by $1,000 for each bond. The $25,000 bond due in one year would have 25,000 bond-year dollars. Another important concept is the *average life*. This is the number of bond years divided by the total number of bonds in an issue. For example, if an issue contains 250,000 bond years, with 25,000 bonds the average life of the issue is 10 years.

Financial Products

The use of derivatives and other financial products by municipal issuers has become an important part of issuers' financial management. This is discussed in Chapter 10.

Bond Insurance

A major decision that issuers must make is whether to use some form of credit enhancement. Bond insurance represents a legal commitment by a third party (the insurance company), to make timely payments of principal and interest in the event that the issuer of the debt is unable to do so. Generally, the issuer will see to it that such payments are made as originally scheduled and that the principal will not be accelerated.

The role of municipal bond insurance in the tax-exempt market is three-fold: to reduce interest costs to issuers; to provide a high level of security to investors; and to furnish improved secondary-market liquidity and price support. Until 2007, many issuers found that their total borrowing costs, including the insurance premium, could be lowered by using bond insurance. The issuer, in making this evaluation, compares the rates on an insured scale with the scale for its own credit. If the issuer is not yet rated, the financial advisor should be able to approximate the rating. The issuer compares the TIC on the insured scale (which incorporates the cost of the insurance) with the TIC on the uninsured scale and then makes the decision whether to use bond insurance.

The financial difficulties experienced by the major bond insurers in 2008 undermined investors' faith in bond insurance. Even though the problems bond insurers encountered had nothing to do with their municipal bond books, many issuers found that they could no longer achieve TIC savings using bond insurance. The proportion of municipal bond issues that carried bond insurance fell from 57.3 percent in 2005 to 6.2 percent in 2010. Investors refocused their attention on the credit quality of the underlying issuers and no longer attributed significant value to insurance for most bond issues. The credit ratings of most major bond insurers active before the financial crisis of 2008 have been downgraded, in some many cases to below investment grade.

Certain issuers may still use insurance for credit support, especially if the underwriter or financial advisor has determined that the best market reception would be for an insured issue. The issuer may nevertheless be constrained by the bond insurer's credit capacity for that issuer's name, state, region, or type of credit. In addition, by 2010, so few creditworthy bond insurers remained active in the market that investors faced capacity constraints on how much exposure they would accept to any one insurer.

STATE AND LOCAL GOVERNMENT ACCOUNTING

Government accounting necessarily differs in several important ways from business accounting. Business accounting is ultimately concerned with the profits of the owners; governments have no such clear-cut measure of success. Businesses must match sales to the expenses incurred in making those sales; governments must be certain that resources are sufficient to meet outlays. Businesses try to maximize profits; governments must meet the annual budget. To the owner of a business, the consolidation of all business expenses and revenues, no matter how diversified, makes sense. Sources of revenue for certain government services, however, often have little to do with revenues raised for other purposes, so that segregated accounts are usually more appropriate and, indeed, are often legally mandated.

Such differences have resulted in a separate set of accounting principles for government, originally developed by the *National Council on Governmental Accounting* (NCGA). The NCGA began to formulate these principles in 1934. In 1984, through an agreement between the Financial Accounting Foundation, which sets business accounting standards; the American Institute of Certified Public Accountants; and the NCGA, the latter was replaced by the *Governmental Accounting Standards Board* (GASB), which now sets standards of accounting and financial reporting for state and local governments. Generally accepted accounting principles (GAAP) promulgated by GASB are widely, but not universally, followed by state and local governments.

Fund Accounting

To account for the diverse activities of state and local governments, accounts are divided into separate funds. As noted previously, statutes and regulations often require that government resources and expenditures be accounted for separately, by area of expenditure. This is called *fund accounting*, which, government officials argue, makes good sense because it gives a clearer picture of how the government's various sources of revenue are used to finance different kinds of expenditures.

Each fund includes a set of accounts to record the revenues, expenses, assets, liabilities, and fund balances of the activities of that fund. The GASB specifies seven major types of funds, which fall into three categories: (1) governmental, (2) proprietary, and (3) fiduciary. A governmental unit may require one or several funds of a single type or, in contrast, may require fewer than seven funds. Six of the seven types of funds are described in the following section. The other fund type is the *internal service fund*, categorized as a proprietary type of fund.

Governmental Funds   Most typical government functions are financed through the following funds:

- *The general fund.* This is normally the largest of the funds. It essentially accounts for all financial resources other than those accounted for in any other fund. Most current operations of the government are recorded here. Such revenue sources as property, income, and sales taxes will typically be recorded in the general fund.
- *Special revenue fund.* This fund records proceeds from specific sources that are usually earmarked for specific purposes, such as the care of parks, museums, or highways. Major capital projects and expendable trusts are recorded in other funds.
- *Capital projects fund.* Any resources used for the acquisition and construction of capital facilities are accounted for here. Exceptions are those projects financed by enterprise funds. The capital projects fund was created because so many capital projects are no longer funded with bonds but from other sources, such as direct revenues and grants. Separate capital projects funds are commonly set up for individual projects.
- *Debt service fund.* This fund records the payment of interest and principal on long-term general obligation debt as well as the accumulation of resources to pay off the debt.

Proprietary Funds   These funds account for government operations that are similar to those of business. The accounting principles for such funds are generally the same as those for business.

   Enterprise fund. This is essentially the fund in which ongoing activities that are operated like those of a business are recorded. Public utilities financed by user charges are one example of such activities. Proceeds from revenue bond issues and their dispositions are usually accounted for here.

   Internal service fund. This is a proprietary fund used to account for internal transfers of goods or other resources within a government.

Fiduciary Funds   These are *trust and agency funds*. They account for money or property that is being held by the governmental unit as a trustee, guardian, or agent for individuals, government entities, or nonpublic organizations. For example, pension funds and investment trust funds are recorded here.

Cash versus Accrual Basis of Accounting

One of the major sources of controversy in government accounting is the question of when to record expenditures and revenues. Businesses do their accounting on an *accrual basis*—that is, revenues are recorded when they are earned, not when the cash comes in, and expenses are recorded when they are incurred, not simply when they are paid. Most governments, on the other hand, use a modified accrual basis of accounting, and it is now required by GASB.

The *modified accrual basis* for governmental accounting is known as *generally accepted accounting principles* (GAAP). Because a government is not trying to measure expenses against sales as a business does, GAAP requires that revenues be recognized only when they are available and measurable, whereas expenditures generally should be recognized when incurred. However, according to GAAP, interest and principal payments on debt should be recorded only when the payment is due. Other expenditures that are not normally liquidated with available expendable financial resources—and therefore are not accrued—include compensated absences, claims, and judgments.

Budgeting

Budgeting is the primary means of financial management and control for governments. The GASB requires that budgets be drawn up annually for all government funds, although there is no enforcement mechanism (e.g., GAAP) for this. The GASB also requires that comparisons between actual and budgeted revenues and expenditures be provided regularly, along with the financial statements.

Financial Reporting

The GASB requires that governmental units prepare both a comprehensive annual financial report and a report that includes a more limited set of *general-purpose financial statements*. The GASB states that the latter type is adequate for official statements as well as for widespread distribution to those not interested in greater detail. The *comprehensive annual financial report*, however, is the official annual report. The GASB also requires that independent audits be undertaken of all state and local government financial statements, although GAAP does not require this.

The GASB requires that general-purpose financial statements include:

- Combined balance sheet of all types of funds and account groups.
- Combined statement of revenues, expenditures, and changes in balances of all governmental funds.
- Combined statement of revenues, expenditures, and changes in fund balances—both budget and actual—of general and special revenue funds and of similar governmental funds for which annual budgets have been legally adopted.
- Combined statement of revenues, expenses, and changes in retained earnings (or equity) of all proprietary fund types.
- Combined statement of cash flows for all proprietary funds (GASB Statement 9).
- Notes to the financial statements.

The GASB requires that the comprehensive annual financial report contain all these statements as well as considerably more detail. All the materials GASB recommends for both the comprehensive report and the general-purpose statements are listed in the *GASB Codification*, published by the GASB.

In June 1999, the GASB issued Statement 34, which established new financial reporting requirements for state and local governments. The new financial reporting was designed to make it easier for users of financial statements to assess whether the government's overall financial position has improved or deteriorated. In addition, citizens should be able to evaluate the costs of providing services, understand how various programs are financed, and analyze the government's infrastructure investment. Basic financial statements and required supplementary information for general-purpose governments consist of:

- Management's discussion and analysis. This comes before the basic financial statements. It gives an analytical overview of the government's financial activities. The analysis includes significant changes in funds and in the budget. Capital asset and long-term debt activity should be discussed, as well as any currently known conditions or facts that may have an effect on operations.
- Basic financial statements. These include government-wide financial statements, fund financial statements, and notes to the financial statements. A major change from the old model for government-wide financial statements is that all capital assets, including infrastructure assets,

are capitalized at their actual or estimated historical cost. In general, depreciation expense is reported in the statement of activities. In addition, the government-wide statement of activities reports the change in net assets for the period. Statement 34 also amended the requirements for proprietary funds and fiduciary funds.

- Required supplementary information. This includes budgetary comparisons. The original budget is compared to the final budget for the general fund and individual major special revenue funds.

These changes were phased in, with larger governments implementing them for the fiscal year beginning June 2001.

Through December 2010, the GASB has published 62 Statements, some of which are technical in nature while others have a broader impact. Among the more important ones that took effect in recent years are Statements 43 and 45, which describe how municipalities should account for postemployment benefits other than pensions, such as retiree health care. Statement 48 requires governments to report securitized future revenue streams (for example, income from the tobacco industry settlement) in most cases as a liability to be amortized over the life of the securitization rather than current revenue. Statement 49 covers remediation costs for existing pollution, such as asbestos removal, which must be expensed rather than capitalized except in limited specified circumstances. Statement 53 sets out accounting and financial reporting standards for derivative instruments, which are widely used by municipal issuers today.

CHAPTER 4

The Primary Market

ISSUANCE TRENDS IN THE PRIMARY MARKET

In 2010, $498.6 billion was raised in the municipal bond markets for state and local governments, compared with $172.7 billion in 1986. Long-term debt issues alone amounted to $433.3 billion in 2010, which included a flurry of activity in the fourth quarter when municipalities scrambled to issue Build America Bonds before the program expired at year end. Table 4.1 details short- and long-term issuance of municipal debt from 1986 to 2010. Volume has fluctuated around a rising trend over this 25-year time period. Volume tends to increase in a low-interest rate environment as well as in response to changes in legislation and the need for infrastructure improvement. A drop in issuance may be attributable to higher interest rates, fewer refundings, the completion of major infrastructure projects, and negative voter sentiment that reduced the number of bond issue approvals.

One of the most important trends of the past 25 years has been the increasing dominance of negotiated underwriting. From 1986 to 2000, the proportion of negotiated issues averaged 74.6 percent and dropped below 70 percent only once, in 1994. In the 10 years through 2010, negotiated issues averaged 81.2 percent of the total, and the preponderance of negotiated over competitive issues increased as the decade progressed. Table 4.2 details the volume of competitive sales and negotiated sales and their percentage of the long-term new-issue market from 1986 through 2010.

At one time, it was axiomatic that GO bonds were sold through the competitive bid process and revenue bonds were sold through the negotiated process. As general obligation deal structures became more complex and issues sizes increased, an increasing proportion of GO bonds were sold through negotiated underwriting in order to ensure the best financing outcomes for borrowers. Based on dollar volume of general obligation bonds from 1986 to 2010, negotiated sales exceeded competitive sales by a comfortable margin

93

TABLE 4.1 Total Short- and Long-Term Municipal Securities Issuance, with Percentage Change in Volume from the Prior Year, 1986 to 2010

Year	Short-Term Volume ($ billions)	Long-Term Volume ($ billions)	Total Volume ($ billions)	Percentage Change from Prior Year (%)
1986	22.0	150.7	172.7	
1987	20.5	105.5	126.0	−27.1
1988	23.6	119.4	143.0	13.5
1989	29.6	125.6	155.2	8.5
1990	34.8	128.0	162.8	4.9
1991	44.4	172.7	217.1	33.4
1992	43.0	235.5	278.5	28.2
1993	47.5	293.0	340.5	22.3
1994	40.4	165.0	205.4	−39.7
1995	38.4	159.7	198.1	−3.5
1996	41.7	184.6	226.3	14.2
1997	46.4	220.4	266.9	17.9
1998	34.7	286.5	321.2	20.4
1999	36.7	227.4	264.0	−17.8
2000	41.2	200.2	241.4	−8.6
2001	56.9	286.8	343.7	42.4
2002	72.4	357.4	429.8	25.1
2003	69.8	382.7	452.5	5.3
2004	56.9	358.7	415.6	−8.1
2005	50.5	408.2	458.7	10.4
2006	44.0	387.9	431.9	−5.8
2007	57.9	429.0	486.9	12.7
2008	60.8	389.6	450.5	−7.5
2009	64.7	409.8	474.6	5.4
2010	65.3	433.3	498.6	5.1

Source: Thomson Reuters.

but, in that same period, negotiated sales were still a far greater proportion for revenue bonds. Table 4.3 shows the volume of all negotiated and competitive sales from 1986 through 2010, categorized by either GO or revenue bond, and the percentage of each category in the whole market.

Based on the number of issues, the pattern is somewhat different. Table 4.4 shows the number of all negotiated and competitive issues from 1986 through 2010, categorized as either GO or revenue bond issues, and the percentage each category represents of the entire market. Most significantly, competitive general obligation issues accounted for 52.7 percent

TABLE 4.2 Long-Term Municipal Debt Issuance, by Competitive and Negotiated Sales, 1986 to 2010

	Competitive Sales		Negotiated Sales		Total
Year	Principal Amount ($ billions)	Percent of New Issue Market	Principal Amount ($ billions)	Percent of New Issue Market	Long-Term Amount ($ billions)
1986	33.0	21.9	114.6	76.1	150.7
1987	23.4	22.2	78.1	74.1	105.5
1988	26.5	22.2	90.6	75.9	119.4
1989	29.7	23.6	92.7	73.8	125.6
1990	30.1	23.5	95.8	74.8	128.0
1991	40.2	23.3	129.3	74.9	172.7
1992	44.2	18.8	188.0	79.9	235.5
1993	55.6	19.0	234.6	80.1	293.0
1994	49.4	29.9	112.8	68.4	165.0
1995	40.8	25.5	115.0	72.0	159.7
1996	47.0	25.4	134.0	72.6	184.6
1997	47.8	21.7	166.2	75.4	220.4
1998	65.3	22.8	215.0	75.1	286.5
1999	52.8	23.2	166.5	73.2	227.4
2000	48.7	24.3	145.3	72.6	200.2
2001	63.1	22.0	220.5	76.9	286.8
2002	71.8	20.1	282.8	79.1	357.4
2003	75.6	19.8	302.9	79.2	382.7
2004	68.8	19.2	287.1	80.0	358.7
2005	76.1	18.6	330.4	80.9	408.2
2006	69.6	17.9	312.5	80.6	387.9
2007	72.8	17.0	351.3	81.9	429.0
2008	53.4	13.7	333.1	85.5	389.6
2009	58.0	14.1	349.0	85.2	409.8
2010	73.2	16.9	357.5	82.5	433.3

Source: Thomson Reuters.

of the number of new issues versus 42.3 percent of the dollar volume of new issues, while competitive revenue issues were 13.8 percent of the number of issues versus 8.7 percent of the dollar volume. During this period, competitive underwriting was used more widely for smaller issues in both categories.

These charts provide the background for the next section, which describes negotiated and competitive underwriting.

TABLE 4.3 Long-Term Municipal Debt Issuance, General Use of Proceeds, 1986 to 2010 (based on volume)

	Negotiated		Competitive		
	Sales ($ billions)	Percent of New Issues	Sales ($ billions)	Percent of New Issues	Total Sales ($ billions)
General Obligation	1,265.7	57.3	932.9	42.3	2,207.8
Revenue	3,939.7	89.3	384.0	8.7	4,409.8
Total	5,205.4	78.7	1,316.9	19.9	6,617.6

Note: Excludes private placements.
Source: Thomson Reuters.

TABLE 4.4 Long-Term Municipal Debt Issuance, General Use of Proceeds, 1986 to 2010 (by number of issues)

	Negotiated		Competitive		
	Number of Issues	Percent of New Issues	Number of Issues	Percent of New Issues	Total Number of Issues
General Obligation	70,367	46.0	80,720	52.7	153,118
Revenue	116,447	80.1	19,983	13.8	145,292
Total	186,814	62.6	100,703	33.7	298,410

Note: Excludes private placements.
Source: Thomson Reuters.

THE BASICS OF UNDERWRITING

The vast number of new municipal offerings each year, originating in every region of the United States, has given rise to a large underwriting industry. The highest volume of underwriting activity is concentrated in national firms and large banks. According to Thomson Reuters, the 25 leading underwriters senior managed 88.6 percent of the total dollar volume of all new long-term issues in 2010. Even greater concentrations exist, with 72.9 percent of the long-term dollar volume senior managed by the top 10 firms. There are also small, local underwriters that primarily handle their own communities' and states' bond offerings.

The Role of Banks in Underwriting

There are four ways that commercial banks can underwrite municipal bonds: (1) through a traditional structure of a bond department within the bank registered with the Municipal Securities Rulemaking Board (MSRB), (2) through a broker-dealer affiliate organized under the Bank Holding Company Act, (3) through an operating subsidiary of the bank, or (4) through a financial subsidiary of the bank.

Until 1999, banks generally could only underwrite general obligation bonds and certain bank eligible revenue bonds. However, the *Financial Modernization Act of 2000* gave banks the authority to underwrite revenue bonds, which had been restricted under the Banking Act of 1933 (the Glass-Steagall Act). The Modernization Act provided that the limitations and restrictions regarding the authority of a bank to deal in, underwrite, and purchase investment securities for the bank's own account do not apply to certain obligations issued by or on behalf of any state or political subdivision of a state or any public agency or authority of any state or political subdivision of a state.

Competitive and Negotiated Underwriting

In principle, the job of the underwriter is straightforward. For a competitive sale, the underwriters bid against each other by submitting to the issuer on a given day at a given time a sealed bid to buy the issuer's bonds and then reoffer them to investors. The underwriter that offers to pay the lowest interest cost for the bonds will win the competitive sale. In a negotiated offering, where there is no sealed bid, the underwriter is chosen before the actual sale date through the competitive Request for Proposal (RFP) process discussed in Chapter 3. Under both procedures, the senior underwriter functions as the quarterback of the deal by coordinating the traders, the salespeople, and all the members of the syndicate.

In recent years, issuers have routinely asked underwriters to indicate their fees in their written or oral proposals. Although the fee is usually a preliminary quote, it has the practical effect of making a "negotiated issue" extremely competitive on price. The underwriter's fee from the bond sale, called the *gross spread*, is the difference between the price the underwriter pays the issuer for the bonds and the price at which the bonds are reoffered to the investing public. The gross spread is also referred to as the *underwriter's discount*. Spreads are usually quoted in terms of dollars per thousand bonds. For example, for each $1,000 the issuer borrows through a negotiated issue, the gross spread that the underwriters get may be $6, with the net proceeds to the issuer $994.

The gross spread is allocated to the various expenses that have been incurred during the financing. Typical underwriter's expenses may include, but are not limited to:

- Underwriter's counsel
- Insurance fee
- Investor information meetings
- Travel
- Advertising
- CUSIP fee
- MSRB fee
- Professional salaries
- Sales commissions
- Overhead
- Cost of capital (including what is called *cost of carry*, the direct costs paid to maintain a securities position)
- Other out-of-pocket expenses

The gross spread less the sum of the expenses is the underwriter's net profit or net loss. This assumes that the bonds are sold at the issue price. Sales at other than issue price may result in a different profit or loss to the underwriter.

The issuer is responsible for certain expenses, many of which can be paid from the bond proceeds. In addition to the capital project costs and reserve funds, the issuer's expenses may include, but are not limited to:

- Financial advisory fee
- Insurance fee
- Rating agency fee
- Issuer's counsel; bond counsel
- Feasibility study/engineer's report/marketing survey
- Printing costs

Table 4.5 details the average gross underwriting spreads for long-term issues from 1986 to 2010. Gross underwriting spreads for both negotiated and competitive sales declined steadily from 1986 through most of this period, reaching a low of 6.1 percent for negotiated issues in 2008 and 6.7 percent for competitive issues in 2007. The decline was greater for negotiated spreads, which used to be 100 basis points higher than competitive spreads. Negotiated spreads fell below competitive spreads for the first time in 2004 and have been equal to or lower than competitive spreads in every subsequent year except 2007.

TABLE 4.5 Long-Term Municipal Debt Issuance: Average Gross Underwriting Spreads, 1986 to 2010 ($ amount per $1,000 bond)

Year	Negotiated Sales	Competitive Sales	All Long-Term Sales
1986	10.8	10.1	10.4
1987	11.0	9.8	10.4
1988	10.9	10.2	10.5
1989	11.1	9.7	10.5
1990	10.9	9.4	10.3
1991	10.6	9.4	10.1
1992	10.0	9.1	9.7
1993	9.5	8.4	9.2
1994	9.1	8.5	8.9
1995	9.0	8.1	8.7
1996	8.5	7.9	8.3
1997	8.4	7.9	8.2
1998	8.5	7.8	8.3
1999	8.4	7.9	8.3
2000	8.1	8.1	8.1
2001	7.8	7.6	7.8
2002	7.7	7.4	7.7
2003	7.6	7.3	7.5
2004	6.9	7.1	7.0
2005	6.8	7.0	6.8
2006	7.1	7.1	7.1
2007	6.9	6.7	6.9
2008	6.1	7.7	6.4
2009	7.3	7.5	7.3
2010	7.4	7.7	7.5

Note: Excludes private placements.
Source: Thomson Reuters.

In both negotiated and competitive sales, underwriters assume complete risk and responsibility for selling the bonds. Competitive underwriting is more risky because, when a bid is made, that bid is final. The underwriter is committed to the price, regardless of whether the market goes up or down. In a negotiated sale, the underwriter negotiates a price when the deal is underwritten based on how the issue is selling, not on a specific time schedule, and the underwriter can adjust the yield to respond to market conditions. Successful underwriting depends on professionals who know all aspects of the primary and secondary market and who keep in touch with what investors need and want for their portfolios at that point in time. Successful underwriters master the delicate balance of finding the yield that produces not only the lowest borrower cost for the issuer but also the highest yield for the investor consistent with the issuer's credit and deal structure. They also generally have enough capital to carry their positions during the selling period, if the issue sells slowly.

For most sizable issues, negotiated or competitive, underwriters join in a syndicate in order to spread the risk of the sale and to gain wider access to potential investors. The composition of syndicates varies from issue to issue. One syndicate comanager might be a major national securities firm, while the other might be a smaller dealer with a strong marketing organization in the region or state of the issuer. Another team might combine a manager specializing in institutional sales with a so-called *wire house*, a firm with many branch offices and a broad clientele of individual investors.

The procedures, rules, and technicalities involved in underwriting an issue are intricate, and the pace is often very fast. Major underwriting firms may bid on and purchase dozens of issues a week while running the books as senior manager on several negotiated issues at the same time.

Advantages and Disadvantages of Competitive and Negotiated Underwriting

The choice between competitive bidding and a negotiated sale offers advantages and disadvantages to the issuer, summarized below.

Advantages of Competitive Bidding

- In theory, the lowest possible capital cost is likely to be achieved because competing underwriters have a strong incentive to find investors willing to pay the highest prices for the bonds.
- Competitive sales insulate municipal officials from potential accusations of favoritism or impropriety in choosing the underwriter for a negotiated offering.
- Underwriters may bid aggressively for a competitive issue in the expectation that they will be better placed to secure future negotiated underwriting mandates.

Disadvantages of Competitive Bidding

- Bidders may factor in a risk premium because they do not know whether they will secure the underwriting mandate.
- An issuer cannot change the sale date or the structure of an issue after the notice of sale is published no matter how market conditions change before the bonds are sold.
- An issuer has no control over the composition of the underwriting syndicate.

- Competing syndicates may lead to trapped bidders (members of a losing syndicate who would have paid more than the winning bid for some bonds), which prevents the issuer from getting the best possible price.

Advantages of Negotiated Sale

- The selected underwriter may be able to perform certain functions carried out by an outside advisor in a competitive issue, eliminating the additional cost.
- The underwriter can do more presale marketing, which increases the likelihood that investors willing to pay the highest prices for the bonds will be found.
- The issuer and underwriter can respond to changing market conditions by altering the terms of the bonds or deferring the sale date.
- The issuer has greater control over the composition of the underwriting syndicate.
- In recent years, the average gross underwriting spread has been slightly lower for negotiated sales.

Disadvantages of Negotiated Sale

- There is no direct competition among underwriters in setting the terms of the offering, which may prevent the issuer from achieving the lowest possible cost.
- The gross underwriting spread covers additional services that may differ from one issuer to another, making it harder to compare costs to determine whether the spread is appropriate.
- Municipal officials may be open to accusations of favoritism toward the selected underwriter.

Numerous academic studies of the relative costs of issuance have not demonstrated a clear advantage to one method of underwriting over the other. Market practitioners see merits in both methods, depending on the circumstances. As a practical matter, issues that are very large, complex, or involve high-risk credits are almost always sold through negotiated underwriting. Issuers have an incentive to choose whichever method they expect to produce the lowest cost in their particular circumstances.

NEGOTIATED UNDERWRITING

By far the most common method of issuing municipal bonds is through the negotiated underwriting procedure described below.

Selection of Managers

Before the sale as described in Chapter 3, the issuer selects the senior manager. The issuer may also select one or more senior comanagers or one or more comanagers or may choose to let the senior manager "sole" manage the issue. For large and frequent issuers, a team of underwriters may be picked to serve for several transactions. In such cases, the senior managers may rotate their positions as each deal comes up, in much the same way as established competitive syndicates operate. When a large new credit makes its debut in the market, it is considered most prestigious to be chosen as the initial senior manager.

Forming a Syndicate

After the issuer selects the managers, it is up to the managers to bring additional members into the syndicate, if necessary. It is the job of the senior manager to make a judgment about the size and composition of the syndicate. The senior manager may want a firm that has a particular distribution capability in the kind of credit being sold, such as health care or high-yield bonds. The issuer may also want certain firms to be in the syndicate, such as other national firms, or local firms that are not large enough to be managers but that have strong local and regional distribution networks. The financial advisor or issuer may believe that including or excluding certain firms for any number of reasons (legal, reputation, etc.) will add to the strength of the syndicate.

There are times when the senior manager may not want to form a syndicate at all, preferring to price and market the bonds solely with the other managers. Reasons for this may include the size of the issue, its prominence, whether it can be sold easily, and its potential profitability. Alternately, the issuer or financial advisors or the underwriters themselves may decide to include a *selling group*, instead of a syndicate, as part of the offering.

Selling Groups

Selling groups are formed by underwriters and syndicate managers to participate in the initial distribution of municipal bonds. In some instances, particularly in smaller offerings, a senior manager will form a selling group rather than a syndicate. Members of a selling group are brokers and dealers who are permitted by the senior manager to acquire underwritten municipal securities for resale on the same terms offered to syndicate members. However, selling group members do not share in the syndicate's net underwriting profits, nor do they assume *pro rata* liability for any underwriting loss or for the purchase of any unsold securities.

Agreement among Underwriters

As part of the syndicate formation, the lead manager circulates the *Agreement Among Underwriters* (AAU), which is the legal document generally used in negotiated sales. The standard AAU was originally developed in 1991 by the Bond Market Association, a predecessor to the Securities Industry and Financial Markets Association, and consisted of two sections: (1) instructions, terms, and acceptance, and (2) standard terms and conditions. In 1997 and 2002, the Bond Market Association released revisions to the original AAU by simplifying the agreement to reflect changes in market practices and legal requirements. The 2002 amendments created two versions of the AAU, one for competitive transactions and the other for negotiated deals. They also switched to an electronic master format, which means once an agreement between any two municipal securities dealers is executed it covers all future underwriting transactions on which they work together. The specific details of each transaction are spelled out in a separate communication that documents each underwriter's participation in that particular deal, to which the terms of the master agreement also apply. The standard forms of master agreement are publicly available at the Securities Industry and Financial Markets Association web site (www.sifma.org).

Credit and Research

In a negotiated sale, the underwriter must obtain the preliminary official statement, which has been deemed final under Rule 15c2-12, and review it in a professional manner. The underwriter is obligated to have a reasonable basis for recommending any municipal security and is responsible for reviewing in a professional manner the accuracy of the offering statements. In negotiated municipal offerings, where the underwriter is involved in the preparation of the official statement, the SEC believes that development of a reasonable basis for belief in the accuracy and completeness of the statements should involve an inquiry into the key representations in the official statement. Here, too, the inquiry must be conducted in a professional manner, drawing on the underwriters' experience with the particular issuer, and other issuers, as well as their knowledge of the municipal markets. Sole reliance on the representation of the issuer does not suffice.

The continuing disclosure agreements required by the Securities and Exchange Commission (SEC) must also be in place. In some firms, the public finance bankers perform these due-diligence and underwriting tasks; in other firms, the credit and research professionals have that responsibility. Chapter 9 contains an extensive discussion of securities law and disclosure.

Marketing the Bonds

One of the major advantages of a negotiated sale is that time can be devoted to presale marketing. Salespeople can concentrate more on a negotiated issue in which their firm is a senior or comanager than on a competitive sale because they are certain that there will be an underwriting and bonds to sell. The salespeople thus work together with the public finance bankers in the early stages of a deal to develop a marketing plan for the bonds. The presale activities can take many forms, depending on the size and complexity of the issue. Often a conference call or webcast will be organized so that the issuer can make a presentation to the underwriters' institutional clients. The investors will have been sent the preliminary official statement, typically in electronic form. Sometimes a presentation book that highlights the key features of the deal is also delivered to investors. Investors then ask the issuer and the investment bankers questions on the credit and other aspects of the offering.

The underwriter may arrange a *road show*, where the issuer travels to meet potential investors. The Internet is sometimes used for financial road shows, which reduces the need for travel and makes the information available to a broader audience. An information meeting where the issuer makes a formal presentation may be part of the road show. A summary analysis of the key features of the deal may be distributed to salespeople with a retail clientele. Again, the purpose is to provide a forum for investors to ask as many probing questions as are needed to fully understand the financing.

Pricing the Bonds

At a propitious time, the senior manager will inform the market that the deal is ready to be priced. Negotiated sales do not usually require the more formal competitive sale notice; a notice to *The Bond Buyer* or other news service is normally sufficient to alert the whole market to the deal (the syndicate has already been formed). The night before the expected pricing of the bonds, the senior manager sends a *consensus scale* to the syndicate members. This scale is a listing by maturity of the prices or yields at which a new issue will be offered. The scale is the result of many conversations among the syndicate members, their salespeople, the public finance investment banker, and the issuer. The next morning, a preliminary scale usually will be distributed to the syndicate. The manager will run the books during the *order period* (a set period of time that depends on market conditions and the issuer). The manager keeps centralized information on which maturities are over-subscribed, meaning more orders received than the par amount, and which are undersubscribed, meaning fewer orders received than the par amount. After the initial order period, the underwriter makes a decision either to extend the order period in order to get more orders or to terminate it. If the order period is extended, the scale is adjusted to market conditions to make some bonds either richer (higher dollar price, lower yield) or cheaper (lower dollar price, higher yield).

At some point during the day, the underwriter proposes a final scale and bid to the issuer. The underwriter then tells the issuer that the deal is *underwritten*. This can, and often does, happen even if all of the bonds have not yet been sold. To attract investors and react to the market, the structure may have been changed, the par amount may have been changed, and the call features may have been changed from the original scale. This flexibility usually gets the best price and structure for the issuer.

After the deal is verbally underwritten and a final pricing communication is sent to the syndicate, the final pricing information is disseminated to the rest of the market through electronic and print media. The formal purchase contract between the underwriter and the issuer, the BPA, is signed. The syndicate desk then processes orders and allocates bonds, as described later in this chapter.

COMPETITIVE UNDERWRITING

A less common, but still widely used, procedure for issuing municipal bonds is through a competitive underwriting, described below.

Informing the Market

The notice of sale. Placing an official *notice of sale* or announcement electronically and in local and national newspapers and in trade publications is the usual way to initiate a competitive sale. Notice to *The Bond Buyer* is virtually a requirement for any significant issue. News services also distribute the information electronically. This electronic notice is often called a summary notice of sale. Active issuers usually send the notice of sale directly to prospective bidders and have the preliminary official statement available on their own web site. Notices are organized in a calendar format, allowing the underwriters to keep close track of all new issues that are coming to market.

The notice of sale typically includes:

- Name of issuer.
- Dollar amount of issue.
- Date, time, and place of sale.
- Purpose, authorization, and security features.
- Dollar denominations.
- Form of bond; name of registration nominee and depository.
- Bond insurance, if available.
- Name of paying agent, bond registrar, or trustee.
- Dated date of bonds.
- Interest payment dates.
- Maturity schedule and call features.
- Basis for bidding and method of award.
- Structure and restrictions on coupon rates.
- Total amount of the bid at par or better or discount if allowed.
- Required amount of good-faith deposit.
- Statement of issuer's right to reject any or all bids.
- Covenant to enter into an *undertaking*, a written agreement or contract to provide ongoing disclosure under SEC Rule 15c2-12.
- Method, approximate date, and place of settlement for the bonds.
- Conditions for delivering the *final official statement*.
- Name of bond counsel and list of opinions and documents that will be provided.
- Name of financial advisor.
- Statement on whether the issue is bank qualified.

Electronic dissemination of the information is the normal method for distributing the notice of sale. Electronic commerce in municipal bonds is discussed in more detail in Chapter 5.

Forming a Syndicate for a Competitive Sale

For small issues, a single dealer may bid on the entire offering. For larger issues, as explained earlier in this chapter, underwriters usually form bidding syndicates. Traditionally, underwriters stay with the group with which their firms bid on the last occasion that the issuer came to market; conversely, most firms are in different syndicates for different issuers. The composition of a syndicate can change, of course. Firms go out of business, new firms are started, and some firms may simply want to drop out of the syndicate for a particular offering.

Syndicates in municipal bonds can have as few as two members or as many as 100 or more members. There may be one manager or several comanagers, although only one of them—the senior or lead manager—actually runs the books of the account, that is, keeps track of sales and the availability of bonds. It is customary for the managers to rotate their positions each time the same issuer comes to market. For example, if Firm A is the senior manager on a deal in March and the same issuer comes to market again in September, Firm B will rotate to the comanager, or senior manager position. If the issuer sells on a regular semiannual schedule and there are three senior comanagers, Firm A will be the senior manager again in September of the next year. However, it remains within each firm's discretion to join or remain in a syndicate. If a firm decides not to be in a given syndicate, or if it wants to bid alone, it is free to do so.

Syndicate Letters and Account Structures

The syndicate members are bound together on any issue by the syndicate letter or contract. This letter specifies the terms under which the account will be managed, including the obligations of all the members. The lead manager sends the letter to each member of the account—typically two weeks before the issue is to be sold. Each member must sign and return to the manager a copy of the syndicate letter, indicating the member's acceptance of the terms. The letters vary, but they generally include:

- Preliminary amount of bonds to be underwritten by each member, called the *participations.*
- Duration of the account.
- Acknowledgment that the bid and offering terms will be set by the majority of the members.
- Obligations of members as to expenses, good-faith deposit, and liability for any unsold bonds.
- Appointment of the manager as agent for the account.
- Granting of rights to the syndicate manager, including rights to borrow, advertise, pledge securities, and make the bid.
- Granting of unspecified authority to the manager where necessary for the proper performance of management functions.
- A provision that no liability is assumed by the manager except for lack of good faith.
- Priority of orders (MSRB requirement).

The most commonly used syndicate account structure is one that is undivided as to sales and liability. Members of the account pool the bonds they have to sell as well as the liability for any unsold bonds. Thus, syndicate members can sell any of the bonds in an account as long as they are available. However, the syndicate profits are divided according to the *participations* agreed on before the sale, no matter how many bonds any individual member sells. If any bonds cannot be sold, all members are liable for a proportionate share of those bonds according to the same participations.

For example, a member might have a 10 percent participation in an account but sell only 5 percent of the bonds. In this case, the member is still entitled to 10 percent of the syndicate's net underwriting profits. However, that same member may sell more than 10 percent of the bonds, while the syndicate as a whole fails to sell the entire issue. In this case, the member is still liable for 10 percent of the unsold bonds, despite its own sales record, and will still receive only 10 percent of any underwriting profits—or be assessed for 10 percent of net underwriting losses. Syndicate managers usually take the largest participations; other members take varying amounts of participation.

The undivided account structure described above was historically known as an *Eastern account* because its roots were in the major national financial centers of the Northeast. It is currently the predominant structure used for competitive bids. The divided, or *Western account*, is another type of structure whose use has declined drastically. In a divided account, members are assigned a portion of each of several groups of bonds. The bonds, for example, might be broken down into several categories (or brackets) of different maturities. However, the account is divided only as to liability, not as to sales. Thus, as in the undivided account, a firm can sell any of the bonds in the issue, according to a priority that is discussed later in this chapter. However, a member is liable for unsold bonds only if it has not sold its full participation in each bracket.

It should be emphasized that net underwriting profits are by no means the only revenues that the members of a syndicate can earn through participation in an underwriting. They receive discounts, known as concessions and takedowns, on bonds they sell or take for their own inventory. If a member can sell bonds for the offering price or at a smaller discount than the member's price, the profit on these sales is part of the firm's revenues. This is discussed more fully later in this chapter.

Credit and Research

An extensive discussion of SEC Rule 15c2-12 is included in Chapter 9, but it is important here to understand how the rule imposes responsibility on the underwriter in the primary market with regard to credit review and disclosure. The SEC has written that in a normal competitive bid offering involving an established municipal issuer, a municipal underwriter generally would meet its obligation to have a reasonable basis for belief in the accuracy of the key representations in the official statement if it reviewed the official statement in a professional manner and received from the issuer a detailed and credible explanation concerning any aspect of the official statement that appeared on its face, or on the basis of information available to the underwriter, to be inadequate.

The job of reviewing official statements for competitive bids is often assigned to the credit and research staffs of the municipal bond dealers. The analysts also check to see that the issuer has committed, in writing, to continuing disclosure. These responsibilities come in addition to the more traditional role of the underwriter, determining through extensive research the relative creditworthiness of an offering. If their own research analysts are particularly confident about the financial health of a municipality, the underwriters may make a more aggressive bid for the offering. However, if a firm's municipal analysts believe that the disclosure is inadequate or that the credit is weak, the firm may not bid at all.

The rating agencies and bond insurers also review the issue before the competitive sale in anticipation of releasing a rating or an insurance commitment. This process is discussed extensively in Chapter 7.

The Preliminary Scale

The formation of the syndicate sets in motion the actual competitive bidding process for the dealer. Typically, on the day before the bid is to be placed, the managers put out a *preliminary scale*, which is a listing by maturity of the prices or yields at which the issue will be offered. Syndicate members are also asked for their preliminary pricing ideas at this time. The preliminary scale is developed with the goal of coming up with the highest dollar bid and lowest interest cost to the issuer while still being confident of selling the bonds at a profitable spread (which is also tested at this preliminary scale). The senior manager must be careful to develop the scale in accordance with the parameters set forth in the notice of sale. This includes the basis of the bid (true interest cost or net interest cost) and whether only par and not discount bonds are allowed.

After the preliminary scale is set, the underwriters at the firms in the syndicate distribute the scale to their own traders and salespeople. This is done to gauge the interest that the market has in the issue and to see how other comparable issues have sold. The salespeople at the firms solicit orders, and frequently, some orders for the bonds have already been lined up before the actual bid.

The manager must also make arrangements for a good-faith deposit to be delivered at the time stated in the notice of sale. The good-faith deposit is a security deposit, which the issuer retains as compensation in the event that the winning bidder fails to pay for the bonds or notes on the delivery date.

The amount of the good-faith requirement is established by the issuer and is stated in the notice of sale. In most cases, the winning syndicate's good-faith deposit is subtracted from the final payment for the issue at the time of delivery and final settlement. The good-faith deposit may range from 1 to 5 percent of the par value of the bonds or notes; it is normally about 2 percent. The good-faith deposits of the losing syndicates are returned to their managing underwriters immediately after the bid award has been made. Instead of the cashier's or certified check that had traditionally been used for the good-faith requirement, issuers can use a financial surety bond. The issuer's bond documents must authorize the use of surety for the good-faith deposit.

Pricing Call on the Day of the Bid

There is a final pricing conference call usually one hour before the bid is due. The call begins with the manager announcing the proposed pricing scale and recommending the size of the spread. If any sales have been made or lined up already, they are announced at this time. The final pricing call can create tremendous tension because there is intense pressure to submit the best bid on time.

During the final pricing call, the senior manager also informs syndicate members of the latest developments in the market. The yields on other issues for sale that day are watched closely as benchmarks for determining yields on the issue being underwritten. The manager then polls the members for their opinions about the scales and the spread. Disagreements among the members often arise at this time. They tend to center on the yields for particular maturities or on the size of the spread. Members may drop out of the syndicate at any time before the bid is placed, and some do so at this time.

During this period, the salespeople at the syndicate firms are working to line up orders and to determine where on the scale demand is strong or weak. The underwriters are continuously informed as those orders are received. In an offering that is going well, some maturities may sell out before the call is over. As orders come in, the members can start to raise their bids by lowering the yields on some maturities. Conversely, the salespeople may be communicating to the underwriter why they are not getting orders. There may be pricing or credit problems or competition with other issues. If few orders come in, the syndicate may become more cautious and raise yields to sweeten the deal.

Sometimes the members decide the spread is too small and try to get the manager to widen, or increase it. Occasionally, a compromise is reached, where the spread is widened while yields on some maturities are reduced. Generally, the manager wields the most influence at the price meetings, but a big order from a member can force a sudden adjustment in the scale. The order period, which usually runs for one or two hours, is also set at the final pricing call. A few minutes before the deadline, the final scale is set and the bid is calculated.

Delivery of the Bid

The senior manager makes the arrangements to deliver the sealed bid before the deadline. The deadline is adhered to very strictly, and any irregularities will disqualify the bidder. Electronic bid submission is now the most common practice. Bids are also sometimes made by phone, fax, or by hand delivery, with the good-faith deposit covered by a surety bond company. If the bid is to be hand-delivered, the senior manager makes sure that someone representing the syndicate delivers the bid properly. If needed, the good-faith deposit is submitted along with the bid form. Because most bidding is now conducted electronically, the results of an auction are known almost instantaneously. Competitive sale results are disseminated immediately through the news wires and are printed in the *Bond Buyer* the following day.

The winning syndicate then immediately works to sell the bonds, although the official award of the bonds usually occurs several hours after the bid, often after the financial advisor has verified that the bid numbers are correct.

ORDERS AND PROCEDURES

There are several types of orders associated with the primary market and several market practices associated with filling those orders.

Types of Orders

There are three types of orders—*net*, *concession*, and *takedown*. The highest-priced order is sold to investors *at the net*, that is, at the price or yield actually shown in the reoffering scale. These prices are always the ones agreed to by the underwriting group, which retains the full spread.

However, an underwriting group or syndicate will generally give up part of its spread to get orders from dealers who are not in the syndicate. These dealers are offered what is known as a *concession*, a fractional discount from the public offering price. The concession works as follows. A typical spread might be $5 per $1,000 bond (one-half point). The concession might be $1.25 (an eighth of a point), so that a nonsyndicate dealer with a municipal bond department would be entitled to buy the bonds for $998.75 and to sell them to a customer for the full $1,000, retaining the $1.25. These bonds are said to be bought at the concession. Since most bonds are sold in lots of 100 or more, the concession can be important to each firm's profit.

Individual members of a syndicate can buy the bonds *at the takedown* for their own accounts, for sale to another dealer, or for sale directly to an investor. The takedown is the fractional discount from the public offering price at which the underwriters purchase the bonds. The concession is a part of the takedown. The takedown might amount to an additional $1.25, the total takedown coming to $2.50. Hence, a syndicate member could buy the bonds at $997.50 and sell them to a dealer outside the group for $998.75; the dealer, in turn, could sell them for $1,000. In this case, the member would keep only the $1.25 for compensation. If the member sells the bonds at the net price to an investor, the syndicate member would then keep the full $2.50 takedown. To summarize, the net is the highest price, the takedown is the lowest price, and the concession is somewhere in the middle.

Priority of Orders

The priority of the types of orders is a critical part of an underwriting. If an offering is oversubscribed, low-priority orders may not be filled. According to MSRB's rule G-11, the priority of orders must be furnished in writing to all syndicate members. The AAU specifies the priority of orders in a negotiated financing as follows:

- *Group net orders.* These are orders taken at the net reoffering price. The spread is retained by the whole syndicate as part of its profit.
- *Net designated orders.* These are orders from investors at the net or concession price. The commission is designated by the investor to the syndicate member.
- *Members orders.* These orders are at the public offering price less the total takedown. They are purchases made by syndicate members for their own accounts or for sale to another dealer or investor.

Within each of these levels of priority, the syndicate may grant preferences in allocation to institutional purchasers, retail purchasers, or other purchasers if such preferences are in the best interests of the syndicate.

An exception can occur in a competitive offering. The difference in designation policy is that in a negotiated issue, the issuer determines designated orders, and in a competitive sale, the buyer makes the designation.

If the issue, or certain maturities of the issue, are oversubscribed, allotments will be made according to the priority of orders, as stated earlier. If given levels of priority bonds are oversubscribed; bonds are fairly allotted to members of the syndicate by the senior manager.

Many MSRB rules relate to the primary offering of securities. The public can access the most current MSRB's rules on the MSRB web site at www.MSRB.org.

Orders are usually confirmed by the manager of the account when the initial order period is over. However, only issues in the greatest demand are typically sold out within the one or two hours of the order period. Subsequently, orders are taken from members on a first-come, first-served basis, regardless of the type of order. When the issue is sold out, the syndicate is disbanded. Most syndicate accounts are set up to run for 30 days.

When an issue proves difficult to sell, the terms of the offering are often revised. Changing the terms usually requires the majority consent of the members, with votes weighted by their respective participations. If the issue still cannot be sold, the bonds may be distributed among the members. The members are free to sell them at whatever price they want or the bonds may be given to one or more bond brokers. The broker then puts the bonds out for a bid. Members of the syndicate also have the right to bid for the bonds, as may any other dealer. The party that produces the best bid for the group of bonds will win them, although the manager retains the right to reject all bids.

Retail Order Period

An exception to the priority of orders is a *retail order period*, during which the issuer requests that retail and smaller investors be allowed to place their orders for bonds before the institutional buyers do so. If an issuer opts to include a retail order period, orders received during that time will have the first priority. The goal is to have bonds available for both in-state and out-of-state investors and to have a fair distribution between retail and institutional investors. The retail investors generally have the ability to cancel their orders if the preliminary institutional price is increased.

In recent years, issuers have increasingly insisted that a retail order period be included in negotiated underwritings. As a practical matter, however, the definition of retail order varies from issuer to issuer, and the line between retail and institutional orders is sometimes nor clear.

After the Sale

After the issue is sold, the manager of the syndicate must undertake a number of procedures to confirm orders, deliver and pay for the bonds, and meet legal requirements. The MSRB Rule G-12 (the Board's Uniform Practice Code) describes the procedures for confirming orders to members in an underwriting. All sales of new issues are made on a "when, as, and if issued" basis. Written confirmations for "when, as, and if issued" orders must generally be sent within one business day following the trade date, according to MSRB Rule G-12(c). Rule G-15(a) establishes the requirements for confirmations to a customer.

Just after the purchase of the issue by the underwriters, the senior manager sends a letter to all members of the account, stating the terms of the issue. The letter sets forth the reoffering terms of the issue, including the spread, takedown, and concession, and confirms the price to be paid to the issuer. It also announces whether and how the issue will be advertised in the financial press, lists the participations of the members in a competitive sale, and includes other relevant information as well. The members must sign and return the letter. In most advertisements, the members of the account are listed in the order of the size of their participations.

MSRB Rule G-32 requires that before or at the time that customers are sent their final written confirmations, the underwriter must make available to each customer a copy of the issue's official statement in final form. In a negotiated sale, information on underwriting spreads, fees, and the offering price for each maturity must also be made available to customers; it is usually included in the final official statements. The rule requires members of the syndicate to promptly provide copies of official statements on request to dealers who have purchased the new-issue securities. It also places other requirements on managers and financial advisors to facilitate distribution of the disclosure documents.

It takes no longer than a month (and usually much less) from the sale date before the bonds are actually ready to be delivered to investors. This allows time for bond counsel to prepare the final opinion and a transcript of proceedings. Up to that point, bond counsel has given only a preliminary opinion and the sale of bonds is conditional on the final opinion. The transcript typically includes a certificate stating that there is no litigation pending against the bonds and a guarantee of the signatures of the officials who signed the bonds.

The senior manager must pay for the bonds when they are available for delivery. The manager may borrow the money to finance the purchase of the bonds. The payment made is the bid price plus accrued interest less the amount of the good-faith deposit. In turn, the bonds are delivered to the members of the account according to the allotments. The members then pay for their shares of the sales. As the payments come in, the manager pays off the loan, usually within a few days.

Once the bonds are paid for and expenses totaled, the senior manager will distribute the profits to members of the syndicate. If there was a loss on the underwriting, the members are assessed for their share. The distribution is accompanied by a final statement of the member participations and the expenses and profits of the syndicate.

Depending on the issue's dated date, investors are not always entitled to the full six months' interest for the first payment period. The interest payment may be a long or short first coupon. The investor must pay the accrued interest to the seller—in this case, the issuer. The investor then receives the accrued interest from the dated date up to but not including the interest payment date. Dealers will simply add on the accrued interest to the price of the bonds.

MSRB Rules adjust to meet changing industry practices and needs. Investors, issuers, and underwriters should consult the MSRB's web site at www.MSRB.org for the most current version of the rules.

CHAPTER 5

The Secondary Market

INTRODUCTION

Secondary markets exist to provide liquidity to investors, enabling them to sell a security after its initial offering. The best-known secondary markets are for corporate equities. Because stocks are not redeemable at a specific date, investors need a secondary market, such as the New York Stock Exchange, in order to convert their investments to cash. Bondholders expect to receive their principal in cash when their bonds mature, but they still want the option of selling their securities before maturity.

A thriving secondary market helps to support the primary market for securities. It also serves investors by providing them with an array of different types of securities at different points in time. The ability to buy or sell quickly enables investors to employ a variety of strategies for maximizing return within their risk constraints.

THE OVER-THE-COUNTER MARKET

Municipal bonds trade in the over-the-counter market, in which transactions are executed among dealers rather than on a central exchange.

Exchange versus Over the Counter

The two broad categories of financial markets are the *exchange market* and the *over-the-counter market*. Equities can be traded in an exchange market where publicly owned corporations meeting certain minimum capitalization and other requirements are listed. The price of the security is shown after each trade. Certain types of equities, including those of newer, smaller companies, are commonly traded over the counter. An over-the-counter market is one where transactions are executed through dealers, not through a centralized exchange.

Municipal bonds are traded in the over-the-counter market, with market participants primarily trading through voice contact. The market has changed in recent years as technology has allowed dealers and customers to interact through electronic trading systems that allow for instantaneous execution of transactions.

Electronic trading systems developed along with the growth of the Internet, which allows for connectivity among nearly all market participants. The minimal cost associated with this connectivity has allowed even the smallest individual investor access to tools and sophisticated information sources that used to be the private domain of institutional investors. In practice, however, most large institutional orders are still handled in the traditional way, while small orders for retail investors often trade on an electronic platform.

Before 1996, the size of the secondary market in municipal securities was hard to determine because there was no central listing of all trades. Table 5.1 shows that annual average daily trading volume grew from $1.1 billion in 1996 to $25.1 billion in 2007, but then dropped back to $12.5 billion in 2009. The complete report, including monthly data for the two most recent years, can be found on www.sifma.org.

Beginning in June 2009, the SEC required all municipal bond transactions to be reported within 15 minutes of the trade time to the MSRB, which

TABLE 5.1 Municipal Bond Market, Average Daily Trading Volume, 1996 to 2010 ($ billion)

	Municipal Bonds
1996	1.1
1997	1.1
1998	3.3
1999	8.3
2000	8.8
2001	8.8
2002	10.7
2003	12.6
2004	14.8
2005	16.9
2006	22.5
2007	25.1
2008	19.4
2009	12.5
2010	13.3

Source: Securities Industry and Financial Markets Association.

displays the information on its Electronic Municipal Market Access web site (www.emma.msrb.org). A sample screen is shown in Figure 5.1. Reading across, it displays the date and time of the trade, CUSIP, a description of the security, maturity date, coupon, price, yield to maturity, principal amount traded, and trade type. The list of transactions can be sorted on any of these items.

Other electronic trading systems offer various types of secondary market information for both the professional investor and for the public, including www.investinginbonds.com, a web site maintained by the Securities Industry and Financial Markets Association.

E-COMMERCE, INFORMATION, AND TECHNOLOGY

The municipal market, along with all other financial markets, has been transformed by the extensive use of technology. Dealers and investors have vast amounts of information literally at their fingertips, which they employ to help them manage positions and portfolios. Both large and small firms maintain their own web sites. They access specific news services with dedicated screens; they use television and radio and print media. Market professionals try to get as much information as they can to get a leg up on their competition, and technology enables them to do their jobs better.

Technology in its many forms does the following things in the municipal market:

- Furnishes data and news in a timely and comprehensive manner.
- Tracks primary and secondary market activity.
- Increases trading efficiency with electronic trading platforms.
- Increases liquidity in the secondary market, as investors and dealers have greater access to information.
- Disseminates key disclosure information.
- Responds to the constantly changing demands of the market by adding new features and products.
- Offers analytical tools to the investor and dealer.

Electronic Trading Systems

Electronic trading has made significant inroads in the municipal bond market, but, unlike most other markets, the penetration is concentrated among retail investors rather than institutions. In 2010, the average trade on TheMuniCenter, a leading electronic trading platform, was for approximately 80 bonds ($80,000 principal amount), a fraction of the size traded

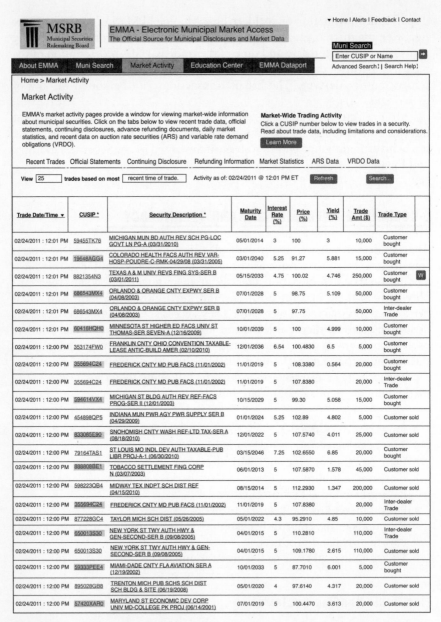

FIGURE 5.1 MSRB Daily Price Report
Source: Municipal Securities Rulemaking Board, EMMA (www.emma.msrb.org).

on the firm's institutional block platform, which averages more than 2,000 bonds ($2,000,000 principal amount).

The nature of the municipal bond market is an obstacle to the widespread use of electronic trading for institutional-size orders. In a large bond issue, a single issuer may sell two dozen or more serial bonds as well as several term bonds. As a result, the secondary market consists of millions of issues—many of which are owned by relatively few holders. It is the exact opposite of the equity markets, in which a few thousand issues are owned by millions of shareholders, so that someone, somewhere is almost always willing to buy or sell each security. In the highly liquid equity markets, electronic trading quickly became the dominant method of execution.

Municipal bonds typically trade actively for a few days to a few weeks after they are issued, but after a month or two most bonds end up in the hands of long-term investors, many of whom plan to hold them to maturity. The smaller serial bond maturities may never trade for months or even years at a time. Posting a bid or offer on an electronic platform is most unlikely to find a match in that environment.

If an institution wants to buy or sell large quantities of municipal bonds through the secondary market, it typically enlists members of the dealer community who are familiar with the bonds. A dealer that was involved in the original underwriting syndicate is the logical choice because it knows which clients bought bonds at the time they were issued. The lead under-writer that ran the syndicate book has even more information: It knows not only where the bonds it sold went, but also who bought every other bond in the entire issue. Secondary market order flow tends to gravitate to that firm, too, so it often has the best picture of who owns the bonds long after the issue date. Traders will call the known holders first as they start searching for buyers or sellers of those particular bonds.

Electronic trading has transformed the market for small retail orders in municipal bonds, however. Individual investors who used to rely on a single broker that had access only to their own firm's order flow can now have access to order flow from multiple sources aggregated on an electronic platform. They can search for bonds that interest them by various criteria, including state, coupon, maturity, yield, and type (general obligation or revenue bonds, for example), pick the one they like best and click through to place an order.

SELLING MUNICIPAL BONDS

The secondary market provides the liquidity for investors to sell their securities before the stated maturity date. Investors who sell may get a higher or a lower price for the bonds than they originally paid, depending on two major factors: market risk and credit risk.

Investors sell securities before maturity for a number of reasons:

- Concerns about unfavorable direction of interest rates.
- More attractive investments in the municipal or other markets.
- Changes in credit quality, including credit rating changes—especially downgrades.
- Mutual fund redemptions may create a need for cash.
- Profit taking if the value of bonds have appreciated.
- Cyclical changes in the investor's primary business may create a need for cash.
- Changes in the investor's financial circumstances.
- Heirs want to convert securities that they have inherited to cash.
- Tax law changes.
- Individual tax considerations.

Market risk is the term given to the potential price fluctuations in a bond that are caused by changes in the general level of municipal interest rates. If the level of these rates has changed since the bonds were bought, the resale value of those bonds reflect that shift. Thus, if interest rates are currently higher than they were when the bonds were bought, the bonds may be worth less; conversely, if interest rates have declined, bond prices generally will have risen and the bonds may be worth more.

Credit risk is associated with the individual issue and issuer. (See Chapter 7 for an extensive discussion of credit.) If the credit standing of the issuer improves, the bonds may be worth more in the market. If the issuer's credit standing weakens, the bonds may fall in value.

The management of market risk and credit risk has become an important aspect of all financial markets, including the over-the-counter municipal market. Investors and dealers alike have placed a greater emphasis on risk management. By measuring how many bonds are owned and how long they have been in an investment portfolio, and by layering the credit risk, investors and their advisors can quantify the risks involved in holding different bonds. The capacity to perform complex risk-management calculations has been spurred on by advances in information technology.

Dealers have developed analytic systems that enable traders and their managers to see the value of a bond at any given time, along with hedging vehicles, and to see profits and losses on a daily basis. This information allows the traders to increase or reduce their market positions as needed. Integrating interest rate forecasts into a firm's inventory position and analyzing how changes in rates will affect a particular bond's performance is another aspect of risk management. Risk-management techniques will continue to evolve with the need to control exposures to market and credit risks and with the development and accessibility of new technology.

THE BASICS OF MUNICIPAL BOND TRADING

The secondary market revolves around trading desks and the people who work on them. The rapid pace of technological advancement that has affected all segments of the economy has increased the efficiency of trading and made enormous quantities of information available to the market.

Key Participants in the Secondary Market

Trading is a fast-paced, risky business where concise communication and quantitative skills are highly valued. Municipal bond traders, the principal market makers, sit on a trading floor with underwriters and salespeople. Their long, connecting desks are crammed with telephone turrets, flashing market screens, computers, news service terminals, bond trader calculators, time stamps, and a *hoot and holler* or *squawk box* for internal verbal communications. The traders who work for full-service securities dealers and for many banks buy and sell securities from institutional and retail investors both for immediate sale and to stock their own inventories. In addition, traders execute transactions with brokers' brokers, other dealers or banks. Municipal traders must have a sense of the kinds of bonds their firms' clients want, so they must have clear and consistent communication with the sales force, which in turn must maintain open lines with the investor clients. Generally, traders try not to be caught with inventory that is hard to sell, since hedging strategies in the municipal market are not as efficient or cost-effective as in other sectors of the capital markets.

Firms that are often called *brokers' brokers* play a significant role in the secondary market. This relatively small group of firms provides anonymity for bond dealers and dealer banks on whose behalf they act. Some maintain full trading operations, and others specialize in certain types of securities, but for the most part, none carries inventories of bonds. They act as agents, not as principals, and do not interact with institutional customers directly.

Brokers perform several services that both create markets and help them to operate efficiently. One of these services is their involvement in the "bid wanted" business. When dealers cannot, or do not, wish to obtain bids directly for bonds they want to sell, they may give them to a broker who will obtain bids from other dealers. Brokers not only identify specific buyers for bonds, they also help dealers find specific bonds from other dealers. If a dealer has an offering that he does not want the whole dealer community to see, a broker may be able to find a buyer by making a few telephone calls. Bond brokers are also occasionally called on to obtain bids for the balance of an underwriting. Brokers are discreet; they do not release the identity of the dealers involved in any transactions without permission.

The brokers continuously communicate with dealers, tracking closely who owns what and who might want to sell or buy bonds. They have a good picture of the market. The anonymity they guarantee to dealers makes the latter more willing to give bond brokers information, and thus, bond brokers often have access to more information than do dealers. Brokers are paid a commission only when they trade bonds.

A firm's salespeople also actively participate in the secondary market. They are on the telephone with hundreds of clients throughout the day, providing updates on developments not only in the municipal market but also in other related markets. The salesperson becomes acquainted with the bonds in the investor's portfolio and is familiar with the account's investment goals and objectives. That way, when the trader either buys bonds or has them in inventory, the salespeople can offer clients the right security to match their needs. Often, the salesperson and the trader will cross bonds between two customers. For example, Investor A holds a block of single-family housing bonds that he or she wishes to sell. The salesperson also knows that Investor B has been looking to buy bonds with those credit and maturity characteristics. With pricing assistance from the trader, the bonds will be crossed from one account to the other.

An investor who is about to circulate a *bid list* often alerts the salesperson. A bid list is a group of bonds distributed by the current bondholder in order to get a current price, or bid, on the bonds. The bondholder asks the salesperson to bid on some or all the bonds by a specified time at prices that will remain firm for a specified time period. The salesperson will consult with the traders and research to arrive at the best price.

MUNICIPAL BOND TRADING

A trader sells securities out of, and buys securities into, the firm's inventory and may also hedge those positions. Traders look at spreads within their own market, as well as the relationships between their market and the other markets. The net revenues from trading come from the relatively small price markups over the trader's initial cost, less any associated costs, which are primarily the cost of carry. The goal of a trader is to turn over their inventory quickly because the cost of carrying inventory for too long can be expensive, as dealers usually borrow funds to finance their inventories.

Financing tax-exempt securities is particularly expensive because tax law constraints limit dealer financing options. Furthermore, holding securities always carries the inherent risk of the securities losing value if interest rates move upward quickly, as prices must then be marked down. Municipal bond trading has five distinguishing characteristics, whose impact will be apparent in the following sections, which describe the factors that go into the decision to trade a bond, how the trade is actually done, and the range of specialists involved in trading. The five distinguishing characteristics of municipal bond trading are: (1) most municipal bonds are traded on the basis of yield to maturity or yield to worst; (2) trades are executed over the counter through dealers acting as principals; (3) there are no set trading hours; (4) there are a vast number of outstanding secondary market issues; and (5) hedging risk and credit risk is an imperfect science.

Factors in a Trade

Market Spreads   Traders are constantly looking at the spread relationships among different securities markets in order to buy and sell securities at the optimal time. For example, the relationship between tax-exempts and Treasuries is monitored to determine when the municipal market is *cheap* to Treasuries and when it is *rich*. In these terms, municipals are cheap when they are trading at a yield that is a relatively high percentage of the Treasury yield, and they are rich when they are trading at a relatively low percentage of Treasuries.

In addition to looking at the spreads between markets, traders always take into account the term structure of interest rates. The shape of the yield curve (see Chapter 8) is crucial to trading decisions, including those based on market spreads and the other factors described below.

Sector Spreads   Traders also look at the spreads between different sectors of the municipal market. For example, a trader may focus on the spread in basis points between *triple-B revenue bonds* and *triple-B hospital bonds*. Triple-B revenue bonds are mostly those of utilities and transportation and exclude those of hospitals. If the spread relationship changes over some period of time, the trader tries to determine why that has happened and then trade in or out of a position based on that knowledge. For example, pending legislation or variations in new bond issue supply may trigger changes in spreads between sectors.

Benchmark yields are often used as a basis to compare sectors of the municipal bond market. One widely used benchmark are the yield and credit curves produced by Municipal Market Data (MMD), a unit of Thomson Reuters. The Securities Industry and Financial Markets Association, in

TABLE 5.2 Composite Municipal Bond Yields for
Revenue Bonds

Month	S&P/Investortools Monthly Total Return (%)	Revenue Municipal Index Ending Yield (%)
Feb-11	1.586	4.707
Jan-11	−1.159	4.841
Dec-10	−2.154	4.667
Nov-10	−2.403	4.322
Oct-10	−0.142	3.892
Sep-10	0.065	3.819
Aug-10	2.445	3.753
Jul-10	1.258	4.264
Jun-10	−0.020	4.403
May-10	0.686	4.374
Apr-10	1.221	4.441
Mar-10	0.114	4.565
Feb-10	0.961	4.501

Source: Securities Industry and Financial Markets Association,
Standard & Poor's.

conjunction with Standard & Poor's, produces benchmark yields for municipal bonds by term, state, type, and purpose as well as composite yield curves
for bonds by rating and by state for certain states. As an example, Table 5.2
shows the 13-month history for the S&P/Investortools Revenue Municipal
Index in tabular form. These indices and yield curves are available on the
web site www.investinginbonds.com.

Credit Spreads   In addition to analyzing sector spreads, traders also look
at credit spreads. These are similar to sector spreads, with the emphasis
on examining spreads within a sector; for example, general-market triple-A
insured hospitals against general-market triple-B hospitals. There are times
when credit spreads are wide—say, 100 or more basis points between a
triple-A and a triple-B bond—and there are times when those spreads narrow to 40 or 50 basis points. When spreads are wide, there is more opportunity to make judgments about the relative value of one type of credit to
another. Looking at these spreads is also valuable to issuers in the primary
market as they make the decision whether to sell bonds with or without
credit enhancement. If the cost of insurance is less than the spread between
generic insured municipal bonds and triple-B municipal bonds there is a
more compelling reason to issue with insurance.

Ratings Changes   Changes in ratings, either upgrades or downgrades, often stimulate trades. If a bond is downgraded, or if it is expected to be downgraded, its spread to others in its rating category and to a triple-A benchmark may widen. Conversely, if a bond is upgraded from Baa1 to A3, the yield spread to a benchmark triple-A bond will narrow. Table 5.3 shows representative quarterly yields from January 2007 through December 2010, on State of Illinois GOs, 5 percent due March 1, 2034, versus the MMD Index for AAA GO municipal bonds.

The spread between the yield on the Illinois GO bonds and the MMD index widened significantly after the third quarter of 2009. In December 2009, Moody's downgraded the State of Illinois GO bonds from A1 to A2; in March 2010, Standard & Poor's placed the state's A+ GO bond rating on Creditwatch with negative implications; in June 2010, Fitch downgraded its rating on Illinois GO bonds from A+ to A and adopted a negative rating outlook; and in September 2010, Moody's shifted its rating outlook

TABLE 5.3   Spread Analysis of State of Illinois General Obligation (GO) Bonds to MMD AAA Municipal Bond Index, 2007 to 2010

		Illinois GOs 5% of 2034* (%)	30-Year AAA MMD Index Yield (%)	Illinois GOs vs. AAA MMD Spread Basis Points
2007	Q1	4.25	4.02	23
	Q2	4.74	4.45	29
	Q3	4.58	4.45	13
	Q4	4.46	4.36	10
2008	Q1	5.04	4.92	12
	Q2	4.99	4.67	32
	Q3	5.43	4.85	58
	Q4	5.33	5.44	−11
2009	Q1	5.22	4.86	36
	Q2	5.25	4.69	56
	Q3	3.85	4.09	−25
	Q4	4.46	4.13	33
2010	Q1	5.00	4.16	85
	Q2	4.96	4.04	92
	Q3	4.15	3.72	43
	Q4	5.43	4.62	81

*Illinois 5% GOs due March 1, 2034, are callable at par on or after March 1, 2014.
Source: Thomson Reuters.

from stable to negative. The deterioration in credit ratings and outlook was reflected in a higher yield spread of Illinois GO bonds against the MMD benchmark, tempered at times by the prospects for legislative action to relieve the pressure on the state's public finances. After the Illinois state legislature passed a package of tax increases and spending cuts in January 2011, all three agencies affirmed their credit ratings and raised the rating outlook from negative to stable.

Material Events   Material events, such as a draw on an issue's reserve fund, may cause some investors to want to trade out of the bonds, while investors on the other side may view any decline in prices as a buying opportunity. Material events must be disclosed to investors under Rule 15c2-12 (see Chapter 9).

HOW A TRADE IS DONE

Municipal bond trading conforms to the normal *bid-and-offer* (or *bid-and-ask*) procedure followed in most over-the-counter markets. The listing of the yield by dealers is always the offered side of the market. Investors, however, may not care to buy the bonds at that yield and may, therefore, bid for them at a higher yield (lower price). A bid yield of 5.25 percent and an offered yield of 5.20 percent means that a dealer is willing to buy the bonds at 5.25 percent and to sell them at 5.20 percent.

In the dialogue that constitutes a trade, the seller of the security will say, "I will sell to you the following," and then give the relevant information on the bonds: name of the bonds; coupon rate; maturity date; par value; agreed yield or dollar price; concession, if any; and CUSIP number. If bonds are callable, the call date, price, and whether the bonds are priced to maturity or a call date must be made known to the buyer. In practice, almost all bonds are assumed to be priced at the yield to worst—yield to maturity if the bond trades at a discount or yield to first optional call date if the bond trades at a premium. The buyer will carefully go over the terms of the trade before confirming. It is common for traders to call back the seller or seller's agent immediately if there is any doubt over the terms agreed on. A trade is consummated with precise information.

Bonds trade this way every day. The market operates on the dictum that "Your word is your bond." If you state that you will buy or sell at a certain price, you must honor that verbal commitment. Electronic bids and offers eliminate the need for verbal commitments, but the basic ethos still applies.

Sometimes offerings are made on an all-or-none basis. These are known as *AON offerings*, where the seller agrees to sell the bonds only if all the bonds on offer will be bought. *Multiples of offerings* are also common, where, for example, sellers offer bonds only in lots of 25, 50, 100, or 200 bonds of $1,000 each.

A frequent practice in the industry is the use of the option to buy. Unlike the case for most securities, this option is free. The seller is asked to make a bona fide firm offering to the prospective buyer, which will hold good for a stated time (usually from one half to a full hour). During this time, the bonds are said to be *out firm*. The prospective buyer uses this grace period to get additional information on the bonds, such as an updated credit opinion, or, if the buyer is a dealer, to find other buyers for the bonds. The buyer thus has the option to get back to the seller and buy the bonds at the agreed-on yield within the set time. If the buyer does not do so, the seller can sell the bonds elsewhere. Essentially, this procedure sets a time frame for the trade, no matter what the market does in the intervening time period. Again, this is where "your word is your bond" is particularly important, as the market can move either up or down while the bonds are out firm, and the commitment to a certain price must remain. As a rule, the option is accompanied by a recall privilege, which gives the seller the right to recall the "firm" bonds in a shorter time period. The amount of time is agreed on beforehand.

Specialists

Some large securities dealers maintain small trading staffs in regional sales offices where municipal bond trading is particularly active. For most issues, trading decisions in these offices are often made independent of the main office, although some firms may refer large or complex trades to the specialists at the main office. There is more than $2.8 trillion dollars in outstanding bonds, and because of this, there are specialists in many segments of the market:

- *General revenue bonds.* Particularly when they are issued by national names in utilities and transportation, general revenue bonds are the bellwethers of the market. They are closely watched to assess the trends in the market.
- *Housing bonds.* These bonds require specialists because of the complex call features that affect their valuations. The traders look at bond prepayments to calculate the average lives of the bonds.
- *Health-care bonds.* A hospital bond trader requires up-to-date information on the financial strength of the borrower. With the continual transformation of health care, the trader must know, for example, whether a hospital is a stand-alone facility or if it has merged into a system, or if a system has merged with another system. Credit ratings range widely

and can change rapidly in this sector, which is therefore more volatile than others.

- *State-specific names.* Local issues can be the province of a trader who may be responsible, for example, for New York State municipalities or California names. Trading operations with broader geographical territories may divide their trading staff by region.
- *High-yield bonds.* High yield bonds are those that are rated below investment grade or are not rated at all. Often these bonds are in the industrial development, health care, and energy sectors. A high-yield trader closely follows the credit stories of these bonds to assess if they are improving, deteriorating, or remaining stable, and will price and trade the bonds accordingly.
- *Short-term products.* Firms also frequently maintain a specialist in the trading of notes, tax-exempt commercial paper, and other bonds that trade like short-term securities such as variable-rate demand obligations (VRDOs). Notes, VRDOs, and commercial paper appeal principally to financial institutions and to money market funds, which typically trade in large denominations and desire liquidity.
- *Odd lots.* A round lot in municipal trading is generally $250,000 or higher. Because of the serial maturity structure of most deals, however, there is not always a $250,000 block of bonds to trade. Odd lots are usually trades of $25,000 or less. These smaller issues generally trade at wider bid-offer spreads than do larger blocks. Since the average new-issue size is less than $35 million, the trading market for these numerous smaller issues is thin.
- *Taxable municipal bonds.* The interest on Build America Bonds and certain other municipal bonds is taxable, which means these bonds appeal to a different set of investors from those who buy tax-exempt municipal bonds. Traders of taxable municipal bonds maintain a separate client list and must monitor developments in other taxable bond markets as well as the creditworthiness of the municipal bond issuer.

MUNICIPAL FUTURES

Traders in most U.S. debt markets are able to maintain short positions. To go short, traders borrow and then sell securities that they do not own, either in anticipation of a decline in prices or to hedge against a long position in other securities. If prices fall, the traders can buy back at a lower price the securities that they sold short, return the securities to the lender with interest, and earn a profit. By going short, these dealers are able to hedge against a loss in their inventory positions that would be caused by a rise in interest rates (and a decline in prices). If prices rise, of course, the dealers cover their short positions by buying back the securities at a higher price and taking a short-term loss. However, municipal dealers and other municipal market participants are prohibited from shorting municipal securities.

From June 1985 until March 2006, municipal bond futures contracts were traded on the Chicago Board of Trade. The contract was based on *The Bond Buyer's* 40-Bond Index. Although municipal futures were designed to provide an effective way for dealers and other market participants to hedge their municipal bond exposures, poor liquidity in the individual components of the index left the underlying index vulnerable to market manipulation, particularly around contract expiration dates. Market participants abandoned the futures contract and began to hedge their positions using other fixed income securities, including U.S. Treasuries, LIBOR swaps, MMD rate locks, credit default swaps, MCDX credit default swaps index tranches and swaps based on the SIFMA Municipal Swap Index instead. Trading volume in municipal futures declined precipitously, and the CBOT eventually withdrew the contract.

PROVIDERS OF DATA IN THE MUNICIPAL MARKET

Municipal market data can be accessed in many ways. It is distributed not only by companies that are dedicated primarily to the municipal market but also by divisions of companies that cover certain facets of many financial markets. The list below is by no means a comprehensive list because this field is constantly changing as new providers enter the field and established providers add new products and services.

- News, both general and financial
- Issuer web sites
- EMMA
- Bond security descriptions
- Disclosure and material event notices
- The former NRMSIRs (Nationally Recognized Municipal Securities Information Repositories)
- State information depositories (SIDs)
- Communication tools, such as syndicate messaging systems
- Broker dealer offerings
- Primary market worksheets
- Pricing and evaluation services
- Active bid-wanteds and offerings

MARKET STATISTICS AND INDEXES

The Bond Buyer Indexes

Some of the most widely watched municipal bond indexes are compiled by *The Bond Buyer*. The 20-Bond Index is composed of dealers' estimates, gathered weekly by *The Bond Buyer*, of the yield that a hypothetical 20-year GO bond would have to offer if that issue came to market during the week. The 20-Bond Index includes GO bonds of 20 actual issuers. The average of the ratings of these issuers is roughly equivalent to Aa2 from Moody's and AA from S&P. The 11-Bond Index is composed of GO bonds of 11 of the 20 issues in the first average, but the quality rating averages Aa1 from Moody's and AA+ from S&P. The Revenue Bond Index includes bonds of 25 issuers of revenue bonds maturing in 30 years. The average rating on the bonds in this index is A1 from Moody's and A+ from S&P. The annual average yield on the 20-Bond Index, the 11-Bond Index, and the Revenue Bond Index from 1985 to 2009 are shown in Table 5.4.

The Bond Buyer ceased to compile its 40-Bond Index, formerly used as the basis for Municipal Futures contracts, when the futures contracts were withdrawn in March 2006.

The Bond Buyer Placement Ratio and Visible Supply   *The Bond Buyer* publishes two measures of the demand for bonds that are widely followed in the industry. These are the weekly *placement ratio* and the daily *visible supply*.

Although these are indicators of the primary market, they are also bellwethers of the demand for municipal bonds in general and good indicators of secondary market demand. A sizable inventory of unsold new issues in the primary market depresses the secondary market, while unsatisfied demand for new issues improves the secondary market.

The Bond Buyer placement ratio is compiled weekly from data as of the close of business on Friday and is reported on Monday. It represents the percentage of the dollar volume of the week's new competitive issues placed with permanent investors during the week. The minimum issue size for inclusion in the ratio is currently $10 million.

In every year since 2000, the highest weekly placement ratio has been 100 percent. Excluding weeks where there were no bond sales, the lowest percentage in this 11-year time period was 50.5 percent in 2001. Previously, the lowest percentage recorded since the initiation of the ratio was 29.2 percent on November 23, 1960, when the ratio was based on combined competitive and negotiated sales. The average annual placement ratio rose from 88.8 percent in 2000 to a peak of 95.2 percent in 2007; it has

TABLE 5.4 Average Annual Yields, 1990 to 2010

Year	*The Bond Buyer* 20-Bond Index	*The Bond Buyer* 11-Bond Index	*The Bond Buyer* Revenue Bond Index	U.S. Treasury 30-Year Bond
1990	7.27	7.13	7.53	8.61
1991	6.92	6.77	7.11	8.14
1992	6.44	6.33	6.59	7.67
1993	5.59	5.49	5.82	6.59
1994	6.19	6.10	6.45	7.37
1995	5.95	5.85	6.20	6.88
1996	5.76	5.66	6.01	6.71
1997	5.52	5.44	5.78	6.61
1998	5.09	5.02	5.32	5.58
1999	5.44	5.37	5.65	5.87
2000	5.71	5.64	5.96	5.94
2001	5.15	5.10	5.44	5.49
2002	5.04	4.99	5.37	5.43
2003	4.74	4.66	5.15	N/A
2004	4.68	4.60	5.09	N/A
2005	4.40	4.32	4.96	N/A
2006	4.40	4.34	4.99	4.91
2007	4.40	4.34	4.64	4.84
2008	4.86	4.76	5.34	4.28
2009	4.62	4.36	5.45	4.08
2010	4.30	4.03	4.88	4.25

Note: The U.S. Treasury did not issue new 30-year bonds from November 2001 through February 2006.
Source: The Bond Buyer; Federal Reserve System.

subsequently declined a little, to 93.2 percent in 2010. Table 5.5 shows the high- and low-placement ratios and their dates for each year since 2000, along with the average placement ratio for the year.

The 30-Day Visible Supply is a chart compiled each day from the "Competitive Bond Offerings" and "Negotiated Bond Offerings" tables. It shows the total dollar volume of bonds expected to reach the market in the next 30 days, including issues scheduled for sale on the publication date of the chart.

The 30-day visible supply of competitive bonds has been reported since 1927. It has ranged from a low of $928,000 on March 3, 1943, to a high of $6.42 billion on June 7, 2005. The 30-day visible supply of negotiated issues has been reported since 1971, ranging from a low of zero on January 4, 1971,

TABLE 5.5 Placement Ratio, 2000 to 2010

		Percentage	Date
2000	High	100.0	12/22/2000
	Low	64.9	4/14/2000
	Average	88.8	
2001	High	100.0	12/21/2001
	Low	50.5	1/12/2001
	Average	86.6	
2002	High	100.0	1/4/2002
	Low	58.2	7/5/2002
	Average	91.3	
2003	High	100.0	8/8/2003
	Low	75.6	3/14/2003
	Average	93.7	
2004	High	100.0	1/2/2004
	Low	61.2	12/24/2004
	Average	94.3	
2005	High	99.9	6/24/2005
	Low	79.6	11/25/2005
	Average	93.5	
2006	High	100.0	1/6/2006
	Low	84.5	1/20/2006
	Average	95.1	
2007	High	100.0	9/7/2007
	Low	68.1	12/21/2007
	Average	95.2	
2008	High	100.0	1/4/2008
	Low	84.0	2/8/2008
	Average	95.0	
2009	High	100.0	8/7/2009
	Low	82.9	2/20/2009
	Average	94.4	
2010	High	100.0	1/1/2010
	Low	83.0	4/16/2010
	Average	93.2	

Source: The *Bond Buyer.*

and December 26, 1989, to a high of $20.8 billion on October 18, 2002. Table 5.6 lists the highs and lows of the total of competitive and negotiated issues for each year from 2000 to 2010, with the date on which the high or low occurred. In six years during this time period, the lowest date of visible supply occurred in late December or early January, while the high point of supply was more evenly spread throughout the year.

TABLE 5.6 30-Day Visible Supply, 2000 to 2010

Year	Total ($ millions)	Date	Competitive ($ millions)	Date	Negotiated ($ millions)	Date
2000						
High	7,364.6	11/14/2000	3,456.1	10/17/2000	4,997.5	2/11/2000
Low	1,028.4	12/22/2000	475.6	12/20/2000	397.4	12/22/2000
2001						
High	14,665.8	12/10/2001	4,615.8	6/5/2001	13,108	12/12/2001
Low	2,285.8	1/2/2001	524.7	12/19/2001	360.2	1/2/2001
2002						
High	23,805.4	10/8/2002	4,787.5	2/12/2002	20,779.2	10/18/2002
Low	2,319.0	12/20/2002	246.4	12/20/2002	1,835.2	11/27/2002
2003						
High	12,882.5	4/25/2003	4,704.4	7/16/2003	9,957.8	2/21/2003
Low	2,594.6	8/15/2003	270.7	12/18/2003	1,668.2	8/15/2003
2004						
High	14,554.7	3/30/2004	3,987.4	7/13/2004	13,082.5	4/30/2004
Low	1,709.5	12/23/2004	294.4	12/17/2004	1,026.9	12/27/2004
2005						
High	15,275.8	7/26/2005	6,420.4	6/7/2005	12,989.7	7/27/2005
Low	1,397.0	12/22/2005	397.5	12/21/2005	946.3	12/22/2005
2006						
High	16,479.8	11/28/2006	4,920.8	11/28/2006	12,058.7	11/29/2006
Low	1,825.4	12/22/2006	404.4	12/20/2006	1,154.0	12/22/2006
2007						
High	20,496	10/10/2007	6,096.7	11/27/2007	17,593.7	10/10/2007
Low	3,278.1	1/2/2007	212.1	12/14/2007	558.9	4/2/2007
2008						
High	21,291.8	12/2/2008	4,486.4	3/7/2008	18,285.8	12/4/2008
Low	8,122.8	1/17/2008	787.3	12/18/2008	6,435.9	1/30/2008
2009						
High	20,426.1	6/9/2009	4,170.2	10/14/2009	17,559.4	6/9/2009
Low	2,984.0	12/18/2009	214.8	12/18/2009	2,636.0	12/29/2009
2010						
High	18,707.7	9/28/2010	4,988.4	11/9/2010	15,085	12/7/2010
Low	4,809.1	9/2/2010	555.8	12/17/2010	3,286.5	2/11/2010

Source: The Bond Buyer.

MSRB RECORD-KEEPING RULES

The MSRB has established several rules governing record keeping for holding securities and for transactions with customers. Rule G-8 is the basic record-keeping rule of the MSRB. It requires every broker, dealer, and municipal securities dealer to maintain account records for each customer, showing all purchases and sales of municipal securities, all receipts and deliveries of securities, all receipts and disbursements of cash, and all other debits and credits to such account.

Subsections of Rule G-8 require that records be kept to show the following information for each security: all long and short positions carried by a municipal securities broker or dealer for its own account or for the account of a customer; the current location of all such securities held in the long position and the offsetting position to all such securities sold short; and the name or other designation of the account in which each position is carried. The securities records should also show any movement of the securities, such as whether securities have been sent out for validation or transfer.

In addition, records of each transaction, whether undertaken as a principal or an agent, must be maintained according to specific subsections of Rule G-8. Trading tickets will suffice for such records. They must show such information as the price and amount of the order as well as the time of the execution to the extent feasible. Some of the other areas covered by Rule G-8 include the types of information to be obtained from customers, customer complaints, and records for put options and repurchase agreements. By and large, the record-keeping regulations do not apply to dealers or brokers who do not do their own clearing, but Rule G-8 does provide that nonclearing dealers and brokers remain responsible for accurate maintenance and preservation of books and records.

Uniform Practices and Confirmation of Transactions

MSRB Rule G-12 establishes uniform practices among municipal securities dealers, and Rule G-15 establishes procedures for confirmation, clearance, and settlement of transactions with customers. Many provisions of the rules are codifications of traditional practices and industry standards that were in existence before the establishment of the MSRB. The Board also has written into the rules standards and procedures to expedite the processing of transactions. For example, the rules require clearance and settlement of most interdealer transactions and most transactions with institutional customers to occur through automated systems operated by clearing agencies registered with the SEC.

The rules allow the settlement date of a transaction—the date used for computing yields and price—generally to be subject to agreement by the parties to the transaction. The rules specify, however, that the settlement date for cash transactions will be the day of trade, while for regular way trades the settlement date will be three business days after the trade date. Firms that engage in transactions that are eligible for automated trade comparison through a registered clearing agency follow the rules for such transactions.

For interdealer transactions not cleared and settled through automated systems, Rule G-12 provides standards for the contents of confirmations and procedures for verifying confirmations sent between dealers. The rule requires confirmations to be sent on the business day after the trade date and to contain certain items of information; dealers receiving confirmations with incorrect information or describing trades that they do not recognize must take specific steps to resolve the discrepancies or trades. Similarly, Rule G-15 requires certain information to be on each customer confirmation and requires the confirmation to be provided at or before the completion of the transaction (if the transaction is *delivery versus payment* or *receipt versus payment,* the confirmation must be sent not later than the day of execution). Information required to be on an interdealer or customer confirmation includes certain items that provide evidence of the contract, a description of the securities, and in the case of customer transactions, certain other items that the MSRB has deemed necessary for disclosure to customers as follows (for more information on MSRB rules, consult the MSRB web site at www.MSRB.org).

CHAPTER 6

Investing in Bonds

INTRODUCTION

A primary attraction that municipal bonds have for investors is that the interest income is exempt from federal income tax (except interest on Build America Bonds and certain other taxable municipal bonds). Interest income from state and local issues is usually exempt from income taxes in their states, although it is generally not exempt from taxes in other states. The major investors in municipal securities have been households and household proxies (mutual funds, money market funds, closed-end funds, and bank personal trusts), property and casualty companies, and commercial banks. The demand for municipal bonds and the relative importance of each of the major categories has shifted over the years. Investors' purchasing patterns are cyclical and depend on factors such as interest rates, tax rates, alternative investments, and profitability.

Municipal bonds are bought and sold with specific investment objectives and goals in mind. The buyer achieves these goals by structuring and managing a portfolio using the basic principles of investing in bonds.

THE BASIC PRINCIPLES OF INVESTING IN BONDS

A fundamental relationship between interest rates and prices exists in all fixed income securities. When interest rates rise, the prices of fixed income securities in the secondary market generally fall to make their yield comparable to that of currently issued securities. When interest rates fall, the prices of outstanding fixed income securities generally rise. Prices are also affected by the supply of and demand for bonds. The relationship between yield and price is not a straight line, but rather, it is convex, or curved like the exterior of a circle or a bow. The degree to which bond prices shift relative to interest rates is affected by several factors. When the bond is *option-free,* meaning that the bond does not contain an embedded put or call (the bond is noncallable or nonputtable), the two most important factors affecting a bond's price volatility (a statistical measure of the variance of price or yield over time) are its term to maturity and its coupon rate. For bonds containing embedded options, those redemption features constitute a third factor in the bond's price volatility.

Term to Maturity

The category of short-term securities includes different products with different terms to maturity. Short-term securities, which mature in 13 months or less, are called *notes.* Commercial paper matures within 270 days, although there have been issues with longer maturities. Short-term bonds, however, can have maturities from one to four years. Medium-term bonds have maturities from 5 to 12 years, while long-term bonds have maturities greater than 12 years.

The longer a bond's maturity, the wider and more volatile are the swings in its price caused by any change in interest rates. For example, a bond with a coupon of 5 percent due in one year would sell at $970 to produce an 8 percent yield to maturity, while a 5 percent bond due in 20 years would have to sell at $700 to produce the same 8 percent yield to maturity. In the first example, a $30 discount over one year is sufficient to bring the yield up to 8 percent. In the second, a $300 discount is required to generate the same yield because the gain is spread over a longer period of time. Short-term bonds of similar structure and credit quality will trade closer to par, because the investor will receive the full amount of the principal sooner.

Coupon Rates

Generally, the higher the coupon interest rate, the smaller the price movements will be for a given change in market interest rates. Conversely, the price volatility is greater for a bond with a lower coupon rate. For example, if interest rates fall 200 basis points from 8 percent to 6 percent on 10-year bonds, the price of a par bond will rise by about 15 points, to 115. On the same drop of 200 basis points, a 6 percent, 10-year bond trading at par would rise more in value than the 8 percent bond from the first example. The price on the 6 percent bond would rise to about $116\frac{1}{2}$ if interest rates fell from 6 percent to 4 percent.

Bonds trading at a discount experience wider price swings for a given shift in interest rates, while bonds trading at a premium shift proportionately less. Consider, for example, two noncallable 20-year bonds, both yielding 6.5 percent to maturity. One, a discount bond with a 2 percent coupon, is selling for 50; the other, with an 8 percent coupon, is selling for nearly 117. If interest rates increase such that the yield to maturity on both bonds becomes 7.5 percent, the price of the discount bond would fall by about $6\frac{1}{2}$ points to $43\frac{1}{2}$. The price of the premium bond will fall by $11\frac{1}{2}$ points. However, the percentage change in the price of the bonds is the key calculation. In the situation described above, the price of the discount bond will have dropped by 13 percent, whereas the price of the premium bond will have dropped by only 10 percent.

The difference in volatility between premium bonds and discount bonds is even more dramatic in the case of so-called cushion bonds—that is, callable bonds selling above the initial call price. In the case of cushion bonds, the volatility will be based on the call date rather than the maturity date, and the bonds will tend to act like shorter-maturity bonds.

These calculations are based on yield calculations alone. The prices of discount bonds will fall even lower than these calculations suggest to compensate for the fact that capital gains and market discount earned on discount bonds are subject to federal income taxation.

Redemption Provisions

Redemption provisions describe the terms and conditions under which an issuer may redeem bonds that contain an embedded call option. Redemption provisions are also discussed in Chapter 2. Investors scrutinize the bond's structure, particularly its call features, for a number of reasons. First, when a bond is called before maturity, the duration of the bond changes, which changes the portfolio's return. Second, when bonds contain a call option and are trading at premium to the call price, those bonds are priced to the call, which is a better statement of their value than if they were priced to maturity. However, if the bonds are called, the investors must replace the income stream generated by the first bond. If interest rates have fallen, it will be hard to replace the bond coupon with one of comparable credit quality. Thus, overall return of the portfolio may suffer. Investors can also purchase market discount bonds with active sinking funds, which are subject to par calls. Purchasing these bonds at prices substantially below par can lead to significant taxable income when the mandatory sinking fund is used to retire debt. This also shortens the duration of the bond. The issue of taxable income is another reason to examine calls as bonds called before maturity may give the investor taxable income or capital losses. While the market discount on a bond that is redeemed is taxed as ordinary income, any capital loss incurred is deductible only against capital gains. Again, because bonds are priced to the call, the call provisions can limit the potential gains on a bond.

Bonds can be called at par, at some premium above par, or in the case of zero-coupon bonds, at the compound or straight-line accreted value. Call protection refers to the bond issuer's inability to exercise a call for some specified period of time. It also refers to the protection a specific bond maturity may enjoy over other bonds in the same issue that are called ahead of it. *First call* refers to the earliest date the issuer can execute a call. Interest accrual or compound value accretion ceases once a bond has been called.

There are three primary types of call features commonly found in municipal bond issues: *optional, mandatory sinking fund,* and *extraordinary* (or special redemptions).

The optional call feature describes the manner in which an issuer may voluntarily redeem bonds. A typical optional call provision allows the issuer to retire serial and term bonds at a price of par or higher ten years from the issue date. If the bonds are subject to premium call, after the first call date, the call price may decline each successive year until it reaches par. There are times when market circumstances allow the issuer to price a new issue so that it does not pay the investor any premium for exercising the call option and other times when investors demand a high premium. Funds for optional calls come from refunding bonds or surplus funds of the issuer.

The mandatory call feature typically describes the way sinking funds work. A sinking fund is used to redeem term bonds on a schedule, enabling the issuer to spread the costs of retiring the term bonds over the life of the issue. Sinking funds add some measure of security on the bonds by avoiding one large payment on the term bond at its final maturity. Sinking funds can be used either to call bonds or in some cases to purchase equal face amounts in the secondary market. Open-market purchases provide price support for sinking fund bonds during periods when such bonds are selling at a discount because of rising interest rates. In a falling interest rate environment, however, sinking fund bonds can be called at par when low rates would otherwise make such bonds worth substantially more. When bonds are called, they are selected on a random basis within each maturity.

Extraordinary or special redemptions are specifically designed to protect the issuer by allowing bonds to be retired in the event extraordinary circumstances impair the issuer's future revenue stream or ability to operate. These provisions are in bonds issued for the construction of capital projects, allowing special redemptions from unexpended monies if the project is not built by a certain time or from insurance proceeds if a catastrophe occurs and the project is damaged or destroyed. They are also found in housing bonds, permitting calls from unexpended bond proceeds, prepayment or sale of mortgage loans securing the bonds, loan insurance proceeds, or excess program revenues.

Extraordinary redemption provisions are often complex and vary considerably among bond issues. They may be mandatory or optional, they can occur at any time after the bonds are issued, and they are usually made at par (or accreted value for original-issue discount bonds). Bond redemptions are most often executed on a *pro rata* basis across all bond maturities in an issue. This means that the redemption funds available are applied to each bond maturity on the basis of what percentage a particular bond maturity bears to the total amount of bonds outstanding. In the case of single-family housing bonds, prepaid mortgage loans are applied to a particular term bond or bonds before any other maturity. This type of bond is known as a *super sinker* and provides call protection for the other term bonds in the issue. The average bond life on a super sinker is substantially shorter than for other term bonds in the same issue, but the yields tend to be only slightly less. Investors must carefully consider the possibility of such a call when evaluating the purchase of premium bonds.

The yield to call shows investors what yield will be earned if the bonds are called at the first call date. It is similar to the yield to maturity, except that it is calculated to the first call date and price. The yield to call, if lower than the yield to maturity, must be cited in written confirmations of orders. Bonds with little time left to the first call date often trade at lower prices and higher yields to maturity than equivalent bonds with ample call protection. This is especially the case when interest rates are high and are expected to fall, a condition that would make redemption likely.

MEASURES OF YIELD AND RETURN

Figuring out yield and return on a municipal bond is not solely a process of checking interest rates and tax deductibility. Professionals in the field use calculations based on finance theory to figure out the most profitable uses of their capital. Below follows a brief review of present value theory and of the measures of returns and yields.

Present Value

Present value is a concept that takes into account the time value of money. One dollar received today is worth more than one dollar tomorrow. Thus, higher value is placed on a three-year investment rather than on six-year investment, for example, even though both promise identical returns. Therefore, the timing of cash flows on an investment is important in any investment including fixed income. The formula for the present value of $1 received at the end of year n is

$$PV = \frac{1}{(1+r)^n}$$

where PV is the present value, r is the discount rate, and n is the number of years.

The formula for the present value of $1 received in one year invested at 5 percent is

$$PV = \frac{1}{(1.05)^1} = \$0.9524$$

The present value of $1 received in two years invested at 5 percent is

$$PV = \frac{1}{(1+.05)^2} = \$0.9070$$

The present value of a series of $1 future cash flows is the sum of each year's present value, which is $1.8594, a sum that is less than the $2 face value. The discount rate and the number of years are the two variables that change the present-value calculation. Given the same number of years, a higher discount rate will generate a lower present value, and a lower discount rate will generate a higher present value. For example, if a 10 percent rate were used in the above example, the present value of the future stream of cash flows for two years would be $1.7325; and if a 3 percent rate were used, the present value of the future stream of cash flows would be $1.9135.

Internal Rate of Return

Present value theory is used in another important way. An issuer may return to an investor one dollar seven years from now on a loan of 75 cents today. Alternatively, another issuer might repay one dollar in six years on a loan of 85 cents today. To select the better investment, the investor compares the two offerings by calculating the internal rate of return. The internal rate of return is the discount rate at which the present value of the cash flow, or series of cash flows, from an investment equals its price. The internal rate of return cannot be computed as cleanly as the present value can. There is no algebraic formula for it. Rather, it is calculated by a trial and error process, where an interest rate is estimated and applied to compute the present value of each cash flow. If the total present value of the cash flows is more than the price of the investment, a higher rate must be used to recalculate the cash flows. If the total present value of the cash flows is less than the price of the investment, a lower discount rate must be used. After a series of trials and errors, when the total present value of the investment equals the price of the investment, the correct discount rate and yield will have been found.

In the above example, the internal rate of return for the 75 cent loan due in seven years is about 4 percent. The internal rate of return for the 85 cent loan due in six years is about 3 percent. Clearly, the first loan offers the investor a higher return, albeit for a longer period of time.

YIELD TO MATURITY AND PRICE

Given the coupon, current price, and time to maturity, the yield to maturity is the internal rate of return an investor earns from payments of bond interest and principal, with interest compounded semiannually. Yield to maturity assumes that interest is compounded semiannually and will be reinvested at the same rate for all present value type calculations. If an investor knows that this will not be the case, adjustments can and should be made to the calculations to get a truer internal rate of return. The formula for yield to maturity is in Chapter 2.

The price of a bond is precisely the present value of all the cash flows—interest and principal—discounted by the yield to maturity or the internal rate of return. For example, if a bond quoted at a 7 percent yield to maturity has a coupon of 6 percent and is due in three years, the price will be the sum of the present values of each semiannual interest payment of $30 plus the present value of $1,000 received in three years, all discounted by 7 percent. What is the price of the bond? The problem can be formulated as shown in the following list.

Time from the Purchase	Cash Received	Present Value at a 7% Discount Rate
6 months	$ 30.00	$ 28.99
12 months	30.00	28.01
18 months	30.00	27.06
24 months	30.00	26.14
30 months	30.00	25.26
36 months	1,030.00	837.91
Total	$1,180.00	$973.36

The total cash payments to the bondholder are $1,180.00, but the sum of the present values, which is the price of the bond, is only $973.36.

To find the yield to maturity when the price is known is the reverse of this process. A discount rate is applied to each semiannual payment to derive the present value. As in the internal rate of return, an interpolation is unavoidable if computed by hand, but is easily calculated on computers and calculators.

Total Return

One way of evaluating a portfolio's performance is to calculate its total return and then compare that total return to some benchmark index. Performance will be discussed more thoroughly after investment objectives, risks, and strategies have been explained. *Total return* is the investment performance measure over a given time period and includes coupon interest, interest on interest, and any realized or unrealized gains or losses. The aggregate or cumulative total return and the average annual total return of portfolios are often calculated. The cumulative or aggregate total return reflects the actual performance of the bond over a stated period of time. That stated period of time could be 1, 5, or 10 years or any other time period that is defined by the investor, an investment manager, or the sponsor of a mutual fund. The average annual total return is a hypothetical rate of return that, if achieved annually, would have produced the same cumulative total return if the performance had been constant over the entire period. Note that the way this is similar to the internal rate of return and to the net present value is that the performance is assumed to be constant. Calculating the average annual total return smoothes out variations in performance and is not the same as an actual year-to-year result. Average annual total return also includes any sales charges that may be involved. Neither average annual return nor cumulative total return take into account the effect of any federal or state income taxes that may be payable when the bond is sold or the fund is redeemed.

Tax-Equivalent Yield

Yield is another measure of performance. Yield, as has been discussed in previous chapters, can be stated as yield to maturity, current yield, yield to first call, yield to worst or in other ways. For an investor in tax-exempt municipal bonds, it is important, no matter which of these yields is used, also to calculate the tax-equivalent yield. This allows investors to make a comparison between the lower yield on a tax-exempt bond and what is usually the higher yield on a comparable taxable bond, enabling them to evaluate equivalent yields on the two securities. The calculation for the tax-exempt/taxable yield equivalent formula is shown in Chapter 2.

INVESTMENT OBJECTIVES

Investment objectives are the goals that an investor sets in structuring and managing portfolio investments. An investor often has more than one investment objective. Sometimes those objectives complement each other, and at other times they may contradict each other. With the great diversity of municipal issues, however, it is nearly always possible to structure a portfolio that fits the investor's criteria. A summary of basic investment objectives follows.

Current Income

Current income is the periodic income stream paid on a bond. In a low-interest rate scenario, premium bonds may improve the current income. For example, a 7 percent, five-year premium bond priced at 108.75 would have a yield to maturity of 5 percent with current income of $70 for every $1,087.50 invested, and a current yield of 6.4 percent. If the investor bought a par bond at the same time with a yield to maturity of 5 percent, the current income would be only $50 per $1,000 invested. While the premium bond enhances the current income, the premium cannot be deducted as a tax loss. The taxation of premium and discount bonds are discussed in greater detail later in this chapter.

Capital Preservation

Capital preservation is the safe return to the investor of the principal amount invested. Some investors cannot tolerate any risk in losing principal; for example, they may have invested funds specifically for retirement or education purposes. There are many ways to maximize capital preservation. The longer the term of the investment vehicle, the greater its potential for price swings, so an investor interested in capital preservation would invest on the short end of the yield curve. Credit risk also plays an important part in capital preservation. All things being equal, a highly rated credit will provide greater safety of principal than a lower-rated credit.

Capital Appreciation

Capital appreciation is the expectation that the investment will be valued more in the future than in the present because current credit, market, or other risks will eventually be resolved. For example, one might purchase a bond trading cheaply compared to others of the same credit quality because of a specific current problem, such as large operating losses, with the expectation that the losses will be reversed. Another way to maximize capital appreciation is to purchase discount bonds. However, the gains earned on discount bonds are taxable as ordinary income. Gains and losses are discussed in greater detail later in this chapter. These bonds can be attractive to investors who will be in a lower tax bracket when the bonds mature. Discount bonds can meet capital appreciation objectives while still providing tax-exempt income before maturity.

Timing the Maturity

Investors can tailor their portfolios to meet specific cash needs at known times by purchasing bonds with specific maturities. For parents who may have children entering college in 10 years, for example, discount bonds that mature at the time the tuition is due may be appropriate. Zero-coupon bonds, which provide no semiannual income but pay out all of the tax-exempt interest in a lump sum at maturity, are one way to accumulate funds for college. Investors can also stagger bond maturities along the yield curve if there is uncertainty when the future cash needs will occur. This is often referred to as *laddering*.

In-State Tax Exemption

Investors in high-tax states that levy an income tax on municipal bonds from states other than their own should generally invest in bonds issued in their own states and in U.S. territories. The interest on bonds issued in these U.S. territories—American Samoa, the Commonwealth of Puerto Rico, Guam, the Northern Mariana Islands, and the U.S. Virgin Islands—is exempt by law from all federal, state, and local income taxes. However, the yields on bonds from these specialty states may be lower than the yield on other issues because the demand for their bonds exceeds the supply of new and outstanding issues. Bonds issued by states with high demand or high state tax rates are called specialty state bonds.

RISK FACTORS

Achieving investment objectives involves undertaking a certain amount of risk. Risk is a way to categorize the degree of uncertainty and the possibility of financial loss on an investment; often, an investment will carry more than one risk.

Credit Risk

Credit risk is the chance that the obligor, or issuer, on bonds will be unable to make debt service payments or will default on the loan because of a weakening of the credit. Credit risk is reflected in a bond's rating. By definition, a bond that carries less credit risk will have a better rating than a bond with more credit risk. Triple-A bonds have less credit risk than double-A credits, and so on all the way down the rating scale. Investors whose objective is preservation of capital generally are averse to credit risk. Such investors may choose to invest only in triple-A issues, or they may prefer only the most highly rated GO bonds.

Event and Political Risk

Event risk is the risk that an issuer's ability to make debt service payments will change because of unanticipated changes, such as a corporate restructuring, a regulatory change, or a catastrophic event. Regulatory changes, which generally take a long time to be enacted, can be included in the total risk profile of an issuer, while unforeseen events or disasters cannot. Political risk in municipal bonds is generally tied to the civic climate in a state or local governmental unit, and may be reflected by tax-limitation referenda or voter rejection of bond issues. Political risk as a subset of credit risk assesses an issuer's willingness to pay. If an investor's goal is in-state tax exemption and voter referenda with negative implications for bonds have been passed in that state, that investor could incur more political risk than an investor with a portfolio of national names not concentrated in any one state.

Market Risk

Interest rate risk involves the potential price fluctuations in a bond that are caused by changes in the general level of interest rates. While every fixed-income investment has some interest rate risk, the price volatility of a bond with a shorter term is lower than one with a longer term. Investors who have a low tolerance for interest rate risk should keep their investment at the short end of the yield curve. Inflation risk is the risk that a bond's value will diminish if there is greater overall inflation. A rise in inflation usually leads to higher interest rates and thus a decrease in bond prices. Liquidity risk is the risk that an investor may not be able to buy or sell a bond because there is no market for that bond at a particular time. Liquidity problems may be macro problems—those affecting the whole market—or they may be specific to one issuer or to one type of credit. Short-term instruments, such as commercial paper and variable-rate demand bonds, usually contain highly rated bank lines of credit to provide liquidity and to reduce the risk that an issuer will not have available cash if bonds are put to them. The banks providing the liquidity may themselves have a problem if their own credit is not favorably perceived, and issuers may end up paying a higher rate on their borrowing than they had originally thought because the market's perception of the liquidity provider's credit has diminished.

Reinvestment Risk

Reinvestment risk is the risk that investors will not be able to invest their interest at the same rate as the original bond rate. Yield calculations assume that coupon interest can be reinvested at the original bond rate. When interest rates are dropping, there is a greater reinvestment risk because it is more difficult to find high-interest coupons.

INVESTOR STRATEGIES

Individuals and institutional investors use various techniques to match their investment objectives with their level of risk tolerance. These are general strategies, and investors should consult with their own advisor as to the applicability to their own situation.

Laddering

One strategy to reduce interest rate risk is to build a *laddered portfolio,* which has maturities that are distributed over time. For example, equal principal amounts of bonds can be purchased with maturities in two, four, six, eight, and 10 years. When the two-year bonds mature, another bond with a 10-year maturity could be purchased, which will continue the ladder. A ladder portfolio reduces interest rate risk and price volatility because prices at the short end of the yield curve are not as volatile as prices at the longer end of the yield curve, but the investor does give up some yield by using this strategy. The investment objectives that can be met with this strategy are current income, capital preservation, and timing of maturities while at the same time controlling interest rate risk.

Barbell

The *barbell strategy* is another technique to manage interest rate risk. Investors concentrate their holdings at both ends of the maturity spectrum rather than in the middle—hence the term barbell strategy. This strategy is used by investors who are uncertain about the course of interest rates. They invest equally in long-term bonds for the higher yields while at the same placing the same portion of their funds in securities with very short-term maturities. This strategy can also limit the risk of fluctuating prices when interest rates turn sharply in either direction. The investment objectives that can be met with this strategy are current income, capital preservation, and timing the maturity while at the same time controlling interest rate risk.

Diversification

Diversification is a strategy to manage credit risk. A portfolio that contains a balanced mix of bonds from many different categories is less likely to lose value if one issue or sector is experiencing problems. Diversifying the portfolio can involve selecting general obligation and other tax-backed bonds and revenue bonds of many issuers in different states. It can mean selecting from within the broad category of revenue bonds a mix of housing, water and sewer, power, and health-care bonds. Within a single state it can mean selecting issuers from levels of government that provide different services that rely on different tax and revenue streams. It can mean building a portfolio with ratings ranging from triple-A to low investment grade or even noninvestment grade. It can also mean having a mix of bond insurers and banks backing bonds in a credit-enhanced portfolio. The investment objectives that can be met with this strategy are current income, capital preservation, and in-state exemption while controlling for credit, event, and political risk.

Bond Swapping

A *bond swap* is the simultaneous sale of one bond and the purchase of another with the proceeds of the sale. Swaps are used to change bond maturities, adjust portfolio credit quality, increase yield, enhance call protection, benefit from interest rate changes, and, most commonly, to generate tax losses. The tax swap is done to produce a loss for tax purposes that can be used to offset capital gains or, to some extent, ordinary income.

The typical tax swap is a two-step process. First, the investor sells a bond that is currently valued below its amortized purchase price. Next, the investor simultaneously purchases a bond with similar but not identical characteristics. For example, an investor owns a $50,000, 20-year, triple-A-rated bond with a 5 percent coupon that was purchased five years earlier at par. As current interest rates have risen to 5.50 percent, the bond price has fallen to $47,500. The $2,500 capital loss incurred when the bond is sold is applied to offsetting the investor's capital gains on other investments or ordinary income. The investor then purchases, for example, a 5 percent triple-A bond from a different issuer, maturing in 15 years, which costs approximately $47,500. The yield, maturity, and bond quality are the same as before, but the unrealized loss was turned into a real loss used to offset taxable gains.

There are several rules about tax swaps that investors must take into consideration. Under current tax law, the maximum tax rate on long-term capital gains is lower than the maximum rate on short-term capital gains, but the investor must hold the bond a year to be eligible for the long-term capital gains rate. In addition, investors should try to avoid a *wash sale,* which is the sale and repurchase within 30 days before or after the trade or settlement date of the same or a substantially identical security. The Internal Revenue Service will not recognize a tax loss generated from a wash sale. While the term "substantially identical" has not been explicitly defined with regard to tax swaps, two bonds have generally not been considered substantially identical if the securities have different issuers or if there are substantial differences in either maturity or coupon rate.

With a swap the investor usually wants to maintain credit quality, keep the total dollar amount of bonds the same, and maintain the same level of current income. Often, to satisfy all of these requirements, the new bond has a longer maturity than the original bond.

TAXATION OF MUNICIPAL BONDS

This section does not cover all of the possible tax consequences resulting from ownership of tax-exempt bonds and the receipt of interest thereon, and it is not intended as individual tax advice. It addresses only beneficial owners who hold such bonds as capital assets and does not address special classes of beneficial owners such as dealers in securities or currencies, banks, life insurance companies, persons holding such bonds as a hedge against interest rate or currency risks or as part of a straddle or conversion transaction, or beneficial owners whose functional currency is not the U.S. dollar. This section is based on the U.S. federal income tax laws as currently in effect and interpreted and does not include any description of the tax laws of any foreign government that might apply to a beneficial owner. Prospective purchasers of tax-exempt bonds should consult their own tax advisors concerning the application of federal and state tax laws to their particular situation.

Capital Gains and Losses

Even though the interest paid on almost all municipal bonds (except for taxable municipal bonds) is tax-exempt, a holder can recognize gain or loss that is subject to federal income tax on the sale of such a bond, just as in the case of a taxable bond. The amount of gain or loss is equal to the difference between (1) the sale price of the bond, and (2) the holder's tax basis in the bond (the amount the holder paid for the bond originally, including any additions to such basis, such as OID, as discussed in the following section). Thus, if a holder purchased a $5,000 face amount municipal bond for $5,000 and then sold the bond for $5,200, the holder would have a capital gain of $200. Typically, the purchase and sale price of a municipal bond includes the dealer's markup; however, in cases where a commission is charged, it should be taken into account by the holder in computing gain or loss.

There are currently two types of capital gains: long-term and short-term. A long-term gain requires that a bond be held for more than 12 months before it is sold; a short-term gain is the result of holding a bond for 12 months or less. The maximum tax rate on long-term capital gains is 15 percent and the maximum tax rate on short-term capital gains is 35 percent (which is also the maximum tax rate on ordinary income).

When a bond is sold, an investor may also recognize a capital loss if the sale proceeds (adjusted for selling costs) are less than the holder's tax basis. In such a case, capital losses are first applied against capital gains of the same type to reduce such gains. Thus, a long-term capital loss will first reduce long-term capital gains, and a short-term capital loss will first reduce short-term capital gains. Any capital losses remaining after offsetting all available capital gains can then be used to reduce ordinary income by up to $3,000 per year, with any losses in excess of that amount available to be carried forward indefinitely to reduce capital gains or ordinary income in future years under the same procedures.

Original Issue Discount

If a tax-exempt bond is originally issued at a price less than par (as distinguished from a subsequent sale of a previously issued bond), the difference between the issue price of such a bond and the amount payable at the maturity of the bond is considered *original issue discount* (OID). For instance, if a $5,000 face amount bond (with a maturity of 10 years and a stated interest rate of 5 percent, payable semiannually) is issued for $4,628, the bond is treated for federal tax purposes as having been issued with $372 of original issue discount ($5,000 minus $4,628). From the bondholder's perspective, OID is simply additional interest that the bondholder will receive on the bond, except that it is paid at maturity instead of annually throughout the life of the bond. In the case of a tax-exempt bond, such OID is treated as tax-exempt interest.

Although the OID is treated as tax-exempt to the holder, it will increase the holder's tax basis in the bond (over the life of the bond) for purposes of calculating gain or loss if the holder disposes of the bond before maturity. In the example above, the value of the bond on the day it is issued is $4,628; at maturity, the bond will be worth $5,000 (assuming it is not in default). If interest rates remain stable, the value of the bond will increase over time from $4,628 to $5,000. If the OID did not increase the holder's tax basis during the period the bond is outstanding, a sale of the bond for an amount in excess of $4,628 would produce taxable capital gain to the bondholder, even if the increase in value arose solely as a result of the accretion of OID. In order to avoid this result, the Internal Revenue Code (the *Code*) provides that the holder's basis will increase over time based on a *constant yield to maturity* (CYM) method.

To determine the constant yield to maturity on a bond, it is necessary to determine a constant discount rate that must be applied to each and every payment on the bond (principal and interest) in order to produce an aggregate value (as of the issue date) that is equal to the issue price of the bond. Using the above example (a bond that will pay $125 semiannually for 10 years, with a final principal payment of $5,000 at the end of such 10-year period), the discount rate that must be applied to each of those payments to produce a value of $4,628 is 6 percent, compounded semiannually. Thus, even though the stated interest rate is 5 percent, the bond actually produces a yield to the bondholder of 6 percent due to its being issued at a discount. This 6 percent CYM will enter into the accretion of the holder's basis, and such basis will increase each year by an amount equal to the excess of the accreted issue price at the beginning of each semiannual period multiplied by the 3 percent yield (6 percent annual yield divided by 2 to reflect semiannual interest payments), over the amount of interest actually paid on the bond during such period. For instance, assume the bondholder purchased the bond upon issuance on July 1, 2010. The holder's basis six months later on January 1, 2011, would be equal to the opening basis of $4,628 plus ($4,628 × 3 percent = $138.84) minus $125 of interest, which will produce a basis of $4,641.84 as of January 1, 2011. Because this calculation is only necessary to determine the bondholder's basis, it need not be done by the bondholder until sale or other disposition of the bond and, if the investor holds the bond to maturity, it need never be done. The basis of a bond purchased at issuance and held to maturity equals the principal amount of the bond at maturity.

In the case of a taxable bond, if the OID is less than one-fourth of one percent ($^1/_4$ percent) of the principal amount of the bond multiplied by the number of full years until the bond's maturity, the OID is treated as de minimis and is ignored. This rule does not apply in the case of a tax-exempt bond to ensure that the full amount of OID is treated as tax-exempt interest to the holder and that the holder does not have an "artificial" gain on the sale of the bond.

Bond Premium

If a tax-exempt bond is purchased at a premium (i.e., at a price in excess of the face amount of the bond), whether at original issue or in the secondary market, the bond premium is amortized over the remaining term of the bond using the same CYM method discussed under Original Issue Discount. The amount of bond premium amortized each year associated with taxable bonds is not deductible by the holder but, instead, reduces the holder's tax basis. For taxable municipal bonds, annual amortization of bond premiums may be deductible, depending on the tax status of the investor.

Amortizable bond premium can also result if a holder purchases a bond that was originally issued at a discount and the purchase price exceeds the issue price of the bond plus any accrued OID on the bond.

Market Discount

Market discount on a tax-exempt bond can arise if the bond is issued at par or at a premium and is later purchased in the secondary market at a price that is lower than the issue price or if the bond is issued at a discount and is later purchased in the secondary market at a price that is less than the original issue price plus accrued original issue discount through the date of purchase. Market discount, unlike OID, is not treated as tax-exempt interest to the holder when recognized because it arises as a result of market forces, not through the action of the issuer.

The effect of this rule is that a taxpayer who purchases a tax-exempt bond subsequent to its original issuance at a price less than its stated redemption price at maturity (or, if issued with OID, at a price less than its accreted value), either because interest rates have risen or because the obligor's credit has declined since the bond was issued, and who thereafter recognizes gain on the disposition of such bond will have part or all of the gain treated as ordinary income.

For example, if a $5,000 tax-exempt bond (issued at par on January 1, 2010) with a 20-year maturity were purchased five years after its issuance (on January 1, 2015) at a price of $4,400, the market discount would be $600. If that bond were sold on January 1, 2020, at a price of $4,700, one-third (five years of owning the bond divided by 15 years from purchase to maturity) of the market discount would have accrued. Thus,

$200 ($\frac{1}{3}$ × $600) of market discount would have accrued, and that portion of the holder's $300 gain would be treated as ordinary income. The remaining $100 of the holder's gain would be taxed as long-term capital gains.

In the above example, the market discount accrued ratably over the remaining term to maturity of the bond, that is, on a straight-line basis. Alternatively, a holder can elect to accrue market discount using the same method that is used for OID (that is, using a CYM method). In general, the effect of the election is to slightly decrease the rate at which the market discount is deemed to accrue, which will generally produce a beneficial result for the bondholder by reducing the amount of ordinary income recognized on a sale of the bond before maturity. If the bondholder retains the bond until maturity, both methods will produce the same result with the entire amount of market discount taxed as ordinary income.

If the market discount is less than a certain *de minimis* amount, it is treated as zero. In the case of a tax-exempt bond, this is beneficial to the holder because, although the discount will be taxable when the bond matures, it will be taxed as a capital gain instead of ordinary income. Market discount is treated as *de minimis* if it is less than one-fourth of 1 percent ($\frac{1}{4}$ percent) of the redemption amount of the bond (typically the par value) multiplied by the number of complete years until the bond matures, measured from the date it is acquired by the holder. For example, if an individual acquires in the secondary market a $10,000 face amount bond (issued at par) on January 1, 2011, for a price of $9,800, and the bond matures on January 1, 2021, the $200 market discount is *de minimis*. This result occurs because the face amount of the bond, $10,000, multiplied by $\frac{1}{4}$ of 1 percent, multiplied by 10 years until maturity, equals $250. Thus, any market discount less than $250 is *de minimis*. If the purchase price had been exactly $9,750, the market discount would not have been *de minimis* and would have been treated as ordinary income on maturity of the bond.

How would market discount be calculated in the case of a tax-exempt bond that was originally issued at a discount? For example, the bond that was discussed in the section on OIDs was issued at $4,628 on July 1, 2010, had a coupon rate of 5 percent, and a yield to maturity of 6 percent. On July 1, 2011, the original holder would have accrued $28.10 in original issue discount (calculated by multiplying the issue price by 3 percent, reducing that amount for the actual interest paid, and repeating the calculation for two semiannual periods). Thus, the *adjusted issue price* would be $4,656.10 ($4,628 plus the accrued OID). Assume the holder sells the bond for $4,456.10 ($200 less than the adjusted issue price). In that case, the new holder has $200 of market discount. The new holder will continue to accrue the tax-exempt OID at the same rate as the prior holder (and for this purpose should consult IRS Publication 1212 and the OID tables available on the IRS web site for the appropriate amount of OID that accrues each period). Those amounts of OID will equal, in the aggregate, $343.90 by the time the bond matures ($5,000 face amount minus the adjusted issue price of $4,656.10). When the second bondholder adds that amount to his cost basis of $4,456.10, he will have a final basis of $4,800 in the bond. If the second bondholder holds to maturity, he or she will thus recognize a gain of $200 ($5,000 proceeds on maturity minus $4,800 basis). Since this gain is wholly attributable to the market discount, the gain will be taxed as ordinary income.

What if the second holder sold the bond before maturity? In that case, he would have to determine his adjusted basis by starting with his cost basis ($4,456.10) and adding to that the amount of OID that has accrued (based on the original discount on the bond). If the holder sold after two years, the amount of OID that would accrue in the above example would be $61.42 in those two years. Thus, the second holder's basis would increase to $4,517.52. If he sold the bond for $4,600, he would have a gain of $82.48. Part of that gain is attributable to the $200 market discount at the time he bought the bond. That market discount accrues on a straight-line basis at the rate of $200 divided by nine years or $22.22 per year. As he has held the bond for two years, $44.44 of his gain is ordinary income and the remaining $38.04 is long-term capital gain.

These calculations are complex. It is possible for an investor who sells or redeems a tax-exempt bond to have earned a combination of tax-exempt interest, capital gain, and ordinary taxable income. Holders who purchase bonds in the secondary market should consult their brokers and tax advisors to ensure that they have adequate information to calculate their correct tax basis, the amount of original issue discount and market discount that accrues during the period they hold the bond, and the appropriate amount of gain on sale or maturity. In many cases, the information supplied on Form-1099 (in the case of a taxable bond) or in IRS OID tables may be insufficient (or inaccurate) in the case of a secondary purchaser of bonds. This will be true with respect to both tax-exempt bonds and taxable bonds. Accordingly, all secondary purchasers of bonds should ensure that they fully understand the information that is supplied to them on Forms-1099 (in the case of a taxable bond) or through IRS Publication 1212 (for both taxable and tax-exempt bonds) so that they or their tax advisors can properly determine the tax consequences of holding or disposing of bonds after purchase in the secondary market.

The treatment of market discount as ordinary income applies to tax-exempt bonds purchased after April 30, 1993. Thus, if a holder bought a market discount bond in the secondary market prior to May 1, 1993, any gain realized on the eventual sale of such bond would be treated as capital gain, not ordinary income, whether or not the gain was attributable to accrued market discount.

Redemption of Bonds at a Premium

An issuer will sometimes be permitted under the terms of a bond to redeem the bond prior to its maturity date at a fixed price. Such a redemption is treated as a sale of the bond by the bondholder. Thus, the holder may recognize a capital gain or loss on such a sale. If the bond is redeemed at a price above the stated face amount of the bond, it is considered to be redeemed at a premium. For instance, assume a holder purchased at original issue a 10-year bond for $10,000 on January 1, 2010, and that the issuer was permitted to redeem the bond on January 1, 2015, for a payment of $10,300. If the issuer in fact chooses to redeem the bond at that time, the additional $300 paid by the issuer to the holder is considered a premium and will produce a $300 long-term capital gain to the holder.

Borrowing to Buy a Tax-Exempt Bond

Taxpayers may, in some instances, claim an interest deduction for debt that is incurred to purchase or carry investments. However, a taxpayer may not deduct interest on indebtedness incurred or continue to purchase or carry obligations that are exempt from federal income tax. Without this *interest disallowance rule*, taxpayers would realize a double tax benefit from using borrowed funds to purchase or carry tax-exempt bonds, as the interest expense would be deductible while the interest income would escape federal tax.

The interest disallowance rule applies whenever a taxpayer uses borrowed funds to purchase or carry tax-exempt bonds. Thus, if borrowed funds are used for, and directly traceable to, the purchase of tax-exempt bonds, or tax-exempt bonds are used as collateral for indebtedness, then no part of the interest paid or incurred on such indebtedness may be deducted. If borrowed funds are only partly or indirectly used to purchase or hold tax-exempt bonds, then the rule will disallow a deduction for that portion of the interest allocable to the tax-exempt bonds. This concept applies generally to institutional purchasers of tax exempt municipal bonds as well as individual taxpayers.

While the interest disallowance rule is broad in scope, it does not automatically deny an interest deduction whenever a taxpayer simultaneously maintains debt and earns tax-exempt income. For example, the rule generally does not apply if an individual, while holding tax-exempt bonds, takes out a mortgage to purchase a residence rather than selling the bonds to finance the purchase. In this circumstance, the personal purpose of the loan predominates, and the IRS considers it unreasonable to deny the mortgage interest deduction. Similarly, the interest disallowance rule will not apply with respect to *bona fide* business loans unless the indebtedness is determined to be in excess of reasonable business needs. For example, the interest disallowance rule generally will not apply if a taxpayer that owns tax-exempt bonds borrows funds to finance a major capital improvement. In addition, a taxpayer may invest the proceeds of *bona fide* business indebtedness directly in short-term tax-exempt bonds for a temporary period while the borrowed funds await their intended use.

The Internal Revenue Service has issued a Revenue Procedure (Rev. Proc. 72-18) that permits individual and corporate taxpayers to avoid the effect of this disallowance rule where the taxpayer's investment in tax-exempt bonds is insubstantial. In the case of an individual, investment in tax-exempt obligations is considered insubstantial if the average amount of tax-exempt obligations (valued at their adjusted basis) is less than or equal to 2 percent of the average adjusted basis of all portfolio investments of the taxpayer. In the case of a corporation (other than a bank or dealer in tax-exempt obligations), investment in tax-exempt obligations is considered insubstantial if the average basis of such investments is less than or equal to 2 percent of the corporation's total assets. The American Recovery and Reinvestment Act specifies that banks could apply the two-percent treatment to tax-exempt bonds acquired between February 17, 2009, and December 31, 2010.

The interest disallowance rule also prevents a bank or other financial institution from deducting that portion of its interest expense that is allocable to tax-exempt interest. The disallowed portion is determined by applying for a particular tax year a ratio of (1) the taxpayer's average adjusted basis of tax-exempt bonds acquired after August 7, 1986, to (2) the average adjusted basis of all assets of the taxpayer. However, a financial institution may deduct 80 percent of its interest expense allocable to *qualified tax-exempt obligations,* which are a special type of tax-exempt obligation issued by qualified small issuers that reasonably anticipate issuing no more than $10,000,000 in tax-exempt obligations during the calendar year or $30,000,000 in 2009 and 2010.

Reporting of Tax-Exempt Interest

Notwithstanding the exemption from taxes for interest on municipal bonds (other than Build America Bonds), taxpayers are still required to report such interest on their federal income tax returns pursuant to section 6012(d) of the Code. The interest is reported for information purposes only and does not enter into the computation of any tax that is due, except as discussed with respect to the alternative minimum tax and the taxation of Social Security benefits.

Alternative Minimum Tax

The tax-exempt status of municipal bonds does not extend in all instances to the *alternative minimum tax* (AMT). The AMT is a separate tax calculation that must be performed by both individual and corporate taxpayers, and the resulting tax is then compared to the regular tax. Whichever tax is higher is the amount that must be paid. The AMT is calculated by starting with regular taxable income and then making certain adjustments to that income. The most common adjustments are the elimination of the personal exemption deduction, the elimination of a deduction for state and local taxes, and the inclusion in income of interest on private activity municipal bonds. In general, the bonds on which interest is taxable for AMT purposes are private activity bonds that were originally issued after August 7, 1986, except for (1) qualified 501(c)(3) bonds and (2) certain refunding bonds. *Private activity bonds* typically include any municipal bond the proceeds of which are used to benefit or finance a facility for the use of a private business and where debt service is secured by a private business (see Chapter 9). Once AMT income is calculated, a taxpayer is permitted to reduce that income by a so-called *exemption amount* before calculating the tax due.

In general, investors in the 35 percent federal tax bracket will not encounter an AMT problem because their regular income tax will exceed their AMT. However, for investors in the 28 percent or 31 percent brackets, especially those with large capital gains that may result in the reduction or elimination of the exemption amount and those who live in states with high income taxes, the AMT may become a problem. An investor who is not otherwise subject to the AMT should take into account the effect of this provision in deciding whether, and to what extent, to purchase tax-exempt bonds that are subject to the AMT. Furthermore, an investor already subject to the AMT should take into account the additional AMT that would be owed as a result of the purchase of otherwise tax-exempt bonds. Municipal bonds subject to AMT generally trade at a discount to similar non-AMT securities. Hence, any investor not subject to the AMT may be able to earn additional yield by buying AMT bonds.

Effect of Tax-Exempt Interest in Calculation of Social Security Benefits Subject to Taxation

Under some circumstances, a taxpayer who receives tax-exempt interest will have a greater portion of his or her Social Security benefits taxed than if he or she received no tax-exempt interest. Although this does not constitute a direct tax on the tax-exempt interest itself, it does increase the overall tax liability of the individual and should be taken into account in making the investment decision of whether or not to purchase the tax-exempt bond.

The calculation of the amount of Social Security benefits subject to tax is governed by Section 86 of the Code and is fairly complex. Because of the complexity of such calculations, individuals subject to Section 86 may wish to consult their own tax advisors to perform these calculations.

State Tax Treatment of Tax-Exempt Bonds

This section is not intended as a comprehensive guide to the state tax treatment of tax-exempt bonds. However, in general, most states do not tax individuals on the interest income arising from tax-exempt bonds issued by that state, its agencies, or its political subdivisions. However, the reverse is true with respect to bonds issued by out-of-state agencies or political subdivisions—virtually all states tax the interest resulting from such bonds. The effect of such disparate treatment is to increase the effective yield on a tax-exempt bond issued in one's own state versus an out-of-state bond. For instance, if an investor pays state tax at an effective 5 percent rate (after taking into account the federal deduction allowed for such state taxes) and the state taxes out-of-state (but not in-state) bonds, an in-state bond bearing a 6 percent interest rate is the equivalent of a 6.32 percent out-of-state bond.

The state tax exemption for interest on in-state bonds will not necessarily extend to capital gain resulting from the sale or disposition of such bonds (or ordinary income resulting from the application of the market discount rules). Thus, a holder who recognizes capital gain (or ordinary income resulting from market discount) may be required to pay state tax and should consult a tax advisor with respect to the state tax consequences of such a sale.

OTHER INVESTMENT FACTORS

Investors often invest in classes of securities whose yields are historically out of line with those of other securities in the market. Sometimes they do so in anticipation of a shift in these relationships caused by changing market conditions.

Spread Relationships

When interest rates are very high and investors are particularly concerned about a weakening in the economy, credit spreads (the gap between the yields of differently rated securities) often widen. Credit spreads generally narrow in a stronger economy, when many investors buy lower rated bonds to increase the portfolio's yield. In addition, investors examine spreads between different sectors of the municipal market for increased yield opportunities. Similarly, the spread between bonds with long maturities and short-term bonds varies under different market conditions.

Investors are often concerned with the spread between tax-exempt and taxable securities, often expressed as a ratio. At times of very narrow spreads—or a high tax exempt-to-taxable ratio—different classes of "crossover" investors may purchase municipal securities. Thus, experienced investors expect the tax-exempt municipal market to outperform taxable bond markets during these periods of narrow spreads. Conversely, when the spread between tax-exempt and taxable instruments is relatively wide—or a low tax exempt-to-taxable ratio—crossover investors may move out of tax-exempt securities. Yield relationships in comparison with taxable investments also help determine the specific maturities that an investor may wish to purchase. Investors monitor the option-adjusted spread, which is the average spread over the triple-A spot curve adjusted to reflect the put and call options that are embedded in a bond.

Measuring Performance

Investors evaluate the characteristics and performance of their portfolios with a wide range of financial and statistical measures that grade and rank the portfolio against itself and against other portfolios or indices.

In accordance with basic principles of investing—term to maturity, coupon rates, and redemption provisions—investors look for bonds that have the most favorable structure and features. They examine both the duration and convexity of the bond. *Duration* (or option-adjusted duration or effective duration) is the discounted, weighted maturity of a bond's cash flows. *Modified duration* is duration adjusted to represent the percentage change relationship of price and yield for noncallable bonds; it measures the price sensitivity of a bond for a given change in interest rates.

Convexity is the mathematical measure of the rate of change in the bond's duration as interest rates change. The more convex a bond is, the more its duration changes with interest rate shifts. *Negative convexity* happens when the bond price moves less, or even in an opposite direction, than the overall market, while in *positive convexity* the bond price moves just as much as, or more than, the overall market. A bond that is noncallable may have greater value to an investor than one of the same maturity and coupon that contains a call option because the call features in municipal bonds may create negative convexity. In a low-interest rate environment, where price volatility is greater than in a higher-interest rate environment, investors often want to avoid negative convexity because it reduces the portfolio's total return.

Investors also manage the portfolio's duration because the greater the duration of a bond, the greater its price volatility. A portfolio manager may employ hedging techniques to keep the portfolio's duration at a level where the total return is maximized.

There are many resources available to compare the performance of institutional investors, particularly for mutual funds. Numerous publications and web sites compare the total return of a fund's portfolio on an annual, three-year, or longer basis. Investors and the fund's competitors can use web sites to sort the performance of funds by sector, by state, by manager, or by other criteria. The fund's performance can also be compared to standard industry indices.

Evaluations for Individual Investors

Because municipal bonds are traded over the counter and because so many issues are traded infrequently, investors often request evaluations of their municipal holdings to determine the market value of their portfolios. Evaluations may also be necessary to satisfy legal or financial requirements for individuals and institutional investors as well as for bond funds.

The types of evaluations vary widely, but essentially they are designed to approximate the price that would be received for each bond in a portfolio if the bond were sold that day. Evaluators generally value a portfolio by comparing each bond with the recent trade prices of matching or similar bonds. Beginning in 2008, daily municipal price and yield reports on actively traded municipal bonds have been posted on EMMA, the MSRB web site (See Chapter 5). Investors can sort the information by state, credit rating, high and low prices, maturities, yield, and other criteria.

INVESTOR CATEGORIES

Table 6.1 shows the holdings of municipal securities by major investor categories from 1955 to 2010. Over time, market share has shifted among investor groups. Household and household proxies represented 27.3 percent of all holdings in 1980, mostly as direct investments. By 2010, these combined categories had more than doubled their share of the holdings to 70.3 percent. Direct household investment peaked in 1990 at 55.0 percent and then declined as growth shifted to investments through various types of funds. Commercial banks were the single largest category of holders in 1980, at 37.3 percent. The 1986 Tax Reform Act made owning bonds by commercial banks less attractive, and by 2010 commercial banks accounted for only 8 percent of all holdings. Property and casualty companies' purchases of municipal bonds fluctuate with their earnings cycle and with tax rates. In 1980, these companies accounted for 20.2 percent of holdings; but by 2010, that share had declined to 13 percent.

TABLE 6.1 Trends in the Ownership of Municipal Securities, 1955 to 2010

	Households (%)	Open-End Funds (%)	Money Market Funds (%)	Closed-End Funds (%)	Commercial Banks (%)	Property and Casualty Insurance (%)	Other (%)	Total Outstanding ($ billions)
1955	42.0	–	–	–	28.2	9.2	20.6	45.7
1960	43.7	–	–	–	24.9	11.4	20.0	71.0
1965	36.4	–	–	–	38.6	44.3	13.7	100.4
1970	24.3	–	–	–	48.2	11.7	7.6	145.5
1975	22.4	–	–	–	46.1	14.9	9.0	223.0
1980	26.2	1.1	–	–	37.3	20.2	8.3	399.4
1985	40.3	4.1	4.2	0.1	27.0	10.3	8.5	859.5
1990	55.0	9.6	7.1	1.2	10.0	11.6	5.6	1,178.6
1995	42.1	16.6	10.1	4.6	7.4	12.7	6.6	1,268.2
2000	35.9	15.6	16.4	4.6	7.7	12.4	7.5	1,480.7
2005	36.9	14.0	15.1	4.0	7.1	14.1	8.8	2,226.0
2010	37.1	18.0	11.4	2.7	10.2	13.1	7.5	2,925.3

Note: Percentages may not add up to exactly 100 percent due to rounding. Dash = categories did not exist at that point in time.
Source: Federal Reserve System, Flow of Funds Data.

Households

Households have been the largest single group of municipal investors since the 1980s. At the end of 2010, households directly held 37.1 percent of municipal securities (excluding mutual funds and other proxies). The activity of these investors in the market fluctuates, depending upon four major factors: the absolute level of interest rates, the relationship of municipal yields to those of taxable securities, competing returns in the equities markets, and income tax rates. Individuals generally purchase the greatest volume of municipal securities when municipal rates are near their highest levels; indeed they are generally the last investor category in the business cycle to buy bonds.

Some observers believe that, based on the progressive nature of tax rates, it would make sense for individuals to own more municipal bonds than they actually do. But many who are eligible because of high incomes have not accumulated the wealth to enable them to make substantial purchases, especially if they want to diversify their assets. The interest of individual investors in municipal securities is also affected by various tax law provisions, including the marginal tax rate of an individual under current tax provisions as discussed earlier in this chapter.

Mutual Funds

There are several types of mutual funds associated with municipal securities.

Unit Investment Trusts The first municipal bond fund appeared in 1961 in the form of a unit investment trust. At that time, Congress did not allow managed mutual funds specializing in municipal bonds to pass tax-exempt interest income on to investors, though unit investment trusts could do so. A unit trust issues a set number of shares to investors and invests that finite sum in a portfolio of municipal bonds. The portfolio purchased by a unit trust is essentially unmanaged and usually held to maturity. The life of these trusts, then, is usually limited to the life of the bonds originally bought.

Investors can buy units in the funds. Although most investors intend to hold on to their investments until the bonds mature, the fund sponsors ordinarily maintain secondary markets for the units. Investors can also redeem the units through the fund trustees, although the price paid for the units varies depending on whether interest rates have risen or fallen since the issue date. As the bonds in the unit trust mature or are called, the investors who have held their units are paid back the principal value. Some fund sponsors reinvest interest income for investors in another fund set up for that purpose.

Managed Funds   In 1976, Congress allowed managed mutual funds to pass on tax-exempt income to investors, and thereafter, this category of funds grew rapidly. Managed funds include both closed- and open-end funds. Closed-end managed funds are similar to unit trusts in that a fixed number of shares are offered to investors and a finite sum is invested in a bond portfolio. However, the portfolios of bonds in closed-end funds are actively managed. Many closed-end funds are listed on an exchange and trade like ordinary stocks. In addition to closed-end funds, some mutual fund companies offer municipal *exchange-traded funds* (ETFs), which are designed to mimic the performance of designated indexes. Open-end bond funds generally issue shares in relation to the demand for their product and the supply of appropriate investments. New investors may be accepted, and the portfolio may be expanded on an unlimited basis at the manager's discretion. Both types of managed funds investing in municipals can buy and sell bonds in the portfolio as often as they deem necessary. The objective is for active professional management to produce a higher return than would be available if bonds were simply bought and held. The prices of the bonds in the portfolio determines the asset value of the funds, which shifts up and down with market conditions and with general changes in interest rates. Some funds carry sales charges, and others are *no-loads*.

The objectives and management styles of managed funds vary widely. Some funds are devoted to short-term municipal bonds and provide investors with liquidity. Maximum liquidity in a tax-exempt instrument is available through the purchase of shares in a tax-exempt money market account. Other funds are dedicated to longer-term sectors of the market and have objectives that range from maximum total return funds (coupled with capital preservation) to high-yield funds, which invest in lower-quality or nonrated bonds and are designed for investors seeking maximum tax-exempt interest income with a higher element of risk.

The philosophies of individual fund managers often differ. Certain bond fund managers try to gauge swings in interest rates and to shift their portfolios among long-term and short-term maturities as well as cash. Other managers seek out undervalued securities as a method of increasing the return on their portfolios. Still others use financial products to increase the portfolio's yield. There is an enormous amount of competition among funds to generate the highest total return or income, and investors can compare the performance of funds in order to make investment decisions. Managed funds also often compare their performance to accepted industry indices.

From their inception, open-end bond funds grew steadily to a peak of 18.5 percent of mutual fund holdings in 1990, but declined throughout the following decade as equity mutual funds gained in both popularity and

TABLE 6.2 Municipal Securities as a Percentage of Mutual Funds, 1986 to 2010

Year	Total Municipal Securities in Mutual Funds ($ billions)	Total Mutual Funds Assets ($ billions)	Percent of Municipals in Mutual Fund Assets (%)
1986	67.0	426.5	15.7
1987	74.8	480.2	15.6
1988	82.9	500.5	16.6
1989	98.6	589.6	16.7
1990	112.6	608.4	18.5
1991	139.7	769.5	18.2
1992	168.4	992.5	17.0
1993	211.3	1,375.4	15.4
1994	207.0	1,477.3	14.0
1995	210.2	1,852.8	11.3
1996	213.3	2,342.4	9.1
1997	219.8	2,989.4	7.4
1998	242.6	3,613.1	6.7
1999	239.4	4,538.5	5.3
2000	230.4	4,433.1	5.2
2001	253.0	4,135.4	6.1
2002	277.3	3,638.4	7.6
2003	290.2	4,654.2	6.2
2004	294.3	5,436.3	5.4
2005	311.7	6,048.9	5.2
2006	344.4	7,068.3	4.9
2007	372.2	7,829.0	4.8
2008	389.6	5,435.3	7.2
2009	480.2	6,961.6	6.9
2010	526.6	7,934.5	6.6

Source: Federal Reserve System, Flow of Funds Data.

market value. As shown in Table 6.2, during the 2000s, the proportion of municipal bonds in open-end funds fluctuated, rising in periods after the equity markets declined (2000 to 2002, 2007 to 2010) and declining when the equity markets rose (2003 to 2007).

Closed-end managed funds owned 0.1 percent of municipals in 1985 and accounted for 2.7 percent of municipal holdings at the end of 2010. As shown in Table 6.3, municipal securities as a percentage of all closed-end funds fluctuated between 28.8 percent and 57.0 percent in the decade through 2010.

TABLE 6.3 Municipal Securities as a Percentage of Closed-End Funds, 1995 to 2010

Year	Total Municipal Securities in Closed-End Funds ($ billions)	Total Closed-End Fund Assets ($ billions)	Percent of Municipals in Closed-End Fund Assets (%)
1995	58.2	136.4	42.7
1996	59.1	144.4	40.9
1997	59.4	145.9	40.7
1998	60.7	148.8	40.8
1999	69.7	152.1	45.8
2000	67.7	141.9	47.7
2001	74.7	139.5	53.5
2002	86.0	150.8	57.0
2003	89.3	205.6	43.4
2004	89.1	245.9	36.2
2005	89.4	271.4	32.9
2006	89.4	294.3	30.4
2007	91.3	317.1	28.8
2008	77.9	202.6	38.4
2009	80.9	227.6	35.5
2010	80.3	242.7	33.1

Source: Federal Reserve System, Flow of Funds Data.

Tax-exempt money market funds were offered beginning in 1979. SEC Rule 2a-7, promulgated under the Investment Company Act of 1940, requires that the average overall maturities of securities held in a tax-exempt money market portfolio be 397 days or less. The average maturity in most money market funds is considerably less than that level. Such funds are created primarily to provide short-term liquidity along with the benefits of tax exemption to investors. The advent of tax-exempt money funds led to the growth and the creation of tax-exempt products such as variable-rate demand obligations and commercial paper. Table 6.4 shows that municipal securities as a percentage of all money market mutual funds declined from 22.1 percent in 1990 to 12.3 percent in 2001, rebounded to 16.8 percent in 2005 and then tapered off to 12.1 percent in 2010.

Following the 2008 financial crisis, interest rates fell to such low levels that most tax-exempt money market funds could no longer generate a positive return after covering their costs. Some managers closed their funds,

TABLE 6.4 Municipal Securities as a Percentage of Money Market Mutual Funds, 1986 to 2010

Year	Total Municipal Securities in Money Market Funds ($ billions)	Total Money Market Funds Outstanding ($ billions)	Percent of Municipals in Money Market Fund Assets (%)
1986	64.1	290.6	22.1
1987	61.8	313.8	19.7
1988	66.1	335.0	19.7
1989	70.1	424.7	16.5
1990	84.0	493.3	17.0
1991	90.6	535.0	16.9
1992	96.0	539.5	17.8
1993	105.6	559.6	18.9
1994	113.4	600.1	18.9
1995	127.7	741.3	17.2
1996	144.5	886.7	16.3
1997	167.0	1,042.5	16.0
1998	192.8	1,327.9	14.5
1999	210.4	1,579.6	13.3
2000	242.5	1,812.1	13.4
2001	276.7	2,240.6	12.3
2002	278.5	2,223.9	12.5
2003	292.1	2,016.4	14.5
2004	313.8	1,879.8	16.7
2005	336.8	2,006.9	16.8
2006	370.3	2,312.1	16.0
2007	471.0	3,033.1	15.5
2008	494.6	3,757.3	13.2
2009	401.3	3,258.3	12.3
2010	334.4	2,755.3	12.1

Source: Federal Reserve System, Flow of Funds Data.

while others chose instead to waive management fees to keep the products alive until interest rates returned to more normal levels.

Commercial Banks

Until 1986, the interest of banks in purchasing municipal bonds was influenced by a combination of factors, including the level of loan demand, overall bank profitability, the attractiveness of municipal bonds versus alternative investments, and the level of interest expense deduction. Banks prefer short- and medium-term bonds because they are better matches for the maturities of the banks' liabilities.

The Tax Reform Act of 1986 diminished the attraction of municipal securities to commercial banks because it eliminated the exemption (which now applies only to the smallest local issues) banks had previously enjoyed from rules that prohibit the deduction of interest paid on debt incurred to purchase or carry tax-exempt securities. Table 6.5 shows that municipal securities accounted for 7.8 percent of commercial banks' assets

TABLE 6.5   Municipal Securities as a Percentage of Commercial Bank Assets Outstanding, 1986 to 2010

Year	Total Municipal Securities Held by Commercial Banks ($ billions)	Total Commercial Bank Assets ($ billions)	Percent of Municipals in Commercial Bank Assets (%)
1986	203.4	2,621.1	7.8
1987	174.3	2,774.4	6.3
1988	151.6	2,952.1	5.1
1989	133.8	3,234.3	4.1
1990	117.4	3,337.8	3.5
1991	103.2	3,443.4	3.0
1992	97.5	3,656.7	2.7
1993	99.2	3,894.3	2.5
1994	97.6	4,163.1	2.3
1995	93.4	4,498.5	2.1
1996	94.2	4,716.5	2.0
1997	96.7	5,182.5	1.9
1998	104.8	5,638.7	1.9
1999	110.8	5,998.2	1.8
2000	114.1	6,708.6	1.7
2001	120.2	7,123.5	1.7
2002	121.7	7,683.2	1.6
2003	132.7	8,229.7	1.6
2004	140.8	9,057.8	1.6
2005	157.7	9,843.7	1.6
2006	180.2	10,886.0	1.7
2007	192.9	11,879.9	1.6
2008	216.7	14,056.3	1.5
2009	218.6	14,288.2	1.5
2010	246.1	14,336.1	1.6

Source: Federal Reserve System, Flow of Funds Data.

in 1986, but the proportion fell in every year thereafter until 2002, when it stabilized at 1.6 percent. It has remained close to that level in subsequent years through 2010.

Property/Casualty Insurance Companies

Investment objectives and high tax rates have encouraged companies in the property/casualty insurance industry to invest in municipal bonds.

TABLE 6.6 Municipal Securities as a Percentage of Property/Casualty Insurance Company Assets, 1986 to 2010

Year	Total Municipal Securities Held by Property/Casualty Companies ($ billions)	Total Property/Casualty Company Assets ($ billions)	Percent of Municipals in Property/Casualty Company Assets (%)
1986	101.9	353.6	28.8
1987	124.8	405.0	30.8
1988	134.1	453.9	29.5
1989	134.8	503.0	26.8
1990	136.9	533.5	25.7
1991	126.8	575.8	22.0
1992	134.3	597.9	22.5
1993	146.1	642.5	22.7
1994	153.8	678.1	22.7
1995	161.0	740.3	21.7
1996	175.4	770.0	22.8
1997	191.6	843.5	22.7
1998	208.1	876.4	23.7
1999	199.0	869.9	22.9
2000	184.1	858.1	21.5
2001	173.8	853.1	20.4
2002	183.0	933.7	19.6
2003	224.2	1,057.1	21.2
2004	267.8	1,159.1	23.1
2005	313.2	1,246.3	25.1
2006	335.2	1,335.8	25.1
2007	371.3	1,385.8	26.8
2008	381.9	1,309.4	29.2
2009	369.4	1,387.6	26.7
2010	348.4	1,403.9	24.8

Source: Federal Reserve System, Flow of Funds Data.

Considerable volatility in the investment activity of insurance companies is due to the cyclical nature of profits within the industry. The level of purchases depends mostly on their taxable profits and cash flows associated with paying claims on insured losses: As profitability levels rise, insurers accelerate their purchases of tax-exempt securities.

The Tax Reform Act of 1986 altered the investment implications of tax-exempt bonds for property and casualty companies with the imposition of an alternative minimum income tax as well as changes in the taxability of loss reserves. However, changes in the way in which insurers' income is calculated may tend to increase their taxable income, thereby generating greater demand for municipal bonds in some cases.

Property/casualty insurers have typically favored long-term maturities for their municipal bond portfolios. They have been interested principally in producing the highest yield possible, given adequate credit quality, and long-term municipal bonds produce the highest returns. Many property/casualty insurers prefer revenue bonds to GO securities to produce higher returns on their investments. However, portfolio managers are always looking for opportunities along the yield curve and among sectors to maximize their performance.

Since 1986, the proportion of municipal securities held by property/casualty companies has fluctuated with the underwriting profit cycle, ranging from a low of 10 percent in 1992 to a high of 14.8 percent in 1998; these insurers held 13.1 percent of municipal securities at the end of 2010. Table 6.6 shows that municipal securities as a percentage of overall property/casualty insurance company assets peaked at 30.8 percent in 1987, dropped to 19.6 percent in 2002 and then rebounded to 29.2 percent in 2008; at the end of 2010 it was 24.8 percent.

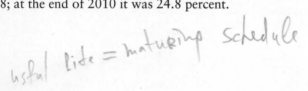

CHAPTER 7

Credit Analysis

INTRODUCTION

Municipal credit analysis assesses both the ability and the willingness of an issuer to repay bonded debt as scheduled. Analysts use quantitative tools and qualitative judgments to evaluate the creditworthiness of an issuer.

Municipal Credit Quality

Up to the mid-1970s, investors and dealers in municipal securities had been accustomed to the comparatively secure payment of principal and interest. There had been few serious municipal credit problems since the Depression in the 1930s, when there were nearly 5,000 recorded defaults. One study found that between 1945 and 1965 only $10 million of principal and interest was permanently lost to municipal investors. Even the Depression defaults were almost entirely corrected by 1945, and most investors were paid what they were owed.

During the 1970s, however, the financial debt environment changed. Beginning with the note defaults by New York City, Cleveland, and the New York State Urban Development Corporation, municipal credit analysis drew increased attention from investors and dealers. This attention was heightened in 1983 by the default of the Washington Public Power Supply System (WPPSS) on more than $2 billion of debt issued to finance the construction of nuclear power plants. The 1994 bankruptcy of affluent Orange County, California, made it clear that no jurisdiction was immune to financial uncertainty.

The now-defunct Advisory Commission on Intergovernmental Relations (ACIR) analyzed the problem in its March 1985 report, *Bankruptcies, Defaults, and Other Local Government Financial Emergencies*. The commission found that the number of municipal bankruptcies grew to 21 between 1972 and 1984, compared with only 10 cases filed between 1960 and 1971.

Changes in bankruptcy laws and the proliferation of special-district and industrial development bonds were partly responsible for this development.
Under the revised Bankruptcy Code, which went into effect in 2005, municipalities have the right to file for bankruptcy protection under Chapter 9.
However, the municipality's state law must authorize a filing, and not every
state authorizes Chapter 9 filings. There can be no involuntary bankruptcy
filings as only the municipality itself can initiate the proceeding. The approval of creditors is no longer required for filing for bankruptcy, so that
some entities—for example, the San Jose School District, California—were
able to file for bankruptcy in order to avoid the burdens of a labor agreement. In 1994, Orange County filed for protection under Chapter 9 as a
result of substantial losses resulting from the county's investment activities. More recently, the city of Vallejo, California, cited its inability to pay
pension obligations when it filed for bankruptcy in 2008.

The number of general purpose government filings has remained small,
but defaults and bankruptcies can move independent of one another. For instance, the WPPSS defaulted on two projects without filing for bankruptcy,
while the San Jose school district did file, although its debt payments
remained intact. Historically, municipal bankruptcy filings have been rare.
Table 7.1 shows that there were only 177 Chapter 9 filings from 1991
to 2009.

This compares to 49,091 business filings in the year 2009 alone.

Tax-supported bonds and revenue bonds are analyzed in different ways
that give greater emphases to different factors. For tax-backed bonds, analysts concentrate on the financial health of the entire entity, noting the extent
of its taxing power as well as the potential of its economic base. These are
the major determinants of the entity's ability to raise the necessary taxes
and fees to support debt service. The political environment, along with the
debt; economic, financial, and management factors; and overall characteristics of the municipalities, are explored in detail by credit analysts. They
seek information about population, wealth, and local industry; they watch
for trends in employment, per capita income, and the assessed valuation of
property; they closely analyze the issuer's financial statements; and they seek
full disclosure of data where necessary.

Revenue bond analysis is a broad field, with as many specializations as
types of revenue bonds that are issued. Analysts tend to specialize, focusing
on utilities, housing, or health care, for example, in order to stay on top
of the trends that occur in each industry on a regional and national basis.
A thorough economic analysis of an enterprise is necessary, as well as an
assessment of the economic strength of the enterprise's service area. The
legal provisions of the trust indenture protect bondholders from such risks
as dilution of security through the issuance of additional bonds, and so the
legal provisions and covenants are also carefully scrutinized.

TABLE 7.1 Chapter 9 Bankruptcy Filings (12 months ended March 31)

Year	Number of Filings
1991	21
1992	18
1993	10
1994	15
1995	13
1996	9
1997	7
1998	8
1999	4
2000	6
2001	9
2002	8
2003	7
2004	8
2005	6
2006	12
2007	5
2008	4
2009	7
Total	177

Source: Administrative Office of the U.S. Courts.

Whether the analyst works on the sell side for a dealer or on the buy side for an investor, for a credit enhancer or for a rating agency, the analyst's job is to evaluate the issuer's creditworthiness. The next section describes the role of the ratings agencies in the municipal market.

THE RATING AGENCIES

Moody's Investors Service, Standard & Poor's Ratings Services, and Fitch Ratings are the three rating agencies that dominate the municipal market. At these three agencies, specialists in all facets of municipal credit evaluate new issues and perform surveillance on outstanding issues. Each agency publishes reports on new and outstanding issues. They provide statistical information such as median debt ratios for states, utilities, health-care institutions, and higher education institutions. They also follow general trends, such as annual rating changes, and specific trends, such as policies on rating new credit structures and publish rating criteria.

In addition to municipal debt, each agency rates many other kinds of debt, such as that of international, corporate, and asset-backed issuers. Each agency has it own rating definitions. Tables 7.2 through 7.4 are the rating definitions of Moody's, Standard & Poor's, and Fitch respectively.

THE RATING PROCESS

Although each rating agency has its own style, the rating process is fairly similar among the three. For a new offering, the issuer sends the rating agency all financing documents, financial projections, audits, and a preliminary official statement. Two or more analysts may be assigned to important issues, and one analyst usually assumes a lead role. The analysts review the documents and prepare questions for the issuer. These may be addressed in a formal meeting at the rating agency, on-site with the issuer, or during a telephone call or teleconference. The issuer's experts, such as the financial advisor, the investment banker, and the feasibility consultant may be present at the meeting.

After all data have been gathered and all questions asked and answered, the lead analyst presents the issue to a rating committee. The committee thoroughly reviews the issue and then assigns the rating. The news is given to the issuer before it is publicly disseminated to the market. Issuers who are dissatisfied with the result may offer new information or clarify existing points in their attempt to raise the rating.

The rating agencies also perform surveillance on outstanding ratings. An issue may be upgraded or downgraded because of long-term trends such as improvement in the local economy or declining debt service coverage. Rating changes may also happen suddenly in the case of extraordinary events such as an unexpected bankruptcy filing. Each agency maintains its own public list of issues that are under review for possible upgrade or downgrade: Moody's Watchlist, Standard & Poor's CreditWatch, and Fitch Alert.

Representatives of issuers also visit the rating agencies on a regular basis to keep analysts up-to-date on developments in their jurisdiction, even when there is no deal currently in the market. Such visits can be part of an issuer's long-term strategy for a rating upgrade. Issuers also meet with agencies to discuss new credit structures, to gauge how those structures would be rated, and to assess their impact on the rating of any existing credit.

From time to time, the rating agencies revise their rating criteria. In 2010, for example, Fitch Ratings and Moody's made changes to synchronize their ratings for municipal bonds with their global ratings scale. For many investment grade municipal issuers, the effect was to upgrade their ratings by half a notch to one full notch on the scale: that is, an issuer previously rated A became either A+ or AA.

TABLE 7.2 Moody's Rating Definitions

Long-Term Obligation Ratings

Moody's long-term ratings are opinions of the relative credit risk of financial obligations with an original maturity of one year or more. They address the possibility that a financial obligation will not be honored as promised. Such ratings use Moody's Global Scale and reflect both the likelihood of default and any financial loss suffered in the event of default.

Aaa

Obligations rated Aaa are judged to be of the highest quality, with minimal credit risk.

Aa

Obligations rated Aa are judged to be of high quality and are subject to very low credit risk.

A

Obligations rated A are considered upper-medium grade and are subject to low credit risk.

Baa

Obligations rated Baa are subject to moderate credit risk. They are considered medium grade and as such may possess certain speculative characteristics.

Ba

Obligations rated Ba are judged to have speculative elements and are subject to substantial credit risk.

B

Obligations rated B are considered speculative and are subject to high credit risk.

Caa

Obligations rated Caa are judged to be of poor standing and are subject to very high credit risk.

Ca

Obligations rated Ca are highly speculative and are likely in, or very near, default, with some prospect of recovery of principal and interest.

C

Obligations rated C are the lowest rated class and are typically in default, with little prospect for recovery of principal or interest.

Note: Moody's appends numerical modifiers 1, 2, and 3 to each generic rating classification from Aa through Caa. The modifier 1 indicates that the obligation ranks in the higher end of its generic rating category; the modifier 2 indicates a mid-range ranking; and the modifier 3 indicates a ranking in the lower end of that generic rating category.

(Continued)

TABLE 7.2 (*Continued*)

Long-Term Issuer Ratings
Long-Term Issuer Ratings are opinions of the ability of entities to honor long-term senior unsecured financial obligations and contracts. Moody's expresses Long-Term Issuer Ratings on its long-term global scale.

U.S. Municipal Short-Term Debt and Demand Obligation Ratings

Short-Term Obligation Ratings
There are three rating categories for short-term municipal obligations that are considered investment grade. These ratings are designated as Municipal Investment Grade (MIG) and are divided into three levels—MIG 1 through MIG 3. In addition, those short-term obligations that are of speculative quality are designated SG, or speculative grade. MIG ratings expire at the maturity of the obligation.

MIG 1
This designation denotes superior credit quality. Excellent protection is afforded by established cash flows, highly reliable liquidity support, or demonstrated broad-based access to the market for refinancing.

MIG 2
This designation denotes strong credit quality. Margins of protection are ample, although not as large as in the preceding group.

MIG 3
This designation denotes acceptable credit quality. Liquidity and cash-flow protection may be narrow, and market access for refinancing is likely to be less well-established.

SG
This designation denotes speculative-grade credit quality. Debt instruments in this category may lack sufficient margins of protection.

Demand Obligation Ratings
In the case of variable rate demand obligations (VRDOs), a two-component rating is assigned; a long or short-term debt rating and a demand obligation rating. The first element represents Moody's evaluation of the degree of risk associated with scheduled principal and interest payments. The second element represents Moody's evaluation of the degree of risk associated with the ability to receive purchase price upon demand ("demand feature"), using a variation of the MIG rating scale, the Variable Municipal Investment Grade or VMIG rating.

When either the long- or short-term aspect of a VRDO is not rated, that piece is designated NR, e.g., Aaa/NR or NR/VMIG 1.

VMIG rating expirations are a function of each issue's specific structural or credit features.

TABLE 7.2 (*Continued*)

VMIG 1

This designation denotes superior credit quality. Excellent protection is afforded by the superior short-term credit strength of the liquidity provider and structural and legal protections that ensure the timely payment of purchase price upon demand.

VMIG 2

This designation denotes strong credit quality. Good protection is afforded by the strong short-term credit strength of the liquidity provider and structural and legal protections that ensure the timely payment of purchase price upon demand.

VMIG 3

This designation denotes acceptable credit quality. Adequate protection is afforded by the satisfactory short-term credit strength of the liquidity provider and structural and legal protections that ensure the timely payment of purchase price upon demand.

SG

This designation denotes speculative-grade credit quality. Demand features rated in this category may be supported by a liquidity provider that does not have an investment grade short-term rating or may lack the structural and/or legal protections necessary to ensure the timely payment of purchase price upon demand.

Source: © Moody's Investors Service, Inc. and/or its affiliates. Reprinted with permission. All Rights Reserved.

Not all municipal issues are rated. Issuers and their financial advisors may decide that the issue is not of sufficient quality to receive an investment-grade rating. They would prefer to market the issue as nonrated as opposed to noninvestment grade. Investors then must be even more diligent in assessing the strengths and weaknesses of the credit. This may involve making a site visit to the facility and questioning the project's management. In other cases, the issue may not be large enough to warrant the expense of applying for a rating or the issue may be marketed to only one or several investors who are already familiar with the credit quality of the issuer. Table 7.5 shows the volume of long-term municipal issuance not rated by both Moody's and Standard & Poor's from 1999 to 2009.

GENERAL OBLIGATION BONDS

Political Mood

One of the important lessons that the municipal market has learned is that changes in the political mood of taxpayers can prove as important for the

TABLE 7.3 Standard & Poor's Ratings Definitions

A Standard & Poor's issue credit rating is a forward-looking opinion about the creditworthiness of an obligor with respect to a specific financial obligation, a specific class of financial obligations, or a specific financial program (including ratings on medium-term note programs and commercial paper programs). It takes into consideration the creditworthiness of guarantors, insurers, or other forms of credit enhancement on the obligation and takes into account the currency in which the obligation is denominated. The opinion reflects Standard & Poor's view of the obligor's capacity and willingness to meet its financial commitments as they come due, and may assess terms, such as collateral security and subordination, which could affect ultimate payment in the event of default.

Issue credit ratings can be either long term or short term. Short-term ratings are generally assigned to those obligations considered short-term in the relevant market. In the U.S., for example, that means obligations with an original maturity of no more than 365 days including commercial paper. Short-term ratings are also used to indicate the creditworthiness of an obligor with respect to put features on long-term obligations. The result is a dual rating, in which the short-term rating addresses the put feature, in addition to the usual long-term rating. Medium-term notes are assigned long-term ratings.

Long-Term Issue Credit Ratings
Issue credit ratings are based, in varying degrees, on Standard & Poor's analysis of the following considerations:

* Likelihood of payment—capacity and willingness of the obligor to meet its financial commitment on an obligation in accordance with the terms of the obligation;
* Nature of and provisions of the obligation;
* Protection afforded by, and relative position of, the obligation in the event of bankruptcy, reorganization, or other arrangement under the laws of bankruptcy and other laws affecting creditors' rights.

Issue ratings are an assessment of default risk, but may incorporate an assessment of relative seniority or ultimate recovery in the event of default. Junior obligations are typically rated lower than senior obligations, to reflect the lower priority in bankruptcy, as noted above. (Such differentiation may apply when an entity has both senior and subordinated obligations, secured and unsecured obligations, or operating company and holding company obligations.)

AAA
An obligation rated AAA has the highest rating assigned by Standard & Poor's. The obligor's capacity to meet its financial commitment on the obligation is extremely strong.

TABLE 7.3 (*Continued*)

AA
An obligation rated AA differs from the highest-rated obligations only to a small degree. The obligor's capacity to meet its financial commitment on the obligation is very strong.

A
An obligation rated A is somewhat more susceptible to the adverse effects of changes in circumstances and economic conditions than obligations in higher-rated categories. However, the obligor's capacity to meet its financial commitment on the obligation is still strong.

BBB
An obligation rated BBB exhibits adequate protection parameters. However, adverse economic conditions or changing circumstances are more likely to lead to a weakened capacity of the obligor to meet its financial commitment on the obligation.

BB, B, CCC, CC, and C
Obligations rated BB, B, CCC, CC, and C are regarded as having significant speculative characteristics. BB indicates the least degree of speculation and C the highest. While such obligations will likely have some quality and protective characteristics, these may be outweighed by large uncertainties or major exposures to adverse conditions.

BB
An obligation rated BB is less vulnerable to nonpayment than other speculative issues. However, it faces major ongoing uncertainties or exposure to adverse business, financial, or economic conditions which could lead to the obligor's inadequate capacity to meet its financial commitment on the obligation.

B
An obligation rated B is more vulnerable to nonpayment than obligations rated BB, but the obligor currently has the capacity to meet its financial commitment on the obligation. Adverse business, financial, or economic conditions will likely impair the obligor's capacity or willingness to meet its financial commitment on the obligation.

CCC
An obligation rated CCC is currently vulnerable to nonpayment, and is dependent upon favorable business, financial, and economic conditions for the obligor to meet its financial commitment on the obligation. In the event of adverse business, financial, or economic conditions, the obligor is not likely to have the capacity to meet its financial commitment on the obligation.

CC
An obligation rated CC is currently highly vulnerable to nonpayment.

(*Continued*)

TABLE 7.3   (*Continued*)

C

A C rating is assigned to obligations that are currently highly vulnerable to nonpayment, obligations that have payment arrearages allowed by the terms of the documents, or obligations of an issuer that is the subject of a bankruptcy petition or similar action which have not experienced a payment default. Among others, the C rating may be assigned to subordinated debt, preferred stock or other obligations on which cash payments have been suspended in accordance with the instrument's terms or when preferred stock is the subject of a distressed exchange offer, whereby some or all of the issue is either repurchased for an amount of cash or replaced by other instruments having a total value that is less than par.

D

An obligation rated D is in payment default. The D rating category is used when payments on an obligation, including a regulatory capital instrument, are not made on the date due even if the applicable grace period has not expired, unless Standard & Poor's believes that such payments will be made during such grace period. The D rating also will be used upon the filing of a bankruptcy petition or the taking of similar action if payments on an obligation are jeopardized. An obligation's rating is lowered to D upon completion of a distressed exchange offer, whereby some or all of the issue is either repurchased for an amount of cash or replaced by other instruments having a total value that is less than par.

Plus (+) or minus (−)

The ratings from AA to CCC may be modified by the addition of a plus (+) or minus (−) sign to show relative standing within the major rating categories.

NR

This indicates that no rating has been requested, that there is insufficient information on which to base a rating, or that Standard & Poor's does not rate a particular obligation as a matter of policy.

Short-Term Issue Credit Ratings

A-1

A short-term obligation rated A-1 is rated in the highest category by Standard & Poor's. The obligor's capacity to meet its financial commitment on the obligation is strong. Within this category, certain obligations are designated with a plus sign (+). This indicates that the obligor's capacity to meet its financial commitment on these obligations is extremely strong.

A-2

A short-term obligation rated A-2 is somewhat more susceptible to the adverse effects of changes in circumstances and economic conditions than obligations in higher rating categories. However, the obligor's capacity to meet its financial commitment on the obligation is satisfactory.

TABLE 7.3 (*Continued*)

A-3
A short-term obligation rated A-3 exhibits adequate protection parameters. However, adverse economic conditions or changing circumstances are more likely to lead to a weakened capacity of the obligor to meet its financial commitment on the obligation.

B
A short-term obligation rated B is regarded as having significant speculative characteristics. Ratings of B-1, B-2, and B-3 may be assigned to indicate finer distinctions within the B category. The obligor currently has the capacity to meet its financial commitment on the obligation; however, it faces major ongoing uncertainties which could lead to the obligor's inadequate capacity to meet its financial commitment on the obligation.

B-1
A short-term obligation rated B-1 is regarded as having significant speculative characteristics, but the obligor has a relatively stronger capacity to meet its financial commitments over the short-term compared to other speculative-grade obligors.

B-2
A short-term obligation rated B-2 is regarded as having significant speculative characteristics, and the obligor has an average speculative-grade capacity to meet its financial commitments over the short-term compared to other speculative-grade obligors.

B-3
A short-term obligation rated B-3 is regarded as having significant speculative characteristics, and the obligor has a relatively weaker capacity to meet its financial commitments over the short-term compared to other speculative-grade obligors.

C
A short-term obligation rated C is currently vulnerable to nonpayment and is dependent upon favorable business, financial, and economic conditions for the obligor to meet its financial commitment on the obligation.

D
A short-term obligation rated D is in payment default. The D rating category is used when payments on an obligation, including a regulatory capital instrument, are not made on the date due even if the applicable grace period has not expired, unless Standard & Poor's believes that such payments will be made during such grace period. The D rating also will be used upon the filing of a bankruptcy petition or the taking of a similar action if payments on an obligation are jeopardized.

(*Continued*)

TABLE 7.3 (*Continued*)

SPUR (Standard & Poor's Underlying Rating)
This is a rating of a stand-alone capacity of an issue to pay debt service on a credit-enhanced debt issue, without giving effect to the enhancement that applies to it. These ratings are published only at the request of the debt issuer/obligor with the designation SPUR to distinguish them from the credit-enhanced rating that applies to the debt issue. Standard & Poor's maintains surveillance of an issue with a published SPUR.

Municipal Short-Term Note Ratings Definitions

A Standard & Poor's U.S. municipal note rating reflects Standard & Poor's opinion about the liquidity factors and market access risks unique to the notes. Notes due in three years or less will likely receive a note rating. Notes with an original maturity of more than three years will most likely receive a long-term debt rating. In determining which type of rating, if any, to assign, Standard & Poor's analysis will review the following considerations:

- Amortization schedule—the larger the final maturity relative to other maturities, the more likely it will be treated as a note; and
- Source of payment—the more dependent the issue is on the market for its refinancing, the more likely it will be treated as a note.

Note rating symbols are as follows:

SP-1
Strong capacity to pay principal and interest. An issue determined to possess a very strong capacity to pay debt service is given a plus (+) designation.

SP-2
Satisfactory capacity to pay principal and interest, with some vulnerability to adverse financial and economic changes over the term of the notes.

SP-3
Speculative capacity to pay principal and interest.

Dual Ratings
Standard & Poor's assigns "dual" ratings to all debt issues that have a put option or demand feature as part of their structure. The first rating addresses the likelihood of repayment of principal and interest as due, and the second rating addresses only the demand feature. The long-term rating symbols are used for bonds to denote the long-term maturity and the short-term rating symbols for the put option (for example, AAA/A-1+). With U.S. municipal short-term demand debt, note rating symbols are used with the short-term issue credit rating symbols (for example, SP-1+/A-1+).

TABLE 7.3 (*Continued*)

The ratings and other credit related opinions of Standard & Poor's and its affiliates are statements of opinion as of the date they are expressed and not statements of fact or recommendations to purchase, hold, or sell any securities or make any investment decisions. Standard & Poor's assumes no obligation to update any information following publication. Users of ratings and credit related opinions should not rely on them in making any investment decision. Standard & Poor's opinions and analyses do not address the suitability of any security. Standard & Poor's Financial Services LLC does not act as a fiduciary or an investment advisor. While Standard & Poor's has obtained information from sources it believes to be reliable, Standard & Poor's does not perform an audit and undertakes no duty of due diligence or independent verification of any information it receives. Ratings and credit related opinions may be changed, suspended, or withdrawn at any time.

Source: Standard & Poor's Ratings Definitions, © 2011. This material is reproduced with permission of Standard & Poor's Financial Services LLC.

Standard & Poor's Financial Services LLC (S&P) does not guarantee the accuracy, completeness, timeliness, or availability of any information, including ratings, and is not responsible for any errors or omissions (negligent or otherwise), regardless of the cause, or for the results obtained from the use of ratings. S&P GIVES NO EXPRESS OR IMPLIED WARRANTIES, INCLUDING, BUT NOT LIMITED TO, ANY WARRANTIES OF MERCHANTABILITY OR FITNESS FOR A PARTIC- ULAR PURPOSE OR USE. S&P SHALL NOT BE LIABLE FOR ANY DIRECT, INDIRECT, INCIDENTAL, EXEMPLARY, COMPENSATORY, PUNITIVE, SPE- CIAL OR CONSEQUENTIAL DAMAGES, COSTS, EXPENSES, LEGAL FEES OR LOSSES (INCLUDING LOST INCOME OR PROFITS AND OPPORTUNITY COSTS) IN CONNECTION WITH ANY USE OF RATINGS. S&P's ratings are statements of opinions and are not statements of fact or recommendations to pur- chase, hold, or sell securities. They do not address the market value of securities or the suitability of securities for investment purposes, and should not be relied on as investment advice.

value of the bonds as the issuer's financial ability to pay. Willingness to pay has always been a focus of municipal bond analysis, but the principle was brought home by several notable instances in the 1990s. The Orange County, California, bankruptcy is a good example. The county, which was wealthy by traditional economic measures, filed for bankruptcy in 1994. Many an- alysts did not question the county's ability to pay the debt but, rather, its willingness to do so. Another example was Brevard County, Florida, where a referendum was held to consider whether the county should decline to appropriate rentals on a new administrative center financed by certificates of participation. Although that referendum was defeated, other COP issuers felt the repercussions over time. These episodes were preceded by events

TABLE 7.4 Fitch Ratings Definitions

International Issuer and Credit Rating Scales
The Primary Credit Rating Scales (those featuring the symbols AAA-D and F1-D) are used for debt and financial strength ratings. The below section describes their use for issuers and obligations in corporate, public, and structured finance debt markets.

Long-Term Rating Scales

Issuer Credit Rating Scales
Rated entities in a number of sectors, including financial and nonfinancial corporations, sovereigns, and insurance companies, are generally assigned Issuer Default Ratings (IDRs). IDRs opine on an entity's relative vulnerability to default on financial obligations. The "threshold" default risk addressed by the IDR is generally that of the financial obligations whose nonpayment would best reflect the uncured failure of that entity. As such, IDRs also address relative vulnerability to bankruptcy, administrative receivership, or similar concepts, although the agency recognizes that issuers may also make preemptive and therefore voluntary use of such mechanisms.

In aggregate, IDRs provide an ordinal ranking of issuers based on the agency's view of their relative vulnerability to default, rather than a prediction of a specific percentage likelihood of default. For historical information on the default experience of Fitch-rated issuers, please consult the transition and default performance studies available from the Fitch Ratings web site.

AAA: Highest credit quality.
AAA ratings denote the lowest expectation of default risk. They are assigned only in cases of exceptionally strong capacity for payment of financial commitments. This capacity is highly unlikely to be adversely affected by foreseeable events.

AA: Very high credit quality.
AA ratings denote expectations of very low default risk. They indicate very strong capacity for payment of financial commitments. This capacity is not significantly vulnerable to foreseeable events.

A: High credit quality.
A ratings denote expectations of low default risk. The capacity for payment of financial commitments is considered strong. This capacity may, nevertheless, be more vulnerable to adverse business or economic conditions than is the case for higher ratings.

BBB: Good credit quality.
BBB ratings indicate that expectations of default risk are currently low. The capacity for payment of financial commitments is considered adequate but adverse business or economic conditions are more likely to impair this capacity.

TABLE 7.4 (*Continued*)

BB: Speculative.
BB ratings indicate an elevated vulnerability to default risk, particularly in the event of adverse changes in business or economic conditions over time; however, business or financial flexibility exists which supports the servicing of financial commitments.

B: Highly speculative.
B ratings indicate that material default risk is present, but a limited margin of safety remains. Financial commitments are currently being met; however, capacity for continued payment is vulnerable to deterioration in the business and economic environment.

CCC: Substantial credit risk.
Default is a real possibility.

CC: Very high levels of credit risk.
Default of some kind appears probable.

C: Exceptionally high levels of credit risk
Default is imminent or inevitable, or the issuer is in standstill. Conditions that are indicative of a C category rating for an issuer include:

a. the issuer has entered into a grace or cure period following nonpayment of a material financial obligation;
b. the issuer has entered into a temporary negotiated waiver or standstill agreement following a payment default on a material financial obligation; or
c. Fitch Ratings otherwise believes a condition of RD or D to be imminent or inevitable, including through the formal announcement of a coercive debt exchange.

RD: Restricted default.
RD ratings indicate an issuer that in Fitch Ratings' opinion has experienced an uncured payment default on a bond, loan, or other material financial obligation but which has not entered into bankruptcy filings, administration, receivership, liquidation or other formal winding-up procedure, and which has not otherwise ceased business. This would include:

d. the selective payment default on a specific class or currency of debt;
e. the uncured expiry of any applicable grace period, cure period, or default forbearance period following a payment default on a bank loan, capital markets security, or other material financial obligation;
f. the extension of multiple waivers or forbearance periods upon a payment default on one or more material financial obligations, either in series or in parallel; or
g. execution of a coercive debt exchange on one or more material financial obligations.

(*Continued*)

TABLE 7.4   *(Continued)*

D: Default.

D ratings indicate an issuer that in Fitch Ratings' opinion has entered into bankruptcy filings, administration, receivership, liquidation or other formal winding-up procedure, or which has otherwise ceased business.

Default ratings are not assigned prospectively to entities or their obligations; within this context, nonpayment on an instrument that contains a deferral feature or grace period will generally not be considered a default until after the expiration of the deferral or grace period, unless a default is otherwise driven by bankruptcy or other similar circumstance, or by a coercive debt exchange.

"Imminent" default typically refers to the occasion where a payment default has been intimated by the issuer, and is all but inevitable. This may, for example, be where an issuer has missed a scheduled payment, but (as is typical) has a grace period during which it may cure the payment default. Another alternative would be where an issuer has formally announced a coercive debt exchange, but the date of the exchange still lies several days or weeks in the immediate future.

In all cases, the assignment of a default rating reflects the agency's opinion as to the most appropriate rating category consistent with the rest of its universe of ratings, and may differ from the definition of default under the terms of an issuer's financial obligations or local commercial practice.

Note: The modifiers "+" or "−" may be appended to a rating to denote relative status within major rating categories. Such suffixes are not added to the AAA Long-Term IDR category, or to Long-Term IDR categories below B.

Source: Reprinted with permission from Fitch Ratings (as of April 2011).

a decade earlier with referenda in favor of property-tax cutbacks, most notably in California and Massachusetts. The limitation that these referenda placed on the tax-raising abilities of localities in these states did not affect their outstanding GO debt because any debt already approved was protected. However, lease-rental bonds, which are paid out of general tax revenues and are usually subject to appropriation, and tax-allocation bonds, which are backed by property tax revenues on increased property values, were affected.

In short, a community's actions can significantly alter the credit of municipal issues that are already outstanding. Although the contractual obligation of issuers to pay off GO debt has been strongly reinforced by the courts, such obligations cannot be met if the funds are not available.

In 2008, the City of Vallejo, California, declared bankruptcy after it was unable to negotiate cuts in pay and pensions with unions representing

TABLE 7.5 Long-Term Municipal Issuance: Nonrated Issues by Moody's and Standard & Poor's, 2000 to 2010

Year	Nonrated Principal Amount ($ billions)	Nonrated Number of Issues	Percent of Municipal Debt Nonrated (%)	Long-Term Municipal Debt ($ billions)
2000	14.6	2,816	7.5	194.1
2001	11.6	2,464	4.1	284.2
2002	9.7	2,360	2.7	355.2
2003	11.8	2,371	3.1	378.6
2004	14.0	2,420	3.9	355.9
2005	15.6	2,514	3.8	406.4
2006	19.8	2,413	5.2	382.1
2007	27.5	1,908	6.5	424.2
2008	9.3	1,577	2.4	386.5
2009	9.9	1,605	2.4	406.8
2010	10.6	1,686	2.5	430.8

Source: Thomson Reuters.

city employees. At the time, it was the largest municipal bankruptcy since Orange County in 1994. A proposed plan of adjustment filed in January 2011 did not affect the rights of retirees and former employees to pensions and health-care benefits, although unsecured general creditors were offered only 5 percent to 20 percent on their claims. Investors who held about $50 million in certificates of participation payable from the city's general fund had to take a loss, but those who owned either $175 million in water revenue bonds backed by a special assessment or certain other special tax obligations secured by the city's restricted funds did not. The difficulties Vallejo encountered after filing for bankruptcy—the city fired almost half the police force, for example—encouraged other municipalities in financial distress and public sector unions to explore negotiated alternatives.

Most revenue bonds are not affected by taxpayer limitations on property tax because these bonds are normally paid from other sources of income. But there is nothing to say that electric utility users, for example, will not stage their own revolt—as they did in the Pacific Northwest during the early 1980s. As a result, assessment of the prevailing political mood of states and localities can prove to be an important part of municipal bond analysis for revenue as well as GO bonds.

Analysts also rely on other information to assess a community's willingness to pay. The details of the state's constitution or of the statutes authorizing bonds and taxes provide an indication of how difficult it is for an issuer to raise more debt. Past action to meet budget deficits is another guide. Over the longer term, analysts prefer to see that the final maturity of bonds does not exceed the life of the project for which the proceeds are used. Future taxpayers may not be willing to pay for a public enterprise that is no longer in use or that is in need of substantial repair.

Debt Factors

Traditional GO bond analysis, where the bond is secured by the issuer's pledge of its full faith, credit, and taxing power, emphasizes the debt burden of the community. The objective is to determine whether the debt of the issuer is at a manageable level in proportion to property values, population, income, and similar data. Measures of debt burden have proved to be inadequate tools in themselves. However, coupled with other information, debt burden is still an important gauge of the ability of communities to pay their debts. Among the other measures most commonly used are a series of debt ratios that can be compared with benchmarks based on averages throughout the country. Trends in these ratios are watched closely for signals of improvement or deterioration. The analysis begins with the computation of the municipality's debt. A sample debt statement for the City of Austin, Texas, is shown in Table 7.6. This table is from the Comprehensive Annual Financial Report that can be viewed on the city's web site.

The first step in the analysis is to compute the municipality's total bonded debt—that is, the total GO debt issued by the municipality, no matter what the purpose. Added to this is any unfunded debt, typically short-term notes. The sum of the two is usually called *total direct debt*. Austin had no outstanding short-term notes as of the date of this table. The next step is to subtract all debt that is not actually a potential burden on the municipality's tax resources. This subtraction includes self-supporting enterprise debt, which is generally issued to support a project and is paid out of the revenues of the enterprise's operation. Austin has general obligation debt for several enterprise activities, which make up this type of subtraction and are not listed in Table 7.6. Analysts should also subtract any sinking funds or reserve funds established to pay off future debt. The buildup in such reserves reduces the burden to the issuer. *Tax anticipation notes* and *revenue anticipation notes* (TANs and RANs) are usually subtracted. *Bond anticipation notes* (BANs), which are ultimately refinanced into long-term debt, are not deducted from total debt in the computation unless they have been issued for a self-supporting enterprise. Again, Austin did not have that type of debt.

When these items have been subtracted from total direct debt, the figure remaining is called *net direct debt*. The debt of overlapping or underlying

TABLE 7.6 Computation of Direct and Overlapping Debt, City of Austin, Texas

Name of Governmental Unit	Net Debt Outstanding as of September 30, 2009 ($ thousands)	Percent Applicable to City of Austin[1]	Amount Applicable to City of Austin ($ thousands)
City of Austin			
General obligation bonds	845,741		
Certificates of obligation	78,525		
Contractual obligations	28,456		
Total City of Austin debt	952,722[2]	100.00	952,722
Greater than 10%			
Austin Community College	95,504	71.12	67,922
Austin Independent School District	742,011	93.97	697,268
Del Valle Independent School District	162,275	68.31	110,850
Eanes Independent School District	125,205	29.89	37,424
Leander Independent School District	949,185	11.07	105,075
Manor Independent School District	194,052	69.65	135,157
Northwest Travis County RD #3	2,780	100	2,780
Pflugerville Independent School District	375,345	37.63	141,242
Round Rock Independent School District	665,862	33.39	222,331
Travis County	522,990	69.92	365,675
Less than 10%			
Williamson County	763,345	9.85	75,189
Total direct and overlapping debt			2,913,635
Ratio of total direct and overlapping debt to assessed valuation[3]		3.8%	
Per capita overlapping debt[4]		$3,782.49	

[1] Source: Taxing jurisdictions, Travis Central Appraisal District and Municipal Advisory Council of Texas.
[2] Excludes general obligation debt reported in proprietary funds.
[3] Based on assessed valuation of $76,752,007,737 provided by the Travis Central Appraisal District and Williamson County Appraisal District.
[4] Based on 2009 estimated population of 770,296.
Source: City of Austin, Texas. Comprehensive Annual Financial Report for year ended September 30, 2009.

units of government is then added. Such units include, but are not limited to, school districts, park districts, and other entities that provide services in which the municipality shares, such as police or sanitation. Because the local population and economic wealth must also support this debt, the *pro rata* or proportional part of the debt of these units is assigned to the governmental unit debt burden. The amount assigned is the proportion of the issuer's full market value to the full market valuation of the overlapping unit, including the issuer. Overlapping and underlying debt is totaled and added to the net direct debt to arrive at the final figure, which is called the *direct and overlapping net debt* or the *overall net debt*. The overall net debt for Austin was more than $2.91 billion as of September 30, 2009.

With overall net debt tallied, the analyst then computes a variety of ratios. One popular measure is the ratio of overall debt to assessed valuation. (This ratio in Austin was 3.8 percent.) Analysts prefer to use full market value of property rather than assessed valuation. The latter is generally a percentage of the full value of the property as set by the municipality or state. Because these percentages vary widely, a comparison based on the assessed valuations of different municipalities is difficult to make. By using full valuation, the analyst does not have to worry about variations in state formulas. In Austin's case, assessed valuation and full valuation were the same. Many municipalities, however, have diversified their tax bases beyond the property tax (collecting sales and income taxes, for example), making debt to valuation a less important measure than it once was. Other debt ratios that incorporate fixed costs such as leases and pensions as a percentage of the operating funds can be more relevant than the ratio of overall debt to full valuation.

One commonly used ratio in credit analysis of local issuers is overall net debt to population, or debt per capita. Ratios can be calculated separately for cities, counties, and school districts according to the population of the governmental units. Ratios can also be calculated on such criteria as specific geographic area and sector. Comparison of per capita debt to per capita personal income is another useful measure in assessing the relative wealth levels of the issuer and its ability to repay the debt.

Debt per capita is also an important tool in analyzing the creditworthiness of the 50 states. Debt for this calculation generally includes all direct GO debt and nonvoted obligations such as appropriation-backed debt, lease-rentals, and COPs. Appropriation debt, which is subject to annual legislative action, is generally considered to be of lesser credit quality than direct GO debt.

Finally, comparing annual debt service to tax and other revenues provides another measure of an issuer's ability to pay. It is a common tool for analyzing the credit of states, where the property tax is not the major source of revenue. Further, this ratio has become a much more common tool in looking at those municipalities that have developed a broader mix of nonproperty tax revenues.

The moral obligation bonds issued by states present a special situation for analysts. While the full backing of the state is implied for these bonds, there is no legal obligation for the state to pay debt service. Thus, there is always some doubt as to how readily states will rescue troubled moral obligation issues. Analysts concentrate, therefore, on the degree to which these bonds are self-supporting.

It has become common for municipalities to issue limited-tax bonds. In these cases the tax that is pledged to the repayment of the bonds is limited with respect to either the rate or amount of the levy. It has also become common for states and local governmental units to issue *appropriation* and *lease-rental* bonds and COPs. Generally, the debt analysis of these issues is the same as that for the full general obligation. The analyst looks at the mechanisms that are in place to assure that sufficient funds are budgeted and appropriated to pay debt service. The analyst also assesses how critical or essential the project is to the government in order to assess the likelihood of default. The legal documents involved in these financings are described in Chapter 3.

The best sources of financial information are the municipality's or unit's official statement and annual report. Much of this information is now available on the issuers' own web sites or on EMMA. Moody's, Standard & Poor's, and Fitch provide both print and electronic services that summarize much of the most important credit data for thousands of issues, some of which are available to the public on a nonsubscriber basis.

Economic Analysis

To many analysts, the current and prospective condition of the local economy is the single most important factor in determining a state or municipality's creditworthiness. Communities at different stages of growth may require more or less debt. A young, booming city often needs to issue more bonds than a mature or deteriorating city. However, an older community that has elected to keep up with capital improvements will probably need to embark on major borrowing to keep its economy healthy—or risk economic decline. A high per capita total debt or rising trends in total debt might be acceptable to investors in the first case and present a danger in the second.

Important indications of a community's economic strength include income levels, population trends and prospects, employment statistics, and industry or employer composition. Per capita income and its rate of growth are among the first measures analysts examine. Some analysts also look at income per household because per capita data can often be misleading. It may be distorted by large student or prison populations, for example.

Analysts caution against relying too heavily on unemployment numbers to measure the strength of employment. Patterns of unemployment can be disguised by a number of factors, including population shifts and changes in the composition of the labor force. Labor force growth is a more accurate measure.

A comparison of a state or local population's income levels and of its labor force growth with national averages can provide analysts with a measure of the community's economic standing. Moreover, comparing a state or municipality with its neighbors along similar lines can help identify problems that might otherwise go unnoticed.

Other readily available data that are good indicators of economic health include the valuation of property per capita, the age and condition of the local housing stock, and the community's rent levels. Population can also be a key indicator. A growing population is usually a sign of strength, although unusually rapid growth could lead to pressures to immediately provide infrastructure and service. A declining population is generally associated with deteriorating cities and regions. Occasionally, however, a city may lose population to its suburbs but retain its economic strength as a place of employment. This is especially relevant if the city has maintained its infrastructure in reasonably good shape.

Once the overall direction of the local economy has been established, scrutiny of the specific industries and companies that dominate the community's employment is important. The two principal questions are whether the main industries are healthy and growing and whether the region is economically diversified so that it does not depend too heavily on any one industry or on one sector, such as manufacturing. Expansion plans for major companies can be important, providing one way of assessing the likelihood of growth in employment. A mix of new, growing companies and mature, steady companies is usually most desirable.

Diversity not only protects a community from deterioration should a major employer leave town or suffer a business setback, it can also help to shield the municipality from a severe downturn during economic recessions. A good yardstick for a municipality's strength is how well it did during the last recession. Did employment recover in line with the rest of the economy? Did personal income hold up? Did the municipality run an operating deficit?

Financial Factors

Analysis of a locality's economic structure must be translated into how that structure affects its tax base. A strong economic structure will normally mean plenty of taxing potential, but there are several factors that should be analyzed further. Again, diversity is key. A single corporation may even be more dominant in terms of the proportion of taxes paid in the region than in the employment it provides.

Major sources of revenues besides the property tax are also positive indicators. How significant are revenues from sales and income taxes, fees, and concessions? Because most states do not levy property taxes, a careful analysis of their various sources of income is important. A well-structured tax system is one that encompasses a wide range of economic activity. For example, if a state's tax structure depends heavily on only one or two industries, budget constraints may occur when that industry enters a downturn.

Most analysts regard too much reliance on intergovernmental aid as a danger. For one thing, the flow of these funds is usually out of the control of the municipality (except in the case of school districts, where the state may supplement local property taxes). For another, the amount of aid can be changed not only by legislative actions but also by administrative decisions, all of which are subject to political vagaries.

Once the sources of revenue have been reviewed, analysts can determine what potential there is for raising or lowering tax rates. Generally, if taxes are already high, the potential for increases is less. The percentage of taxes collected in some state and local governments can run dangerously low, even when other factors look good. A poor collection rate, especially compared to rates in adjoining regions, could reflect either economic shifts or simply an inefficient government. A drop in property taxes may sometimes occur as a result of property revaluation, a problem that afflicted municipalities across the entire country after the 2008 financial crisis.

Long-term factors are an important credit consideration in determining municipal financial health. The current financial status of the municipalities and their methods of reporting are also important in credit analysis.

Deficits in any of the various funds municipalities use to account for their finances are red flags that require more investigation. The cause of any deficit, and whether the factors are temporary and easily remedied or chronic and longer term, must be understood. An occasional operating deficit is not necessarily a problem. A dip in the economy, a change in intergovernmental aid, or a local corporate bankruptcy could tilt a municipality's main operating fund into temporary deficit. A large or ongoing structural deficit, however, must be investigated further.

Analysts look carefully at the volume of short-term financing because it may indicate a weakening financial position. Many state and local governments have adopted active short-term financing programs to provide funds when the timing of revenues and expenditures does not match. Annual increases in the magnitude of such cash management financing may indicate that a government is finding it difficult to control expenditures against revenues. The volume of short-term notes or commercial paper can reach dangerously high levels, as in the case of New York City in the 1970s and of California in the early 1990s.

An operating deficit or surplus must be analyzed in light of a municipality's past operations. The surplus or deficit in the final balance is the sum of past surpluses and deficits. A surplus in that figure may more than compensate for an operating deficit in any given year. Balance sheets must also be examined. A healthy level of working capital and highly liquid current assets are beneficial. Reserves for items such as uncollected taxes and accounts payable should be adequate.

Close analysis of the budget is another valuable tool. How many years into the future is a budget prepared? Has the municipality stayed within its budget in the past? If not, what specific items account for the cost overruns or excesses? What measures can be used to balance the budget?

Management Factors

Analysts try to assess the general capability and responsibility of a state or local government's fiscal officers. Increasingly, analysts have come to examine how well a city or state is managed, how carefully programs are documented, and how diligently and imaginatively the future programs of the municipality are planned. Political structure can be particularly important. For example, a strong mayoral system or a council-manager form of government is often able to control finances better than a weak mayor system. Analysts are placing increasing weight on such factors, however subjective they may be. In addition, better-managed governments are developing performance objectives that are both measurable and reported to their constituencies. It is beneficial to examine any such reports.

The state or municipality's investment and debt policies should be evaluated. Does the issuer have a written investment policy for its various (nonbond) funds, including the general fund and the pension funds? Does the issuer use derivatives, and if so, is this program managed prudently? Does the issuer have a debt policy that describes how much debt can be issued, and in what manner? All of these factors are used in assessing management strength.

Analysts also study the pension fund liabilities of municipalities. They generally want to know how pension obligations will affect expenditures over both the short and the long term. Does the municipality have a defined benefit plan or a defined contribution plan? If it has heavy unfunded liabilities, will the state or local government be obliged to increase annual retirement expenses substantially? If pension liabilities are actuarially funded, are actuarial assumptions about inflation and investment returns on the funds realistic, or is funding set too high or too low? If the pension system is overfunded, who is entitled to the surplus?

Many municipalities have substantial unfunded liabilities for future pension costs and other postemployment benefits, such as retiree health care. Disclosure of these costs has improved in recent years, but credit analysts have to determine whether municipalities can meet their obligations and what they have done to curb future growth in these liabilities. A municipality that no longer offers such generous benefits to new employees and is making catch-up payments to amortize pension fund deficits over a reasonable period will be a stronger credit than a similar municipality in which unfunded obligations continue to grow.

Analysts examine issuers' audits carefully. The Governmental Accounting Standards Board (GASB), the Government Finance Officers Association (GFOA), and rating agencies recommend that governments undertake independent audits of financial statements annually. To the analyst, the independent audit helps ensure that the financial data being presented are accurate and consistent with prior financial statements. If the audit is in accordance with the GASB's generally accepted accounting principles, the uniformity and consistency of accounting methods can be relied on. Municipal audits that are supervised by state officials—most states require some kind of audit—or are made to ensure compliance with a government program will not necessarily address the same areas as those covered in an audit conducted by an independent accountant using GASB principles.

Litigation that is material to the issuer's credit is examined to determine current and potential funding needs and expenditures. Some examples of material litigation include challenges to the basic systems of raising revenue, employment issues, and the general structure of the government. Analysts use issuers' official statement, annual financial statements, and the general news media to research any pending litigation. It is quite serious if material litigation is not disclosed to the market; government officials are subject to the SEC antifraud provisions.

REVENUE BONDS

Revenue bond analysis differs in many ways from the analysis of GO bonds. Although analysts apply the basics—examining the debt, along with the economic, financial, and management/legal structure of the issuer—there are differing emphases for revenue bond analysis than for general obligation bonds. An economic analysis of the demand for services, the level of costs, operating efficiency, and actual and potential competition is imperative to revenue bond analysis. The economic health of the service area is an important and complicated factor.

The Bond Resolution or Indenture

Most revenue bonds are traditionally protected by a number of legal and financial agreements that can often be as important to bondholders as the project itself. The first step in an analysis is close examination of the provisions of the bond resolution. The provisions are summarized in the issuer's official statement, but analysts focus on the full text of all legal documents. It is important to keep in mind that final documents may differ in material respects from preliminary information in connection with the offering of new debt.

Revenue lien. From the beginning, analysts determine what security is available for the bonds. Traditionally, revenue bonds are secured by a first lien on net revenues. This means that debt service is paid out of the *net revenues*, the funds that remain after the normal operating costs have been paid. A *gross lien bond*, on the other hand, is one where debt service is paid directly from the gross revenues before the payment of operating expenses. Most analysts do not give significantly higher ratings to gross lien bonds because it is healthier for the enterprise to operate effectively and to run a surplus in order to survive in the long term. Some contract obligations have priority over even first-lien bonds; for example, a power supply contract for a public utility is usually treated as an operating expense and paid before debt service. First-lien bonds are also called senior-lien bonds. Bonds that enjoy the same lien are said to be on *parity* with each other.

Subordinate-lien bonds, which are also called junior-lien bonds or second- or third-lien bonds, may be issued for any number of reasons. The senior-lien bonds may have been issued under a closed-end resolution (see following), meaning that any new bonds must have a subordinate position. Another reason to issue junior-lien bonds is that, over time, the credit quality of the senior-lien bonds may have risen. While bonds with second or third liens are generally rated significantly lower than those with first liens, the issuer may determine that the senior-lien credit is so strong that a well-structured junior-lien bond will be rated relatively close to a senior bond.

Mortgage pledge. In addition to a claim on revenues, some bonds are also secured by a mortgage pledge on the facilities that are being financed. This means that in the event of default, the bond trustee can seize the property for the benefit of the bondholders. With bonds that have a mortgage pledge, usually there is also some kind of revenue pledge. In recent years, fewer bonds have contained mortgage pledges, primarily because municipal facilities have somewhat limited use outside of the purposes for which they were built.

General obligation. Revenue bonds can also be backed by a GO pledge of the issuer. This means that the issuer does not dedicate specific revenue to the repayment of the bonds but, rather, pledges its general credit, similar to the way a municipality pledges its general obligation. The essential difference is that the independent agencies that issue the revenue bonds do not have the ability to raise taxes that are unlimited as to rate or amount. It is common for colleges and universities to issue bonds backed by their general credit, especially if the university or college has a large endowment. It has also become increasingly common for highly rated health-care issuers and strong state housing agencies to issue bonds with a GO pledge.

Flow of Funds

The flow of funds described in the bond resolution sets forth the order in which funds generated by the enterprise will be allocated to various purposes. In general, funds are used to pay for operations and debt service and to establish reserves. Different kinds of bonds require different flows of funds, but generally, all funds are first recorded in the revenue fund. The flow of funds described in Figure 7.1 is typical of many revenue bonds. When an issuer has several series of bonds, there may be separate debt service funds

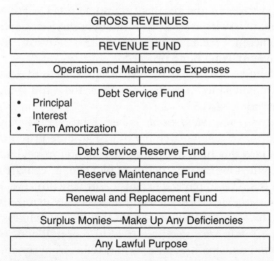

FIGURE 7.1   Typical Revenue Bond Flow of Funds
Source: Securities Industry and Financial Markets Association.

established for each series. This may happen even if all bond series are on parity with each other.

Operations and maintenance expenses. The money necessary to meet the ongoing budgeted expenses of the enterprise is placed in the enterprise's operations and maintenance fund. Normally, one-twelfth of an enterprise's annual budget is shifted from the revenue fund to the operations and maintenance fund each month. From there, expenditures are made to meet expenses. Occasionally, enough money is placed in the fund both to cover budgeted expenses and provide a reserve.

Debt-service fund. Issuers set aside monthly that will equal, over the course of a year, the amount necessary to meet annual debt service. This fund frequently maintains separate accounts for principal and interest. In some resolutions, cash is transferred to the debt-service fund immediately before the semiannual coupon is paid. Sometimes, issuers set up separate bond-redemption funds or accounts. There may also be a note-repayment fund or account and a sinking fund account.

Debt-service reserve fund. This fund can be set up initially out of bond proceeds or be built up over time. If the latter, issuers apportion funds to the debt-service reserve fund after annual debt-service payments are ensured. Issuers tap reserve funds only if the debt-service fund itself is insufficient to meet annual payments. The reserve fund is usually set at an amount equal to six months' or one year's debt service, with the smaller reserve fund used by stronger credits. Debt service can be defined as the maximum annual payment, the average annual payment, or some other negotiated amount. Many high-quality issuers are able to forgo debt service reserves, and other issuers may sometimes use a surety bond or other substitute for the reserve fund instead of employing bond proceeds.

Reserve maintenance fund. Issuers make allocations to this fund to meet unanticipated maintenance expenses, usually at the recommendation of the consultants providing advice.

Renewal and replacement fund. Issuers establish this fund to replace equipment and make repairs over the life of an enterprise and make regular payments into this fund according to the enterprise's budget for such replacements. When more construction is planned, a separate construction fund is normally set up to pay for expansion or new projects.

Surplus monies. Most bond resolutions carefully itemize where issuers may direct the balance of revenues should they exceed what is required for all funds. These funds are sometimes used to redeem bonds or reduce tax payments. Many municipalities take surplus funds from revenue enterprises for use in their own general fund. The resolution also specifies what kinds of securities can be bought with the excess funds.

Covenants

A well-designed flow of funds and ample reserves are not the only assurances investors seek. In the case of user-charge bonds, rate covenants are important. Under a rate covenant, an issuer pledges that rates will be high enough to meet operation and maintenance expenses, renewal and replacement expenses, and debt service. Another form of rate covenant requires that rates be set so as to provide a safety margin of revenues above debt service, after operation and maintenance expenses are met. Rate covenants vary greatly among different types of bonds. Bonds issued for stable and monopolistic enterprises, such as water systems, have lower rate covenants than bonds issued for less stable enterprises that face competition, such as health-care institutions. There has been a general trend in most revenue bond sectors toward loosening, or lowering the margin, in the rate covenant.

Additional covenants might include a provision for insuring the project, requirements for a periodic review by a consulting engineer, or guarantees that no free services will be offered to municipalities or favored customers and that separate books will be kept to record the accounts of the project. Other covenants contain provisions for independent audits and prohibitions against the sale of the project or of its facilities before the bonds are paid off. In some cases, a covenant stipulates the retention of an outside expert for periodic reviews of the enterprise's operations or maintenance.

Additional bonds. Once the claim on revenues has been established, an important covenant written into most revenue bond resolutions involves provisions for issuance of additional bonds. If the issuer retains the right to offer at a later time bonds that have an equal or prior claim on revenues, bondholders may be placed in a riskier position. Most issuers provide one of two types of protective bond clauses. The less common one stipulates that any additional bonds will be junior and subordinate to the current bonds except for bonds that may be necessary for the completion of the enterprise. This is called a closed-end provision; the drawback is that because the new bonds are subordinated, they may be more difficult to market.

An open-end provision allows for the issuance of bonds of equivalent lien on earnings, subject to certain requirements. Generally, the limitation is that the earnings coverage of debt service, including that for the new bonds, may not fall below a set minimum—for example, 125 percent. Earnings of the enterprise can be defined in several ways to meet this test. Some define the earnings as the most recent fiscal year's earnings or the average of earnings over the preceding 24 months. The latter is the most conservative of the methods commonly used. Another method is to base the test on future estimates of earnings, which usually requires reports by consultants with specific industry experience. Some methods permit adjustment of test period revenues to reflect planned rate increases or the anticipated expansion of the customer base.

Economic Analysis

Most revenue bonds are supported by enterprises that are subject to the same analysis as other business ventures. Of course, the factors affecting various kinds of revenue enterprises differ markedly from enterprise to enterprise. Two key factors are whether the enterprise enjoys a monopoly and how essential is the service being provided. Issuers generally provide a great amount of data to investors through preliminary official statements, feasibility and other engineering studies, and annual reports.

Financial and legal considerations are often paramount in the analysis of this kind of debt. However, the effective demand for the service—which includes the ability of customers to pay for it—is a key consideration. Some of the most important factors affecting the credit of different kinds of revenue bonds are outlined below.

Utilities   *Electric utility bonds.* The strength of an area's economy and the cost of the service are key factors in determining that area's effective demand for electricity. With the deregulation of investor-owned electric utilities, and with particular reference to the U.S. Energy Policy Act of 1992, analysts place an even greater emphasis on comparing the costs of the electric utility and its competitors. Analysts prefer to see that sources of power generation are diversified among different types of fuels. The power supply itself must be adequate to support the area's projected growth, and the analysis should consider any future capital outlays. However, underutilization of generation facilities can become a burden.

Water and sewer system bonds. Water bonds usually relate to the supply of water for a community. This is an issue of importance both to established cities, where often the water supply system has to be either enlarged or renovated, and to new cities or communities, where water supply may have to be newly constructed. Sewer system bonds relate largely to the disposal of wastewater. Sewer bonds often finance wastewater treatment plants that treat the sewage prior to its disposal into a river, lake, or ocean as well as conduits and related facilities associated with moving sewage to the plants. Treatment plants have to meet federal environmental standards, and this may require special and expensive technologies. The economic base of the area being serviced and the potential for growth are factors important in determining demand for either water supply or wastewater disposal. Reduced direct federal financial support, especially in wastewater treatment, spurred the development of state revolving funds for wastewater treatment.

Solid waste bonds. Solid waste bonds finance the disposal of nonsewage waste generated by industrial, commercial, and residential usage. The economic analysis of solid waste bonds focuses on the likelihood that the service area will generate enough solid waste to make the project feasible. Analysts consider factors such as price competitions among solid waste facilities in neighboring areas, flow control, and alternative methods of waste disposal, such as landfill. Pledged revenues may include tipping fees. If the facility is a waste-to-energy plant, where electric power is generated as a by-product of burning the trash, the market for that power is reviewed. Municipal guarantees, if any, are examined in light of the strength of the guarantee and the municipality's creditworthiness. Questions about the technology and the project operator, who is generally from the private sector, focus on experience and financial stability.

Health Care, Higher Education, and Other Not-for-Profits *Health-care bonds.* Health-care bonds are among the most complex bond issues. The location, level, and quality of services offered are important. Competition among health-care institutions has intensified tremendously over the past 20 years. How the institution has responded to a changed health-care environment, where the low-cost provider has an important advantage under managed care, is a major part of the analysis. Most hospitals are affiliated with other hospitals, other health-care institutions, or medical schools either through formal systems or through informal arrangements. Those affiliations may be within the same service area, in neighboring areas, or even in other states. Stand-alone facilities are less common.

In addition to traditional bonds issued for hospital construction, bonds are issued for facilities that provide a continuum of care for patients, including assisted living, continuing care, and nursing home facilities. Not-for-profit physician practices and health maintenance organizations have issued tax-exempt bonds for capital projects. For all health-care bonds, the level of services, competition, and cost structure are the key economic factors. Both inpatient admissions and outpatient visits and procedures are measured.

College and university bonds. Private and public colleges have issued a significant amount of debt, either directly or through state-established finance authorities. The bonds are usually direct financial obligations of the institution itself and may be either a GO of the institution or a revenue bond for housing, a stadium or other facilities. Because state-supported institutions receive a substantial part of their budget from appropriations and other state resources, the extent of the state's commitment is a key analytical factor. Private institutions that successfully manage their endowments and their education programs are highly regarded in the bond market. Enrollment trends, diversity of curriculum, the demand for admission as evidenced by the institution's application pool, and the strength of an institution's asset base provide the major clues to its financial health and prospects. Private primary and secondary institutions are analyzed in a similar way.

Bonds for other not-for-profits. Not-for-profit issuers, including cultural institutions, research institutes, philanthropic foundations, membership groups, and service providers can also issue bonds. The economic analysis for these issuers focuses on market position and competition. Is there a positive trend in donations to the institution? Does a museum, say, rely solely on large exhibits to generate revenue, or is there a steady stream of revenues? What other organizations, both local and national, does the institution compete with for philanthropic or research dollars?

Student-loan bonds. Education loans are typically issued through a separately organized entity to meet students' needs for aid in covering tuition costs. Most of these student loan bonds are structured, in that they are based on assumptions regarding prepayments, delinquencies, investment income, insurance coverage, and guarantees.

Housing Bonds   There are essentially two types of housing revenue bonds: multifamily and single-family.

Multifamily housing revenue bonds. These bonds finance rental housing developments for low- and moderate-income families and the elderly. Multifamily bonds are usually secured by the principal and interest payments on a mortgage. These payments consist of the aggregate of monthly rental payments. Earlier multifamily issues were typically subsidized or insured under federal housing programs. As the federal government has reduced its direct involvement in housing construction programs, multifamily issues have come to use market-based rental units to subsidize a dedicated portion of units at below-market rents for defined beneficiaries. Credit enhancements such as bond insurance, surety bonds, collateralized mortgage pass-through certificates, and letters of credit are employed. Key analytical variables related to multifamily bonds include the occupancy rate and the ability of the occupants to pay. Proper construction of the housing as well as the quality of ongoing management are also important; maintenance of reserves, for example, should be adequate. Legal documents relating to redemption provisions and credit enhancement must be studied. Some highly rated state housing authorities have issued general obligation bonds meaning that all resources of the authority are pledged to the repayment of the bonds. These are not, however, general obligations of the state.

Single-family housing revenue bonds. These bonds provide mortgages at below-market rates to qualified individual borrowers financing one- to four-family owner-occupied dwellings. Security for these bond issues is derived from individual monthly mortgage payments generated by a portfolio

of mortgages. Delinquencies, foreclosures, and prepayments are key considerations in analyzing these bonds. The level of reserves, type of mortgage
insurance coverage, and investment policies of an issuer help to define credit
quality. The demand for mortgages in the area served is also an important point to be assessed, as a lack of demand can mean that a portion
of the bond issue will have to be called, resulting in a lower coverage of
program costs.

Transportation   *Toll-road bonds.* Once potential traffic for a highway is
estimated, the major question for the success of this kind of enterprise concerns the elasticity of demand. In other words, if toll rates increase, would
the amount of traffic decrease substantially? A mix of different types of
users, especially if this includes heavy usage by commercial vehicles, helps
ensure stable demand levels, but competition from other roadways, particularly those without tolls, should be a consideration. Bond resolutions may
contain provisions calling for limitations on the construction of potentially
competitive projects by the same issuer. For new toll roads, the timely completion of the construction on budget is important to the issuer's ability
to meet traffic and revenue projections. Economic trends in the area being
serviced need to be analyzed, as do the price and availability of fuel. Bridge
and tunnel authority bonds are often examined using these same criteria.

Transit revenue bonds. Both new and older public transportation systems have developed revenue bond programs to build, expand, or renovate
their systems. As no public transit system in the United States is able to
support itself entirely from fares, other financial resources are generally provided. These additional funds include ongoing federal and state capital and
operating subsidies and taxes such as a sales or gasoline tax. Security for a
debt financing may take the form of a gross revenue pledge from fares together with either a special sales tax pledge, or revenues from gasoline taxes
and vehicle-related license and registration fees. Key factors in such cases
are the security offered, the need and demand for the service, the importance
of the service to the local economy, the outlook for nonfare revenues, and
management factors, particularly labor relations.

Airport bonds. Generally, a feasibility study is a must in analyzing the
prospects for an airport. The potential traffic through the airport is the main
consideration. Will the airport's traffic be generated primarily by residents of
the metropolitan area around the airport, or will the airport be a hub, where
passengers fly in to make connections with flights to other destinations? The
economics of these two kinds of airports are significantly different. Another
question is, are there competing airports in the same region? Some airport
revenue bonds (special facilities bonds) are secured directly by leases with
participating airlines and should be analyzed much like industrial revenue

bonds. More often, revenues are derived from contracts with many airlines, based on usage, and from other airport services such as car rental and parking facilities. The economy of the service area and pricing policies of the airlines that fly to and from the airport are also factors.

Industrial Revenue and Pollution Control Bonds These bonds are usually analyzed as unsecured corporate debt even though they may be backed by leases of highly rated corporations. Often, however, the bonds are guaranteed by a corporate subsidiary and not by the parent company. In the more secure issues, the investor has a first mortgage on the property involved.

Structured Bonds Efforts have been made to create asset-backed municipal bonds, although they are still rare. Asset-backed bonds are secured by pools of municipal assets, which can be leases, tax receivables, or other receivables. Analysts look at the underlying strength of the pooled assets as well as the legal and financial structure of the issue, including how isolated the bonds are from financial troubles of the governmental issuer.

Financial Factors

Financial ratio analysis is a useful way to assess the strength of a revenue project. Analysts are interested not only in a single year's results but also in the year-to-year trend of results. Analysts look at the ratios in both income statements and balance sheets. The most frequently used measure of an enterprise's well-being is the *coverage ratio*—the ratio of revenues (less operation and maintenance expenses but before provision for depreciation) to debt service—which uses figures from the income statement. Projecting future debt service coverage is important. This coverage may be adequate when bonds are issued, but if additional bonds are planned or if revenues decline, the ratio could drop sharply. Analysis of the efficiency of current facilities and of the potential need for new facilities plays a role here.

In addition to coverage, the analyst looks at trends in operating ratios. For example, the trend of days in accounts receivable would show how efficient the issuer is in collecting money. Balance sheet ratios, such as days cash on hand, show how liquid the issuer is and how much financial cushion exists.

The rating agencies annually publish financial ratios for revenue bonds. These ratios are helpful in comparing an issuer against its peer group or against a group that is rated higher or lower. Analysts can also create their own universe of ratios from issuers that they have examined and from other data sources to which they have access.

Electronic delivery of municipal credit information is based on documents (both official statements and continuing-disclosure documents) submitted by the issuer and on other available third-party information. Analysts use the data to evaluate credit quality and to make comparisons to other credits in its sector, region, or rating category or however the user sees fit. Some credit analysis systems embed the issuer's financial statements and official statements directly into the software to maximize the amount of information available and to enhance the user's flexibility.

OTHER FACTORS AFFECTING CREDIT

In assessing how sound certain securities are, analysts must also take into account two final factors: the letters of credit backing an issue and any bond insurance policies, which perform much the same function. States also have enhancement programs for specific public purposes. These programs tend to be linked to the credit of the state.

Letters of Credit and Lines of Credit

Letters of credit (LOCs) are used to increase market access for an issuer that may have difficulty in selling its bonds due to a perceived weakness in its ability to meet its obligations. A letter of credit is generally issued by a commercial bank and represents a contract between the issuing bank and the bond trustee. Under the letter, the bank irrevocably agrees to pay to the trustee on demand monies in an amount necessary to cover all payments due on the bonds. As with all contracts, the specific terms are negotiated and can vary with each bond sale. Within the context of the municipal market, however, terms and conditions tend to be standardized, especially as far as the investor is concerned.

Letters of credit are used for two purposes: to enhance credit and to enhance liquidity. To enhance credit, the bank issuing the LOC irrevocably pledges to provide funds to meet debt service payments in the event that the bond issuer cannot do so. The terms of the LOC empower the bond trustee to draw on the letter of credit directly if the bond issuer fails to make deposits sufficient to provide for timely payment of interest or principal or both. Thus, the letter of credit is used to protect investors from a default.

The expanded use of tender or put option bonds spawned the second use of the LOC: to increase liquidity. Under the terms of this kind of contract, the bank issuing the LOC agrees to advance any funds necessary to purchase bonds tendered by investors. The bank, in effect, provides for extraordinary demands for cash if a substantial number of bonds are tendered.

An LOC is normally issued for up to 10 years, while the bonds may have a maturity of 20 to 30 years. It is necessary, therefore, that the letter be renewed periodically or a substitute obtained. The bond indenture typically provides that if the letter of credit is not renewed or if a suitable substitute cannot be found, the bonds must be redeemed before the expiration of the letter of credit.

Hence, the question of timely payment, while reduced, continues to exist. At the time of the bonds' issuance, a substitution of credit took place—the bank's for the issuer's. A credit analysis should therefore pay attention to the creditworthiness of the bank itself, since a rating change for the bank's obligations would affect all financings supported by the bank. It is important, therefore, that the bank issuing the LOC has a sound financial history and a diverse loan portfolio and that it has adequate assets.

Lines of credit are used mainly to provide liquidity for commercial paper and other short-term programs. The critical difference between the letter of credit and the line of credit is that in a line, there are conditions under which the provider would not have to advance funds under a draw. These conditions can include default on other debt of the borrower, bankruptcy of the borrower, or a rating change, to name only a few. The analyst must look at each individual line of credit to assess the degree of credit enhancement it provides.

Bond Insurance Policies

A municipal bond insurance policy is a noncancellable guarantee designed to protect the bondholder from nonpayment on the part of the issuer. In the event that an issuer fails to meet a scheduled principal or interest payment, the insurer, acting as a third-party guarantor, will make service payment directly to the paying agent or trustee. The insurer receives an up-front premium for the guarantee, the amount of which is determined primarily by the perceived risk associated with the financing. Factors included here are the analyst's credit assessment, current market conditions, and other factors such as competition among the bond insurers for the business.

Analysts for bond insurers require much of the same information from issuers as do other credit analysts in order to approve an issuer's application for credit enhancement on a new issue. In addition to analyzing the credit, bond insurers may propose and negotiate specific covenants they may want added or changed in the indenture. The insurers want to strengthen the credit because they will be taking on the credit risk for the lifetime of the bond. Not all insured issues have underlying ratings, although many do.

In the event of a default, either technical or otherwise, a bond insurer generally works closely with the issuer to solve the problems that caused the default. Often, insurers will require that issuers bring in financial consultants and other experts to offer suggestions on how to improve operations.

The bond insurer's ratings are their most important asset to investors and issuers. Their credit quality is monitored by the rating agencies to detect declines, weaknesses, or improvements. In late 2008, most bond insurers encountered severe financial difficulties as a result of insurance they had written against structured debt securities unrelated to municipal bonds. The rating agencies downgraded the troubled firms, which affected the quality of their guarantees of municipal bonds, too. Investors began to place less value on bond insurance in evaluating credit risk, looking at the credit quality of underlying issuers instead. Insurance companies that had not previously been in the market began to offer bond insurance, but most issuers found they could no longer save enough on the interest rate to justify the insurance premium. The use of bond insurance declined precipitously; the proportion of new issues covered by bond insurance fell from 47.2 percent in 2007 to 8.7 percent in 2009.

It is important to remember that even for an insured bond, the issuer remains the first source of payment of principal and interest. Hence, the underlying credit characteristics of the issuer remain very important.

States also have enhancement programs for specific public purposes. These programs tend to be linked to the credit of the state. A state may withhold state aid payments for education, for example, to enhance the value of a school district's bonds. A state may also use its moral obligation to enhance its authorities' or localities' debt.

CHAPTER 8

Understanding Interest Rates

INTRODUCTION

To the professional municipal underwriter, trader, salesperson, or investor, fluctuations in the price of securities seem a constant, everyday affair. However, underlying the short-term shifts in securities prices and interest rates are less transitory factors that have a profound effect on long-term trends in interest rates. The basic factors that determine interest rates in general also determine the level of municipal rates; municipal bond yields tend to rise and fall in accordance with rates on other fixed-income securities, at least over time. A comparison of the 30-year *Bond Buyer* Revenue Bond Index with the rates on 30-year U.S. Treasury bonds clearly demonstrates the close relationship between markets for these securities (see Table 8.1).

Over shorter periods of time, however, municipal interest rates can move independent of general market rates. The supply of new issues and the cyclical buying habits of the principal investors particularly affect municipal rates. The tax exemption (except on Build America Bonds), as discussed in Chapter 6, limits the market to those who can best take advantage of it: households and household proxies, property and casualty insurance companies, and to a greater extent in the past, commercial banks.

Before 2008, municipal rates were usually lower than rates on other securities of equivalent maturity and risk because of the tax exemption. After the 2008 financial crisis, however, interest rates on Treasury securities fell to unprecedented lows, and while municipal rates also declined, they did not drop as much. Tax-exempt municipal rates generally traded at a premium to equivalent Treasury rates from mid-2008 through early 2011, a period during which short-term interest rates were close to zero.

TABLE 8.1 Average Annual Yields, 1990 to 2010

Year	The *Bond Buyer* Revenue Bond Index (%)	U.S. Treasury 30-Year Bond (%)
1990	7.53	8.61
1991	7.11	8.14
1992	6.59	7.67
1993	5.82	6.59
1994	6.45	7.37
1995	6.20	6.88
1996	6.01	6.71
1997	5.78	6.61
1998	5.32	5.58
1999	5.65	5.87
2000	5.96	5.94
2001	5.44	5.49
2002	5.37	5.43
2003	5.15	N/A
2004	5.09	N/A
2005	4.96	N/A
2006	4.99	4.91
2007	4.64	4.84
2008	5.34	4.28
2009	5.45	4.08
2010	4.88	4.25

Note: The U.S. Treasury did not issue new 30-year bonds from November 2001 through February 2006.
Source: The Bond Buyer; Federal Reserve System.

DETERMINANTS OF THE OVERALL LEVEL OF INTEREST RATES

Several factors determine the level of interest rates and their market impact.

The Business Cycle

One well-established observation of most economists is that as economic activity picks up, borrowing demand increases and interest rates rise. Financial institutions and capital markets compete with each other for a limited supply of funds. Consequently, banks raise both the rates they are willing to pay to lenders and the interest rates they demand from borrowers. To attract more capital to the money and bond markets, rates then have to rise further.

This process has been borne out in business cycle after business cycle. Interest rates peak at about the same time that the rate of real (inflation-adjusted) economic growth begins to decline. In inflationary periods, interest rates have generally peaked a little later in the cycle. Therefore, efforts to forecast the business cycle play an important part in interest rate forecasting.

The Federal Reserve

The nation's central bank is the *Federal Reserve*, or the *Fed,* one of the most powerful forces in the economy. It has considerable influence over key interest rates, both directly, in its ability to raise or lower the discount rate it charges to lend money to member banks, and indirectly, in its ability to add to or subtract from the nation's money supply. To many economists, the growth of the money supply and interest rates are the most important variables in determining the growth of aggregate spending. Others claim that fiscal policy—the primary tools being government tax and spending policies—is also influential.

The Federal Reserve has several methods by which it can influence interest rates and the money supply. It sets the discount rate, which is the rate at which banks that are members of the Federal Reserve System can borrow directly from the Fed. It also establishes reserve requirements for its members: banks must keep a set portion of every deposit or loan on hand as a reserve. The Fed's most flexible means of control, and the one it most frequently uses, works through the policy directions of its *Federal Open Market Committee* (FOMC). The FOMC is a 12-member committee made up of the seven members of the Board of Governors, the president of the Federal Reserve Bank of New York, and on a rotating basis, the presidents of four other Federal Reserve Banks. It meets eight times per year to set guidelines regarding the Fed's purchase and sale of government securities in the open market as a means of influencing the volume of bank credit and money in the economy. It also establishes policy relating to the operations of the Federal Reserve System in foreign exchange markets.

Through guidelines established by this committee, the Fed buys, sells, and repos U.S. government securities and sometimes other securities in order to add to or to withdraw from reserves in the banking system. These actions directly affect the federal funds rate, which is the interest rate on overnight loans among banks and is the key for determining short-term rates. Although the Fed also controls the discount rate, the federal funds rate is adjusted more frequently and it is the Fed's main way to influence interest rates.

In the early 1980s, the Fed focused on controlling the money supply. Since the mid-1980s, however, the Fed has been most focused on controlling the federal funds rate. The economists known as monetarists maintain that the Fed should, by and large, not attempt to control interest rates but, rather, concentrate on controlling the money supply. However, many other economists hold that the level of interest rates, which is partly determined by the federal funds rate, is more important than the money supply.

When the economy or inflation are growing too quickly, the Fed wants overall interest rates to move higher. It will attempt to accomplish this by raising the federal funds rate. FOMC decisions regarding interest rates have been announced immediately since the early 1990s.

From an operational perspective, following a decision to raise the federal funds rate, the Fed often directs its open-market operation to sell government securities. This added supply of securities should drive prices down and yields up. At the same time, the Fed drains bank reserves from the system through the cash it receives in payment for the securities it is selling. This process can reduce the money supply. Conversely, if the Fed wants to drive down rates or to boost the money supply, it will usually buy government securities.

The Fed also implements its monetary policy in large part through open-market operations using repurchase agreements, or repos. A *repo* is an agreement between a seller and a buyer, typically of U.S. government securities, although it is also used for other securities. The seller sells the securities to the buyer, with a simultaneous agreement to repurchase the securities at an agreed on price at a future point in time. With a reverse repo, the buyer buys the securities from the seller and, at the same time, agrees to resell them at a future point in time. If the Fed wants to expand the money supply, it purchases securities in repo transactions from the nonbank dealers who deposit the proceeds into commercial banks, which increases reserves in the banking system. Conversely, if the Fed wishes to tighten the money supply, it will sell securities to nonbank dealers, who will draw on their reserves to purchase the securities.

An entire industry of Fed watchers has grown up over the past four decades. These economists try to anticipate the Fed's activities and explain the reasoning behind what the Fed does. In the late 1970s and early 1980s, the securities markets became very sensitive to Federal Reserve policy. Often, the market would rise or fall on the announcement of the weekly change in the money supply. If the money supply rose unexpectedly, interest rates rose in anticipation that the Fed would withdraw funds from the market and push rates up. An unanticipated drop in the money supply, however, sent rates lower in anticipation that the Fed would buy securities. From the mid-1980s through the present, almost the opposite is true; investors pay less attention to money growth and the focus is on movements in the federal funds rate.

In late 2008, the Fed and the Treasury Department implemented several emergency programs to bolster liquidity in the financial markets after a severe financial crisis caused banks to pull back from lending even to each other. The Fed also embarked on a program of asset purchases, known as *quantitative easing*, to relieve the strain on banks and stimulate economic activity. After the credit crisis eased in 2009, many emergency liquidity programs were withdrawn but interest rates remained at historically low levels. In late 2010, the Fed began another round of quantitative easing intended to keep interest rates low.

Inflation

Many economists believe that inflation expectations are built into interest rates. The theory is that there is a basic, real rate of interest that would prevail if prices were stable, and that nominal interest rates (the rates actually paid by borrowers and received by lenders) will be equal to the sum of this real rate and the expected rate of inflation.

For example, even if there were no inflation, lenders would demand compensation for giving up current purchasing power, while borrowers would be willing to pay for the credit in the expectation that they could use the money productively. History suggests that the real rate of interest for long-term corporate borrowing in the United States has averaged approximately 3 percent, with considerable variation around that average. For short-term securities, the real rate has been much lower.

When prices are rising, lenders demand a higher rate to compensate for their lost purchasing power. Borrowers are willing to pay higher rates because they will be paying back the loan in the future with money that has lost value. If investors expected inflation to stay at 4 percent for the life of a bond, for example, they would demand an additional 4 percent in interest on top of the real rate. According to this view, the 4 percent *inflation premium* plus the real rate of interest would approximate the long-term nominal interest rate under these conditions.

Because future inflation cannot be known with certainty, the degree to which inflation is built into nominal interest rates reflects investors' and borrowers' long-run expectations of inflation. Even short-term interest rates respond to these expectations. Most economists do agree that, for whatever reasons, as the inflation rate rises, so do interest rates. A clear indication of the direction of inflation is one of the most important factors in forecasting the level of interest rates.

The Nation's Flow of Funds

Interest rates are essentially the prices of different kinds of credit. These prices tend to equalize the supply and demand for credit throughout the economy. If there is a high demand for credit, interest rates will rise. This simultaneously makes it more expensive to borrow (thereby reducing credit demand) and attracts prospective lenders (increasing credit supply). If demand for credit falls, interest rates will fall. This makes it less expensive to borrow, so credit demand increases, and the supply of credit decreases because the lower rate is less attractive to prospective lenders.

Changes in the supply of credit affect interest rates in the opposite way. If there are more funds available to buy fixed income securities, rates will be pushed down. If there are fewer funds available to buy these securities, rates will be pushed up. Many economists at brokerage firms and banks closely analyze the nation's capital flows to forecast interest rates. The object is to project the major demands for borrowing, on the one hand, and to project the major sources of the supply of lending, on the other. The projections, of course, are closely related to forecasts of the business cycle in general.

The Federal Reserve publishes an invaluable series of accounts to facilitate such an analysis. It is called the *Flow of Funds Accounts of the United States* and traces just how money flows through the entire economy. Economists use this tool to forecast the various components of the supply and demand for credit. Unusually heavy needs on the part of municipalities or the federal government, for example, can be assessed in this light. Heavy demand from these borrowers may be offset by diminished borrowing needs on the part of corporations. Regarding credit supply, economists can get a better notion of just how much strain will be placed on different kinds of financial institutions, as well as on the direct money and capital markets themselves. Any great increase in the demand for money by major institutions would lead to a tightening in the availability of credit and higher interest rates.

Flow of funds statistics are published quarterly in the Fed's Z.1 release. The data are also available electronically on the Fed's web site.

TERM STRUCTURE OF INTEREST RATES

Why do fixed-income securities of about the same risk but with different maturities trade at different yields? The relationship between yield and maturity among bonds of different maturities is known as the *term structure of interest rates*. This relationship can be represented graphically by what is known as a *yield curve*.

TABLE 8.2   U.S. Treasury Yield Curve (June 1, 2005)

Maturity	Yield June 1, 2005
3-month	3.04
6-month	3.22
1-year	3.36
2-year	3.64
5-year	3.77
10-year	4.00
30-year	n/a

Normal Yield Curve 6/1/2005

Source: Federal Reserve.

   The Treasury yield curve for June 1, 2005, is shown in Table 8.2. This curve is representative of a normal, positive, upward-sloping yield curve. The vertical axis represents increasing yields, and the horizontal axis marks the years to maturity. The points that make up the curve are the actual yields for securities with the stated numbers of years left to maturity. Following the curve across to the vertical axis, one can see that on June 1, 2005, a security maturing in three months yielded 3.04 percent, and one maturing in 10 years yielded 4 percent. At this time, the U.S. Treasury was not issuing 30-year bonds. The difference in yield between the three-month maturity and the 10-year maturity was 96 basis points.

   On January 1, 2011, the prevailing yield curve had a very steep upward slope (see Table 8.3). Following the curve across to the vertical axis, a

TABLE 8.3   Steep Upward-Sloping Yield Curve (January 1, 2011)

Maturity	Yield January 1, 2011
3-month	0.15
6-month	0.18
1-year	0.27
2-year	0.61
5-year	1.99
10-year	3.39
30-year	4.52

Steep Upward-Sloping Yield Curve 1/1/2011

Source: Federal Reserve.

security maturing in three months yielded 0.15 percent, one maturing in five years yielded 1.99 percent, and one maturing in 30 years yielded 4.52 percent. There was a 437 basis point spread between the three-month and the 30-year maturities, a stark contrast to the flatter yield curve on June 1, 2005. The yield curve usually exhibits a more positive slope when the economy is closer to a cyclical low during a recession or the early stage of a recovery. The yield curve shown in Table 8.2 is flatter than this curve. That is, there is less slope or difference between yields in the short and long ends of the curve. Conversely, a steeper yield curve such as the one in Table 8.3 has a greater difference between yields in the short and long ends of the curve.

When the economy is at its peak growth rate and starting to put a strain on resources, the yield curve may be inverted. The yield curve was inverted

TABLE 8.4 Inverted Yield Curve (November 1, 2006)

Maturity	Yield November 1, 2006
3-month	5.07
6-month	5.15
1-year	5.01
2-year	4.74
5-year	4.58
10-year	4.60
30-year	4.69

Source: Federal Reserve.

in November 1, 2006. Short-term rates became higher than long-term rates as money tightened at the height of economic growth. Short-term rates tend to fluctuate much more widely over an interest rate cycle than do long-term rates. Table 8.4 shows an inverted yield curve from 2 years to 30 years. Following the curve across to the vertical axis, one can see that a security maturing in three months yielded 5.07 percent, one maturing in two years yielded 4.74 percent, and one maturing in 30 years yielded 4.69 percent. The yield on three-month Treasury bills exceeded the yield on 30-year bonds by 38 basis points.

Several theories attempt to explain the shape of the yield curve. A summary of the most important ones follows.

Expectations

A theory to which most economists subscribe in one form or another is that investors' and borrowers' expectations of future changes in interest rates are the primary determinants of the term structure of rates. The theory in its pure form assumes that investors seek to maximize their returns, regardless of the maturity of the fixed income securities they buy. Borrowers, too, are considered indifferent to the maturity of their debt. As a result, the long-term interest rate becomes the average of the current short-term rate and the expected level of future short-term rates. As expectations of short-term rate levels change, so do current levels of both short-term and long-term rates.

For example, an investor expects short-term rates to rise more than the general market does, they might buy short-term securities and sell longer-term securities, reasoning that they will earn a better return by rolling over their short-term investments than by keeping their funds in long-term securities. Their action forces current short-term yields to decline as they buy and long-term yields to rise as they sell. On the other side, using the same logic, borrowers seek out longer-term loans in anticipation that short-term rates will be higher in the future. These moves on the part of borrowers and investors have the effect of driving long-term rates up and forcing short-term rates down. The result is that the yield curve slopes upward more steeply, reflecting expectations that interest rates will indeed be higher in the future.

When investors and borrowers expect short-term rates to decline more than the general market does, the opposite result occurs. Investors sell their short-term securities and buy longer-term securities because they want to lock in high rates. Over the long run, they believe the return will be greater. Borrowers defer their longer-term debt issues and instead borrow short term. Their combined actions cause short-term rates to rise and longer-term rates to fall, so that the yield curve flattens or turns downward.

Liquidity Preference

One major problem with the expectations theory, say many economists, is that longer-term securities fluctuate more in price than short-term securities when interest rates shift. If interest rates rise, the price of a long-term security falls much more than that of a short-term security. Thus, the long-bond investor who wants to sell may have to take a significant loss.

Many of these economists subscribe to the liquidity preference theory, which suggests that, to make up for the risk of interest rate fluctuations, yields for longer-term securities must be higher than is implied by the expectations theory described above. The longer the maturity, the greater this premium will be. If investors and lenders all believe that future short-term rates will equal current short-term rates, the expectations theory predicts that the yield curve will be flat. Those who believe there must be a risk premium, however, argue that the curve will still be sloped upward.

Market Segmentation

At the other end of the theoretical spectrum are those economists who believe that interest rates are primarily a function of the supply and demand for bonds at different maturities. These economists argue that most investors and borrowers are not willing to shift into different maturities simply because yields change. They tend to buy and sell within a range of maturities for a variety of reasons, including legal constraints, regulatory constraints, habit, strategies that match the duration of an institution's assets with its liabilities, portfolio requirements, or market conditions. Banks, for example, tend to lend in the shorter-term ranges regardless of level of interest rates. The supply of, and demand for, funds at those maturities would then be the principal determinant of rates.

At one point, for example, there may be a very light investment demand for securities with maturities between 5 and 10 years. Or it may happen that very few borrowers come to market with issues that mature in more than 20 years. In each of these so-called segmented markets, according to proponents of this theory, rates will be set independent of what is going on in other maturities. The greater the supply of bonds compared to the demand in a maturity, the higher the rate will be, regardless of rates for other maturities. Conversely, the lower the supply, the lower the rate. In this view, then, the shape of the yield curve will depend mostly on the supply and demand for securities at different maturities.

MUNICIPAL BOND RATES

Economists generally take all the above factors into consideration when making forecasts of the overall level and term structure of interest rates. The municipal bond market, however, has several special features that affect prices and yields. By far the most important of these is the unusual nature of the demand for tax-exempt municipal securities. The advantages of the tax exemption generally limit municipal bond purchases to higher-income households and their proxies, property and casualty insurance companies, and commercial banks.

Supply and Demand

Because of the specialized nature of the market for tax-exempt securities, highly cyclical demand factors are probably more important in determining municipal rates than in determining the rates of most other types of fixed-income securities. The particular characteristics of the major buyers of municipal bonds make for a cyclical pattern of demand.

Capital Gains Tax Effects

One other factor that has a different effect on municipal rates than on the rates of other securities is the treatment of capital gains. Although municipal bond interest payments are tax-exempt, capital gains and market discount earned from selling bonds are taxed. The buyers of discount municipal bonds, for example, receive their interest payments tax-free. But when the bonds are redeemed at maturity, the difference between the par value and the original purchase price of the bonds—market discount—is subject to federal income tax at the applicable ordinary tax rate.

Volatility

In percentage terms, municipal rates are generally less volatile than rates on equivalent Treasury securities. A look back at Table 8.1 reveals the wider range of yield fluctuations for U.S. government securities compared to municipal revenue bonds. Despite this general pattern, municipal securities can be more volatile than Treasuries or corporate bonds when income tax rates change. Tax rates have no effect on the large institutional investors that dominate taxable bond markets, but for the individuals who buy most tax-exempt municipal bonds, tax rates directly affect the after-tax yield on their investments.

Intermarket Yield percentage

The difference in yield between municipal securities and U.S. government securities is one of the most closely watched indicators in the municipal market. The spread is expressed in basis points, with municipals usually lower than Treasuries, and the ratio of municipals to Treasuries is expressed as a percentage, usually less than 100 percent. The higher the percentage of municipal yields to Treasury yields, the greater is the relative value of municipals.

Table 8.5 shows two municipal intermarket yield curves. One is from December 31, 2009; the other is from December 31, 2010. Many spread

TABLE 8.5 Active U.S. Treasury Yield Curve versus AAA GO Municipal Bond Yield Curve, December 31, 2009, and December 31, 2010

Maturity	Active U.S. Treasuries		AAA GO Municipals		Spread Munis to Treasuries	
	12/31/09	12/31/10	12/31/09	12/31/10	2009 (%)	2010 (%)
1-year	0.44	0.26	0.31	0.46	71.2	175.5
2-year	1.14	0.59	0.62	0.79	54.6	133.1
5-year	2.68	2.00	1.66	1.75	61.9	87.2
10-year	3.84	3.29	3.26	3.44	84.9	104.4
30-year	4.64	4.33	4.47	4.90	96.3	113.1

Source: Federal Reserve.

relationships can be measured, including changes over time and differences on one day along the yield curve. On December 31, 2009, a 30-year AAA general obligation municipal bond yielded 96.3 percent of the return on a 30-year Treasury, a discount of 17 basis points. On December 31, 2010, a 30-year AAA general obligation municipal bond yielded 113.1 percent of the return on a 30-year Treasury, a premium of 57 basis points. This means that during the course of 2010, municipal yields as a percentage of Treasuries rose or Treasury yields fell or both, with the municipal investor getting a higher relative yield in December 2010 than in December 2009. The municipal bond market sold off in late 2010 after Congress allowed the Build America Bonds program for taxable municipal bonds to expire, which meant that the supply of traditional tax-exempt municipal bonds was expected to increase in 2011. Traders look at these intermarket relationships throughout the day to spot buying or selling opportunities.

On any day, different relationships between securities can be observed all along the yield curve. For example, on December 31, 2010, two-year AAA GO bonds yielded 20 basis points more than two-year Treasuries, a 33.1 percent premium. One year earlier, the relationship was reversed: AAA GO bonds yielded 54.6 percent as much as two-year Treasuries, a 52 basis point discount. Municipal professionals are acutely aware of these spread relationships and also monitor the differences between municipal and other markets to create trading and investment opportunities.

Upward-Sloping Yield Curves

The yield curve for municipal bonds is almost always upward sloping, as seen in Table 8.3, and steeper than the Treasury curve even when interest rates are near cyclical peaks. Short-term instruments trade very close to the after-tax return for corporations and individuals in the highest tax brackets, except during brief periods of abnormally heavy supply of short-term instruments or seasonal withdrawal of assets from money funds.

Long-term municipal securities often trade at somewhat higher relative rates. Even if the market expects rates in general to fall (when the corporate yield curve would be downward sloping), the municipal yield curve generally slopes upward. The primary reasons are: (1) the heavy supply of intermediate- and long-term bonds as a percentage of the total market, (2) the relatively limited demand for longer-term securities by corporate purchasers of tax-exempt bonds, and (3) individual investors are more concerned about income from their municipal bond portfolios than the total return.

CHAPTER 9

Regulatory and Disclosure Requirements

INTRODUCTION

Until the late 1960s, the municipal securities market was relatively free from federal regulation. Despite the enactment in 1913 of the Sixteenth Amendment to the U.S. Constitution (which permitted the establishment of the modern federal income tax system), each version of the Internal Revenue Code enacted by Congress expressly exempted interest on municipal securities from federal income taxation. Similarly, when Congress enacted the Securities Act of 1933, the Securities Exchange Act of 1934, and related laws governing securities transactions, the lawmakers expressly exempted municipal securities and their issuers from the registration, reporting, and regulatory requirements imposed in connection with the issuance of securities by private corporations. However, issuers, underwriters, and other participants in a municipal securities transaction remain subject to the antifraud rules of the securities laws.

Federal involvement in the municipal securities markets began its significant increase with the enactment of legislation and with the promulgation of Treasury regulations in the late 1960s that imposed conditions for the interest on municipal securities to enjoy the federal tax exemption. The new federal tax restrictions were followed by the enactment in 1975 of federal securities laws that provided for the development of a comprehensive regulatory scheme under the jurisdiction of the MSRB to oversee the activities of brokers and dealers in municipal securities transactions.

The SEC adopted rule 15c2-12 in 1989 to impose express disclosure document review and distribution requirements on underwriters of municipal securities. In 1994, the SEC added a requirement for underwriters to determine, as a condition to underwriting certain municipal issues, that borrowers agree to a commitment to provide continuing disclosure. The SEC made various amendments in subsequent years that expanded the scope and refined the particulars of what underwriters must demand from issuers.

The Dodd–Frank Wall Street Reform and Consumer Protection Act of 2010 substantially augmented both the powers of the MSRB and the SEC's oversight of the municipal bond market. Municipal advisors, who provide services and advice related to bond issuance and other functions, had to register with the SEC for the first time; by March 2011, more than 840 individuals and firms had done so.

THE BASIS OF FEDERAL TAX EXEMPTION

The tax-exempt status of municipal securities is closely intertwined with the development of the federal income tax system. The historical basis for the exemption initially rested on an application of the constitutional doctrine of "intergovernmental tax immunity." The 1895 case that applied this doctrine to municipal securities, *Pollock v. Farmers' Loan and Trust Company*, also produced the need for the Sixteenth Amendment to the Constitution, which authorized a modern income tax system.

At issue in *Pollock* was whether the Wilson-Gorman Tariff Act of 1894, which levied a federal tax on certain types of income, including interest on municipal securities, was constitutionally valid. Article I, Section 2 of the U.S. Constitution requires that direct taxes among the states be apportioned according to population; and Article I, Section 8 of the Constitution requires that indirect taxes, such as duties and imports, be uniform throughout the United States.

In *Pollock*, the Supreme Court decided that the 1894 Tariff Act was unconstitutional because taxes levied were not apportioned according to population. The Court also ruled that interest on municipal securities was not subject to federal income taxation because a tax on interest would impermissibly burden state government and interfere with its power to borrow money. Applying the doctrine of intergovernmental tax immunity, the Court reasoned that the states were immune from federal interference with their borrowing power. That doctrine, established in the landmark case of *McCulloch v. Maryland* (containing Justice Marshall's famous dictum, "The power to tax involves the power to destroy"), limits the ability of federal and state governments to levy taxes on each other that impermissibly intrude upon governmental sovereignty.

The *Pollock* decision produced the necessity for the Sixteenth Amendment to the U.S. Constitution in order to permit an effective federal income tax structure that would not be constrained by apportionment and population requirements. The amendment, which was enacted by Congress and ratified by the required number of states in 1913, states that "The Congress shall have the power to lay and collect taxes on incomes, from whatever source derived, without apportionment among the several states, and without regard to any census or enumeration."

During the ratification process, an issue arose over the wording of the Sixteenth Amendment and its potential effect on the municipal securities tax exemption established by the *Pollock* decision. The concern was that the words authorizing a tax on incomes "from whatever source derived" expanded the areas of potential federal taxation to include the income on municipal securities. Several U.S. congressmen, including sponsors of the Sixteenth Amendment, disputed that interpretation and disavowed any congressional intent to achieve that result. Thus, for example, Senator William E. Borah of Idaho stated in the *Congressional Record* that

> To construe the proposed amendment so as to enable us (the Congress) to tax the instrumentalities of the state would do violence to the rules laid down by the Supreme Court for a hundred years, wrench the whole Constitution from its harmonious proportions and destroy the object and purpose for which the whole instrument was framed.

The Sixteenth Amendment, in the form proposed, was eventually ratified by the states. The question of whether the term "from whatever source derived" expanded the substantive areas of federal taxation was addressed by the Supreme Court in *Evans v. Gore*, decided in 1920, in which the Court concluded that

> the genesis and words of the amendment unite in showing that it does not extend the taxing power to new or excepted subjects, but merely removes all occasion otherwise existing for an apportionment among the states of taxes laid on income, whether derived from one source or another. And we have so held in other cases.

Although *Pollock* established the constitutional basis of tax exemption and later cases made clear that the Sixteenth Amendment did not expressly eliminate it, federal efforts to restrict or significantly limit the exemption have been made through the years, as discussed in the next section. Moreover, subsequent to *Pollock*, several Supreme Court decisions in other areas of federal-state relationships significantly limited the scope of the intergovernmental immunity doctrine, producing strong debate on the continuing vitality of *Pollock*, particularly as federal tax restrictions on municipal securities increased.

That debate eventually led to a challenge of federal restrictions and a re-examination of the *Pollock* holding in *South Carolina v. Baker*, decided by the Supreme Court in 1988. In that case, South Carolina contested the provisions of the Tax Equity and Fiscal Responsibility Act of 1982 that required most municipal securities to be issued in registered form and conditioned tax exemption on compliance with the registration requirement. The Supreme Court upheld the validity of the provisions and, in doing so, expressly overruled the *Pollock* holding that municipal bond interest is immune from a nondiscriminatory federal tax.

The *South Carolina v. Baker* decision removes the claim to historical constitutional protection for the municipal securities tax exemption and makes the continuation of that exemption and the nature of tax restrictions subject to the political dynamics of the federal legislative process. The Court's ruling in *South Carolina* produced discussion among some state and local governments about the need for a constitutional amendment expressly protecting the municipal securities tax exemption from federal intrusion.

HISTORY OF FEDERAL TAX LEGISLATION AFFECTING MUNICIPAL SECURITIES

Although the first Internal Revenue Code enacted after the adoption of the Sixteenth Amendment contained a specific stated exemption for interest on municipal securities, federal efforts to constrict or eliminate that exemption began soon after that enactment and have continued ever since. For example, the House of Representatives passed a proposed constitutional amendment in 1923 to authorize the taxation of income derived from future issues of municipal securities, but the proposal failed to pass the Senate. Other federal attempts to tax municipal bonds were made in the 1930s and 1940s without success. During consideration of the Revenue Revision of 1942, the Treasury Department strongly urged the imposition of a tax on the interest on all state and municipal bonds including both present and future issues. This proposal was rejected by the U.S. House of Representatives' Committee on Ways and Means but was accepted by the Senate Finance Committee with respect to future issues. After extensive debate on the floor of the Senate, the proposal was defeated and stricken from the bill. In 1969, the House passed a bill that included interest earned on all municipal securities within the Internal Revenue Code's minimum-tax provisions. The Senate did not accept the measure. Finally, in the late 1970s, a number of proposals were made in Congress to give municipal issuers the option of issuing taxable securities and receiving an interest subsidy from the federal government. At the time, proposals of this nature (called the taxable bond option) were opposed by municipal issuers, who feared that federal intervention would accompany the subsidies.

The taxable bond option was revived in 2009 when Congress passed the American Recovery and Reinvestment Act, which permitted municipalities to issue Build America Bonds through December 31, 2010. Interest payments on Build America Bonds are taxable to investors, but issuers receive a federal subsidy equal to 35 percent of the interest paid. At a time of intense pressure on state and local government budgets, municipalities embraced a program that allowed them to tap investors who buy taxable bonds, a larger pool than those who buy traditional tax-exempt municipal bonds. During the 21 months the program was in force, a total of $181.4 billion of Build America Bonds were issued.

Since the taxable bond option proposals of the late 1970s, there have not been any general federal legislative attempts to eliminate completely, or to provide a complete substitution for, the municipal securities tax exemption. Nevertheless, during that same period, the federal statutory authorization for such exemption has been the subject of significant restrictions. This process began in 1968, when Congress passed a law restricting the uses for which industrial development bonds could be issued and still retain the federal tax exemption. The list of eligible uses included in that law, as amended, included residential real property for family units; sports facilities; convention or trade show facilities; airports, docks, wharves, mass-commuting facilities, parking facilities, or storage or training facilities directly related to any of the foregoing; sewage and solid waste disposal facilities; facilities for the local furnishing of electric energy or gas; air and water pollution control facilities; facilities for the furnishing of water under certain conditions; development of industrial parks; and "small issue" industrial development bonds that are subject to dollar-amount limitations.

In 1969, Congress eliminated the statutory exemption for interest on *arbitrage bonds*, which are municipal securities the proceeds of which are used to acquire other securities with a yield higher than the yield on the municipal securities. Congress was concerned that some state and local governments were misusing the tax exemption for municipal securities by issuing arbitrage bonds solely for the purpose of investing their proceeds in higher-yielding federal or other obligations. The difference between the yields was pure profit to the municipalities. In addition, both the industrial development bond law and the arbitrage bond law have spawned extensive and intricate Treasury regulations governing the statutory concepts and their application to particular circumstances.

Further and increasingly extensive federal tax regulation of municipal securities occurred in 1980, with the enactment of the Mortgage Subsidy Bond Tax Act, which imposed substantial limits and requirements on tax-exempt residential mortgage bonds; in 1982, with the enactment of the Tax Equity and Fiscal Responsibility Act, which imposed additional restrictions on industrial development bonds and arbitrage bonds and required all municipal securities to be issued in registered form; and in 1984, with the enactment of the Deficit Reduction Act, which imposed volume limitations on *private activity bonds* (PABs), among other restrictions. With the enactment of the Tax Reform Act of 1986, Congress further restructured and added additional restrictions to the provisions governing the issuance of tax-exempt municipal securities and on the tax-exempt nature of municipal bond interest.

THE CURRENT STATUTORY EXEMPTION

The Internal Revenue Code of 1986 continued the basic tax exemption for interest on municipal securities set forth in Section 103 of the Internal Revenue Code of 1954. However, the 1986 Code significantly changed prior law by imposing new restrictions on all types of municipal securities, by further limiting the availability of tax-exempt bonds to finance private activities, by further restricting the aggregate volume of private activity bonds, and by imposing additional arbitrage-related restrictions and procedures.

Although any discussion in full detail of the provisions of the 1986 Internal Revenue Code applicable to municipal securities is beyond the scope of this book, certain basic concepts are important and can be broadly, if somewhat imprecisely, summarized. In general, Section 103 of the 1986 Code exempts interest on municipal obligations except for arbitrage bonds and certain private activity bonds.

Private Activity Bonds

Under the 1986 Code, private activity bonds are defined as any municipal obligation, irrespective of the purpose for which it is issued or the source of payment, if (1) more than 10 percent of the proceeds of the issue will finance property that will be used by a nongovernmental person in a trade or business, and (2) the payment of debt service on more than 10 percent of the proceeds of the issue will be (a) secured by property used in a private trade or business or payments in respect of such property, or (b) derived from payments in respect of property used in a private trade or business. These two tests—the private business use test and the private payment or security test—must be examined in connection with the issuance of any municipal security. For example, it is important that municipal securities issued to finance a government office building do not violate the tests by virtue of underlying leases to, or operating arrangements with, nongovernmental persons. Interest on a municipal security that is a PAB will not be tax-exempt unless it is a *qualified bond* under the 1986 Code and meets certain other requirements.

Qualified private activity bonds encompass municipal securities that meet specific requirements of the tax law, including securities issued to finance residential mortgages, qualified veterans' residential mortgages, qualified industrial development projects for manufacturing and certain farming purposes, qualified student loans, qualified redevelopment projects, and qualified expenditures of 501(c)(3) organizations such as hospitals and educational institutions. Qualified bonds also include those issued to finance exempt facilities such as governmentally owned airports, docks, wharves, and mass-commuting facilities; water-supply systems; sewage facilities; certain solid waste disposal facilities; qualified hazardous waste facilities; qualified residential rental projects; facilities for the local furnishing of electric energy or gas; and local district heating or cooling facilities. Exempt facility bonds must meet a higher threshold, too: At least 95 percent of the net proceeds must be used to finance the exempt facility.

Among the additional restrictions that apply to qualified private activity bonds are specified state volume limitations imposed on an annual basis, a limitation on maximum bond maturity, public hearing and approval requirements, informational reporting requirements, and limits on the amount of proceeds that can be used for other than qualifying expenditures. In addition, certain restrictions applicable to all municipal securities, such as the arbitrage and rebate requirements discussed below, also apply to PABs.

Arbitrage Restrictions and Rebate

Another major area of restriction that is applicable to all municipal securities involves arbitrage and rebate. The arbitrage restrictions essentially preclude investment of the proceeds of municipal securities in higher-yielding securities. There are limited exceptions to this general rule for temporary periods, for reasonably required reserve funds not exceeding 10 percent of bond proceeds, and for a minor portion of the overall bond proceeds. In addition, under the 1986 Code, with limited exceptions, arbitrage earnings on bond proceeds must be paid ("rebated") to the federal government at specified intervals to the extent that such earnings exceed the earnings that would have been derived if the proceeds had been invested at the bond yield. This rebate requirement includes an exemption for certain small-volume issuers and an exception for municipal securities issues where all the proceeds are expended for the applicable governmental purpose within specified periods after the date of issuance.

Other Restrictions

The 1986 Code also imposes restrictions on the advance refunding of municipal securities—that is, securities issued more than 90 days prior to the application of the proceeds of the securities to retire an outstanding issue of securities. Among other things, the 1986 Code prohibits the advance refunding of private activity bonds (except for obligations issued for 501(c)(3) organizations) and restricts the number of times and conditions under which all other municipal securities can be advance refunded.

In addition to the restrictions summarized above on the types of municipal securities eligible for the federal tax exemption and the use of the proceeds of those securities, the 1986 Code also imposes a number of related restrictions affecting the municipal securities market. Thus, under the 1986 Code, interest on private activity bonds (other than 501(c)(3) obligations) issued after August 7, 1986, is treated as a preference item for purposes of computing the corporate and individual alternative minimum tax. Similarly, interest on all municipal securities (whenever issued) is required to be entered into the minimum tax computation for corporations through the adjusted current earnings provisions of the 1986 Code. With limited exceptions, the 1986 Code also eliminated the prior provision that permitted financial institutions to deduct 80 percent of the amount of interest attributable to purchasing or carrying tax-exempt obligations. The effect of these and other provisions of the 1986 Code has been to alter significantly the type of investors participating in the municipal securities markets.

Recent Changes

The tax-exempt bond provisions of the 1986 Code have been revised by subsequent tax acts, including limitations on pooled financing bonds (1988) and *hedge bonds* (bonds issued for the purpose of hedging against potential future increases in interest rates) (1989). Arbitrage and rebate regulations have been amended from time to time, too. In general, the changes have targeted specific perceived abuses; nothing comparable to the wholesale overhaul wrought by the 1986 Code has been implemented since it became effective.

From time to time, restrictions in the tax rules governing municipal bonds have been relaxed to facilitate public policy objectives. In 1997, for example, Congress created Qualified Zone Academy bonds (QZABs), which are designed to allow schools located in certain underprivileged neighborhoods to borrow at zero or nominal interest cost to finance improvements to school buildings, equipment, the development of course materials, and teacher training. Although attractive in theory, in practice the structure authorized for QZABs—tax credit bonds—have not proven to be successful. A similar program, Clean Renewable Energy bonds, was created in 2005 to foster the development of electricity generated from "clean" energy sources; it was expanded in 2008 through the Energy Conservation bond program.

The 1986 Code has also been relaxed to foster economic recovery after natural disasters and other catastrophic events. Congress authorized Liberty Zone bonds in 2002 to finance redevelopment near the World Trade Center site in New York City; Gulf Opportunity Zone bonds in 2005 to finance reconstruction in Alabama, Louisiana, or Mississippi after those states suffered devastating hurricane damage; and Midwest Disaster Area bonds in 2008 to assist areas in seven Midwestern states struck by severe storms, tornadoes and flooding as well as counties in Texas and Louisiana affected by Hurricane Ike. In general, the disaster recovery bond programs relax the limits on tax exemption for private activity bonds for projects located in the specified areas.

APPLICATION OF FEDERAL SECURITIES LAWS TO MUNICIPAL SECURITIES

The Securities Act of 1933 established the SEC as the federal agency with regulatory authority over the issuance and trading of securities in the U.S. capital markets and imposed registration requirements governing the issuance of such securities. Congress, however, specifically exempted municipal securities from the registration and reporting requirements of the 1933 Act. Similarly, Congress exempted persons issuing municipal securities or engaging in municipal securities transactions from the reporting, registration, and related requirements of the Securities Exchange Act of 1934. The legislative history of the 1933 and 1934 Acts indicates that the municipal securities exemption stemmed not only from potential constitutional questions over the ability of Congress to regulate state and local governments in the issuance of securities but also from a sense that the municipal securities markets did not require the same type of regulation and oversight as the corporate capital markets.

In the early and middle 1970s, however, Congress refocused its attention on the municipal securities market as a result of the "boiler room" sales and questionable trading practices of a few municipal securities dealers. This renewed federal oversight resulted in the enactment of the Securities Acts Amendments of 1975. These amendments imposed the requirement that municipal securities dealers register with the SEC and provided for the establishment of the MSRB to regulate municipal securities transactions effected by brokers, dealers, and municipal securities dealers.

An important issue during congressional consideration of the Securities Acts Amendments was whether the legislation should permit regulation of issuers of municipal securities. This raised the possibility of the promulgation by the SEC of specific disclosure requirements for municipal bond issues and registration of offerings by municipal issuers. In response to those concerns, the proposed amendments were modified to prohibit the SEC and the MSRB from requiring an issuer, directly or indirectly, to make any filing with the SEC or MSRB before the sale of its securities in connection with their issuance, sale, or distribution. In addition, the Tower Amendment was added, prohibiting the MSRB from requiring an issuer of municipal securities, directly or indirectly, to furnish any information with respect to the issuer to the MSRB or any purchaser or prospective purchaser of its securities. There was reserved to the MSRB, however, authority to require municipal securities brokers and dealers to furnish to the MSRB information with respect to the issuer generally available from a source other than the issuer.

Even though the imposition of federal disclosure requirements for issuers was thus restricted by the Securities Acts Amendments of 1975, those amendments confirmed the applicability to municipal market participants and transactions of the antifraud provisions of the federal securities laws. The most frequently referenced of the antifraud provisions, Rule 10b-5 promulgated pursuant to Section 10(b) of the 1934 Act, provides in part, that

> *it shall be unlawful for any person . . . (b) to make any untrue statement of a material fact or to omit to state a material fact necessary in order to make the statements made, in the light of the circumstances under which they were made, not misleading . . . in connection with the purchase or sale of any security.*

The definition of a person under the 1934 Act was modified by the Amendments to include definitively municipal market participants for the purpose of §10(b) of the 1934 Act and of Rule 10b-5.

Specific disclosure practices in the municipal market were first addressed by SEC rule making in 1989 when the SEC, invoking its rule making authority under the antifraud provisions, adopted Rule 15c2-12 effective January 1, 1990. Rule 15c2-12 imposed for the first time express disclosure document review and distribution responsibilities on municipal securities underwriters. In practical effect, the rule indirectly requires any issuer that wishes to sell securities covered by the rule through an underwritten primary offering to prepare and distribute an official statement for the offering. Rule 15c2-12 was amended in 1994, effective generally for primary offerings sold on or after July 3, 1995, and for issuer fiscal years ended on or after January 1, 1996, to require underwriters to obtain commitments from issuers (or other obligated persons) to provide continuing disclosure for so long as the securities remain outstanding.

In conjunction with the launch of EMMA by the MSRB, the SEC amended Rule 15c2-12 to require that, effective July 1, 2009, continuing disclosure information must be provided to the MSRB instead of to multiple nationally recognized municipal securities information repositories and state information depositories. Amendments to Rule 15c2-12 generally effective on August 9, 2010, require notice to the MSRB of specified events listed in the continuing disclosure commitment to be provided in a timely manner not in excess of 10 business days after the event occurs. The SEC also amended the list of events for which a notice must be provided and deleted a blanket provision that the event must be material before notice to the MSRB is required. The designated events must now be reported in every instance unless the revised description of the event specifically incorporates a materiality standard to trigger a notice.

The 2010 amendments revised an exemption from Rule 15c2-12 for certain offerings of municipal securities with put features. As a result, underwriters of VRDOs are no longer exempt and must ensure that issuers agree to the same continuing disclosure provisions as issuers of fixed rate municipal bonds.

Disclosure and the Antifraud Laws and Regulations of the Federal Securities Laws

Although the federal securities laws do not directly require municipal issuers to register or provide particular disclosure when offering municipal securities, several factors have caused municipal issuers and other municipal market participants to take greater care that their disclosure information is accurate and complete. First, the financial difficulties of some issuers in the 1970s stimulated investor requirements for greater disclosure in connection with the primary offering of municipal securities. Investor requirements, together with industry concerns about potential federal imposition of regulatory and disclosure requirements, prompted municipal market participants to develop recommended disclosure practices.

The GFOA (then the Municipal Finance Officers Association or MFOA) led the development, in 1976, of "Disclosure Guidelines for State and Local Government Securities" (last revised in January 1991), which have become industry standards for municipal securities disclosure documents. In 2001, the GFOA published "Making Good Disclosure," a handbook for state and local officials that describes their disclosure obligations under the federal securities laws. From time to time the GFOA also issues best practice bulletins and advisories on specific topics, including disclosure.

Other industry initiatives, including improvements in government financial accounting and reporting under the auspices of the GASB, have also contributed to improved and more standardized disclosure practices. From 2000 through 2006, The National Federation of Municipal Analysts published its recommended best disclosure practices for 13 different types of municipal securities.

A second major factor influencing the nature and extent of disclosure in connection with municipal securities are the antifraud provisions of both the Securities Act of 1933 and the Securities Exchange Act of 1934 and the increasing commitment of the SEC to enforce adherence to those provisions by municipal issuers and officials. The SEC Staff Report concerning the Washington Public Power Supply System (WPPSS), released in September 1988, refocused industry and federal agency efforts on improving disclosure practices for municipal securities and developing more effective means for assuring the availability, review, and distribution of disclosure information. Although enforcement actions against market participants were not recommended, the SEC Staff Report was critical of the disclosure practices for the WPPSS financings. The findings reflected in that report prompted the SEC to publish, and finally adopt, Rule 15c2-12 in 1989 (effective January 1, 1990), imposing specific disclosure document review and distribution requirements on municipal securities underwriters in connection with the primary offering of municipal securities.

In general, Rule 15c2-12 requires all underwriters participating in a primary offering of municipal securities with an aggregate principal amount of $1 million or more to obtain and review a nearly final official statement before bidding for, purchasing, offering for sale, or selling the securities. An offering of securities is exempt from the Rule if the securities are in minimum authorized denominations of $100,000 and the securities (1) have a maturity of nine months or less (no longer applicable except to issues outstanding as of November 30, 2010), or (2) are sold to 35 or fewer investors that the underwriter reasonably believes to be sophisticated and not to be purchasing for more than one account or with a view to distributing the securities. The Rule also requires each participating underwriter in negotiated offerings to deliver or make preliminary official statements available to potential customers by the first business day following a customer request and to contract with an issuer for the receipt by the underwriter of final official statements in sufficient quantity and time to permit the underwriter to include or make available a copy of that document with customer payment confirmations and to comply with MSRB Rule G-32. A participating underwriter also has an obligation under Rule 15c2-12 to deliver or make available a copy of the final official statement to each potential customer on request until the end of specified periods following the underwriting period.

The SEC release proposing original Rule 15c2-12 also set forth the staff's view of a municipal underwriter's responsibilities in connection with the delivery of primary offering documents to investors (Release No. 34–26100; S7–20–88; September 27, 1988). The staff modified its interpretation slightly in the release adopting Rule 15c2-12 (Release No. 34–26985; S7–20–88; June 28, 1989), but confirmed its view that by delivering offering documents to an investor, an underwriter implicitly represents that "it has a reasonable basis for belief in the accuracy and completeness of the key representations contained in the documents." The releases discuss factors to be considered in determining whether the investigatory activities undertaken by an underwriter with respect to an offering would be sufficient to provide the requisite reasonable basis for belief in the accuracy and completeness of key representations. The interpretation acknowledges that an underwriter's investigation in a competitively sold offering is likely to be less extensive than for a negotiated offering because the underwriter is presumably involved in the preparation of the offering document for a negotiated offering.

The requirement for continuing disclosure was added by amendments to Rule 15c2-12 effective generally for primary offerings sold on or after July 3, 1995, and for fiscal years that ended on or after January 1, 1996. With certain exceptions, the Rule now requires an underwriter to determine, as a condition to participating in the underwriting of a primary offering, that the issuer or obligated persons—that is, certain persons obligated with respect to payment of debt service—have agreed to provide, as long as the securities are outstanding, certain financial information and operating data annually and notice of the occurrence of specified events, if material, when and as they occur and to have a reasonable basis to believe the borrower will comply with that agreement. Primary offerings exempt from the requirements of Rule 15c2-12 also are exempt from the continuing disclosure requirements.

The specific continuing disclosure requirements vary depending on the amount of nonexempt securities an issuer or obligated person has outstanding and the term to maturity of the securities being issued. If an obligated person with respect to an offering has outstanding more than $10,000,000 of nonexempt securities (including the proposed offering and any outstanding securities subject to the Rule or that would have been subject to the Rule if the Rule had been effective when they were issued), an underwriter must determine that the issuer or obligated person has agreed to provide to the MSRB annual financial information and operating data of the type included in the final official statement for the primary offering, as well as audited financial statements (if and when available), for each obligated person. The commitment may set forth an objective standard for determining whether, for a particular fiscal year, continuing disclosure must be provided as to certain obligated persons. This approach would commonly be used in connection with pool financings in which the relative magnitude (and materiality) of a particular obligated person's payment obligations could vary over time.

The issuer or obligated person must also commit to provide notice of the occurrence of any one of the following 14 events:

1. Principal and interest payment delinquencies.
2. Nonpayment-related defaults, if material.
3. Unscheduled draws on debt service reserves reflecting financial difficulties.
4. Unscheduled draws on credit enhancements reflecting financial difficulties.
5. Substitution of credit or liquidity providers or their failure to perform.
6. Adverse tax opinions, the issuance by the Internal Revenue Service of proposed or final determinations of taxability, Notices of Proposed Issue (IRS Form 5701-TEB) or other material notices or determinations with respect to the tax status of the security, or other material events affecting the tax status of the security.
7. Modifications to rights of security holders, if material.
8. Bond calls, if material, and tender offers.
9. Defeasances.
10. Release, substitution, or sale of property securing repayment of the securities, if material.
11. Rating changes.
12. Bankruptcy, insolvency, receivership, or similar event of the obligated person.
13. The consummation of a merger, consolidation, or acquisition involving an obligated person or the sale of all or substantially all of the assets of the obligated person, other than in the ordinary course of business, the entry into a definitive agreement to undertake such an action or the termination of a definitive agreement relating to any such actions, other than pursuant to its terms, if material.
14. Appointment of a successor or additional trustee or the change of name of a trustee, if material.

The continuing disclosure requirements are more limited if no obligated person has more than $10,000,000 of nonexempt securities outstanding (including the offered securities) or if the stated maturity of the issue is 18 months or less. Those obligated persons must commit to provide notice of the occurrence of any of the events described above, if material, and must also commit to provide either to a state information depository annually or to any person upon request, if the stated maturity of the issue is greater than 18 months, the financial information customarily prepared by the issuer and publicly available.

Effective October 1, 2010, the Dodd–Frank Act imposed for the first time a requirement for municipal advisors to register with the SEC. The SEC adopted a broad definition of *municipal advisor* on a preliminary basis:

- A person (who is not a municipal entity or an employee of a municipal entity) that (i) provides advice to or on behalf of a municipal entity or obligated person with respect to municipal financial products or the issuance of municipal securities, including advice with respect to the structure, timing, terms, and other similar matters concerning such financial products or issues; or (ii) undertakes a solicitation of a municipal entity.
- Includes financial advisors, guaranteed investment contract brokers, third-party marketers, placement agents, solicitors, finders, and swap advisors, if such persons are described in any of clauses (i) through (ii) above.
- Does not include a broker, dealer, or municipal securities dealer serving as an underwriter (as defined in section 2(a)(11) of the Securities Act of 1933) (15 U.S.C. 77b(a)(11)), any investment advisor registered under the Investment Advisors Act of 1940, or persons associated with such investment advisors who are providing investment advice, any commodity trading advisor registered under the Commodity Exchange Act or persons associated with a commodity trading advisor who are providing advice related to swaps, attorneys offering legal advice or providing services that are of a traditional legal nature, or engineers providing engineering advice.

Municipal disclosure practices will continue to be the subject of industry and federal regulatory focus. The SEC has become more aggressive in its enforcement activities relating to municipal bonds in recent years, and the expansion of its oversight under the Dodd–Frank Act is likely to prompt further changes in disclosure practices.

THE MUNICIPAL SECURITIES RULEMAKING BOARD

As noted above, the MSRB was created by Congress in 1975 as an independent, self-regulatory organization charged with primary rule-making authority for the municipal securities market. The MSRB's regulatory authority covers dealers, dealer banks, and brokers in municipal securities and municipal advisors, but as discussed earlier, its jurisdiction does not extend to the issuers of municipal securities. All market participants subject to MSRB jurisdiction are required to register with the SEC. As a self-regulatory organization, the MSRB is financed solely by the municipal securities industry. Its operations are supported by fees and assessments paid by firms and dealer banks engaged in the municipal securities business. These payments include an initial fee paid by a firm or dealer bank before commencing municipal securities activities, an annual fee, and an assessment based on the volume of new-issue underwriting and trading in which a firm or dealer bank participates.

The Regulatory Structure

The MSRB was designated by Congress as the rule-making body for the municipal market with a view to the unique nature of the municipal market and its diverse participants—banks, securities firms engaged in a general securities business, and firms whose sole business is municipal securities. The MSRB currently has 21 members, a majority (11) of whom, the *public representatives*, are independent and cannot be associated with or controlled by a municipal securities broker or dealer. One of the public representatives must represent investors, and another must represent issuers of municipal securities. The minority board members include three bank representatives, three municipal advisor representatives, and four securities firm representatives.

The initial Board members (15 in number at the time, with a majority of industry participants) were appointed by the SEC in September 1975. Subsequently, new Board members have been nominated and elected by the MSRB under a procedure that allows for recommendations of individuals for nomination by the industry and by interested members of the public. While not involved directly in the election procedures, the SEC must, pursuant to statute, approve the selection of public MSRB members.

The Securities Acts Amendments of 1975 grant the MSRB general rule-making authority over municipal market participants and specify several areas of mandatory rule making in which the board is required, as a minimum, to propose and adopt rules. These enumerated areas include standards of operational capability and professional qualification, rules of fair practice, record keeping, the minimum scope and frequency of periodic compliance examinations, the form and content of quotations relating to municipal securities, sales of new-issue municipal securities to related portfolios during the underwriting period, the definition of "separately identifiable department or division" as it relates to banks for purposes of SEC registration and enforcement of MSRB rules, the internal operation and administration of the MSRB, and assessments.

The MSRB's rule-making procedures involve several steps. Typically, the board drafts proposals for rule changes and then requests public comments for a period of 60 days. On adoption by the MSRB in final form, rule proposals are filed with the SEC and the federal bank regulatory agencies. Each proposed rule is published in the *Federal Register* and is subject to a public comment period of up to 35 days from the date of publication. The MSRB's rules are ordinarily subject to approval by the SEC before becoming effective. Exceptions are rules relating solely to the administration of the MSRB and to assessments that are effective on filing but that may be rescinded by the SEC within 60 days.

Even though the MSRB is charged with primary rule-making responsibility over municipal market professionals, the SEC retains ultimate regulatory authority and may add to or delete from the MSRB's rules if it finds such action necessary or appropriate.

In recognition of the existing regulatory structure for banks and securities firms, the MSRB does not have inspection or enforcement authority. Instead, the Financial Industry Regulatory Authority (FINRA), or its members, and the three federal bank regulatory agencies, as appropriate, are charged with the responsibility for inspection and enforcement of the board's rules, which have the force of federal law under the legislation.

The Rules

The MSRB wrote most of its rules in the first two years of its existence. Since then, the board has been concerned primarily with amendments to and interpretation of the existing rules. These rules are separated into three major categories, the first two of which are administrative and definitional. The third group, the general rules, are the substantive rules of the MSRB. The details of the most important of these rules have already been discussed. A brief summary of the major rules is given below, but the descriptions are at best simplifications, meant only as a guide. According to the MSRB's Rule G-29, each broker and dealer must keep a copy of the rules in each office in which municipal securities activities are conducted and make the rules available for examination by customers promptly on request.

Administrative Rules The administrative rules, A-1 through A-17, cover such areas as membership, powers, meetings of the board, and arbitration, fees, and deposits. The rules outline the rule-making procedures and set fees for registered dealers as well as rates for underwriters' assessments. Assessments are charged on the underwriting of primary offerings. In addition, the MSRB also assesses fees on secondary market transactions between dealers, and between dealers and customers.

Definitional Rules A short set of rules (D-1 through D-11) provides formal definitions of certain key but legally ambiguous terms. A bank dealer, a customer, and a discretionary account, for example, are carefully defined.

General Rules As of December 31, 2010, there were 41 general rules. Many of the key rules have been discussed in previous chapters of this volume. Rule G-1 defines exactly what operations qualify, under the rules, as independent dealer departments or divisions in banks. Professional qualifications, disciplinary actions, and fidelity bonding and other insurance coverage requirements are generally covered in Rules G-2 through G-7.

Rule G-3 is a far-reaching rule, classifying employees and establishing qualifying examinations. The Board has established four distinct classes of municipal securities employees—municipal securities representatives, municipal securities principals, municipal securities sales principals, and municipal securities financial and operations principals—and has developed a different qualifying exam for each class.

Most employees are classified as municipal securities representatives. They include anyone who (1) underwrites, trades, or sells municipal securities; (2) provides financial advisory or consultant services to issuers; (3) does research or offers investment advice; or (4) is involved in "any other activities which involve communication, directly or indirectly, with public investors in municipal securities" as it relates to activities described in (1) or (2). Clerical personnel are not, in general, included in this group. An important exemption from the qualifications test exists for anyone who has already passed the FINRA examination for general securities representatives. New employees of securities firms may take the general securities exam in lieu of the municipal securities exam. In addition to taking the qualifying exam, all new municipal securities representatives must serve a minimum apprenticeship of 90 days before they can transact business with any member of the public. The passing score for the exam is set by the MSRB. An apprentice must pass the exam before the end of a 180-day time limit or cease to perform the functions of a municipal securities representative.

The three other classes of municipal securities employees are municipal securities principals, municipal securities sales principals, and financial and operations principals. Rule G-27 requires the designation by each dealer of one or more persons as municipal securities principals, municipal securities sales principals, financial and operations principals, or general securities principals to be responsible for supervision of its municipal securities activities. The municipal securities principal is a person who has a supervisory role with respect to one or more areas of activity, and each firm must have at least one municipal securities principal; many firms have more. A municipal securities sales principal is a person whose supervisory activities are limited to supervising only sales to and purchases from customers of municipal securities. A financial and operations principal is a person designated to be in charge of preparing and filing financial reports with the SEC or any other regulatory agency for a securities firm. There are separate exams for municipal securities principals, municipal securities sales principals, and financial and operations principals. (Financial and operations principals who are qualified as such under the FINRA examination are exempted from taking the exam.)

The principal record-keeping rule is G-8. Rule G-9 specifies how long records must be preserved, and Rule G-27 requires the adoption, maintenance, and enforcement of written supervisory procedures of the books and records required to be maintained and preserved by Rules G-8 and G-9 (including procedures for maintenance and supervision) by a designated principal.

Rule G-11 lists the MSRB's requirements for syndicate practices. The MSRB established uniform practices for clearing, processing, and settling transactions under Rule G-12. Rule G-15 lists requirements for written confirmations to customers.

Rule G-13 requires that all quotations by dealers must represent actual bids and offers—that is, the dealer must be prepared to make the trade at the yield or price quoted at the time the quotation is made. Dealers can, however, give mere indications of yields or prices when requested, as long as they make it clear that these indications are not actual quotations. Rule G-16 requires the examination of every municipal securities dealer for compliance with the rules by the assigned enforcement agency at least once every 24 months.

Most of the remaining rules—G-17 through G-41—are known as the fair-practice rules. In the words of the MSRB legislation, these are designed

> to prevent fraudulent and manipulative acts and practices, to promote just and equitable principles of trade, to foster cooperation and coordination with persons engaged in regulating, clearing, settling, processing information with respect to, and facilitating transactions in municipal securities, to remove impediments to and perfect the mechanism of a free and open market in municipal securities, and, in general, to protect investors and the public interest.

The first of these rules (G-17) simply states:

> In the conduct of its municipal securities business, each broker, dealer, and municipal securities dealer shall deal fairly with all persons and shall not engage in any deceptive, dishonest, or unfair practice.

Although simple, Rule G-17 has far-reaching implications. The rule has been supplemented numerous times with interpretive guidance detailing its application in specific circumstances.

An equally important rule is Rule G-19, on suitability, which requires that a dealer make suitable recommendations to customers. Some of the other fair-practice rules involve gifts, relationships between underwriters and issuers, dissemination of official statements or similar disclosure documents, advertising, the fairness of prices and commissions, quotations, and the improper use of assets.

Rule G-35 establishes arbitration procedures for dealers and customers who have disputes or claims involving municipal securities transactions. The MSRB has written an arbitration code that provides a procedure for the resolution of municipal securities disputes. The code covers the initiation of proceedings by a dealer or a customer, the conduct of hearings, and awards. A simplified procedure has been established for claims of $10,000 and less. Under Rule G-35, a customer or dealer may compel another dealer to arbitrate a dispute.

On May 31, 1990, the SEC approved Rule G-36, which required underwriters to forward to the MSRB copies of official statements and advance refunding documents for bond issues subject to SEC Rule 15c2-12 and certain other issues if an official statement is prepared for the issue. This rule was rescinded on June 1, 2009, and replaced by amended Rule G-32, which requires underwriters to provide the information to EMMA. Underwriters must also provide by no later than the settlement date either copies of these documents or a notice advising how to obtain them from EMMA to customers who purchase bonds.

On April 7, 1994, the SEC approved Rule G-37, which prohibits a broker or dealer from engaging in municipal securities business with an issuer within two years after a political contribution has been made by the broker or dealer, any associated municipal finance professional, or a controlled political action committee for any particular officials of the issuer, under certain circumstances. This rule also requires the regular reporting of such contributions as well as any payments to political parties.

On January 17, 1996, the SEC approved Rule G-38, which requires the disclosure by a broker or dealer to an issuer of the retention by the broker or dealer of any person to obtain or retain municipal securities business through direct or indirect communication with that issuer. Any such retention must be evidenced by a written agreement, and reports of such arrangements are required to be made to the MSRB. Subsequent amendments to Rule G-38 require the reporting of political contributions by any such consultants retained by a broker or dealer.

On December 16, 1996, the SEC approved Rule G-39, which expressly regulates the telemarketing activities of brokers and dealers. The prohibitions do not apply generally to calls placed for the purpose of maintaining and servicing the accounts of existing customers. The placement of calls by brokers and dealers is also potentially subject to Rule G-17, which addresses fair dealing with investors as described previously.

On June 6, 2002, the SEC approved Rule G-40, which requires municipal securities brokers, dealers, and advisors to maintain an email account dedicated to communications with the MSRB, designate a municipal securities principal as the primary email contact for the account and notify the MSRB of these arrangements and any changes no later than 30 days after the change becomes effective.

On July 11, 2003, the SEC approved Rule G-41, which requires brokers and dealers to establish and implement an anti-money laundering compliance program reasonably designed to achieve and monitor ongoing compliance with the requirements of the Bank Secrecy Act.

Effective October 1, 2010, the Dodd–Frank Act imposed a fiduciary duty on municipal advisors toward the municipalities they advise. The MSRB subsequently amended its rules to require municipal advisors to act in good faith and in the best interests of a municipal entity, to provide written disclosure of any possible conflicts of interests to the municipal entity and to receive written consent to any such conflicts. Municipal advisors must also provide their services in a competent manner, consider alternative financing options, and conduct a reasonable inquiry into a municipal entity's financial circumstances before providing advisory services. The MSRB's review and implementation of Dodd-Frank provisions under its jurisdiction are ongoing as of mid-2011.

CHAPTER **10**

Financial Products

INTRODUCTION

The use of financial products such as derivatives has become integral to financial and risk management for both municipal issuers and institutional investors, allowing them to manage their assets and liabilities more effectively. Some products help lower interest rate costs on the liability side of the balance sheet, while others provide hedges or reduce risks on investments. Financial products are chosen in light of each organization's own needs and the demands of the market. This chapter incorporates a basic discussion of financial products, with a focus on those most commonly used by issuers.

A *derivative* is a financial contract that derives its value from an underlying security or index. In the tax-exempt market, both issuers and investors use derivatives to manage risk and return. Examples of derivative contracts used in the municipal market include interest rate swaps, caps and floors, and credit default swaps.

The municipal market includes both interest rate-focused and credit-focused derivative products. Interest rate derivatives such as floating-to-fixed interest rate swaps are used by municipal issuers to hedge interest rate risk or minimize financing costs. Credit-focused derivatives such as credit default swaps are usually used by investors or dealers to hedge risks or amplify returns. In addition, some issuers may use specialized financial products as investment vehicles.

The following sections include an introductory discussion of interest rate swaps and options, credit default swaps, and certain investment-related products.

INTEREST RATE SWAPS

An issuer uses interest rate swaps to manage the balance sheet and to lower overall interest costs. An *interest rate swap* is a contract between two

247

counterparties, usually a state or local government or private, nonprofit issuer and a swap dealer or other institutional user. An issuer's counterparty can be any of a number of financial institutions including banks, insurance companies, and broker-dealers who agree to swap interest payments for a set amount of time based on a notional, or hypothetical, amount of money. If the swap is entered into at the time of a bond sale, the notional amount can be a percentage or the full amount of the bond issue.

Municipal interest rate swaps can be categorized as fixed rate to floating rate, or floating rate to fixed rate. The issuer may enter into a swap to convert existing fixed rate debt synthetically into floating rate debt, or vice versa. Issuers do this to change the existing mix of fixed and floating rate debt without refunding the existing debt or to take advantage of opportunities to lower their interest costs. Most commonly, issuers execute swaps at the same time that they issue new bonds to create a "synthetic" financing, but other uses are also common.

Assume that the issuer has fixed rate debt and wants to add some variable exposure to its liability mix, but does not want to refund a portion of the outstanding debt. The issuer could enter into a fixed to floating rate swap with a counterparty, as shown in Figure 10.1. The counterparty can be a dealer, an insurance company, or other financial institution. The issuer pays the counterparty the current SIFMA Municipal Swap Index, a floating rate index (discussed in the next subsection). The counterparty pays the issuer an agreed-on fixed rate. The issuer would continue to pay the bondholders the normal interest rate associated with their bonds, but those payments would be fully or partially offset by the fixed payment received from the counterparty. Interest payments between the issuer and the counterparty would be netted out, with only one payment made for the larger amount. The issuer now has increased the variable rate exposure in its liability profile.

Now, assume the issuer would like to convert synthetically a portion of its new or existing floating rate debt to a fixed rate. With an agreed-on notional amount, the issuer would enter into a floating to fixed rate swap. Figure 10.2 diagrams the flow of payments of a floating to fixed rate swap.

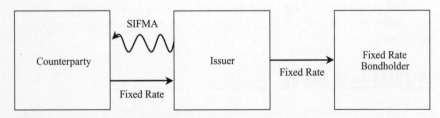

FIGURE 10.1   Fixed to Floating Rate Swap

FIGURE 10.2 Floating to Fixed Rate Swap

The issuer pays the counterparty a set fixed rate based on the current market. The counterparty pays the issuer a floating rate, typically either SIFMA or London Interbank Offered Rate (LIBOR). Again, the payments are netted out.

Swaps may become attractive when there is a significant differential between interest rate markets, such as the municipal fixed rate bond and the SIFMA Index swap markets. For instance, assume that in the previous floating to fixed rate swap the issuer has two alternatives for creating fixed rate debt. The issuer can either sell 20-year fixed rate debt in the bond market at 5.50 percent, or can enter into a fixed rate to SIFMA Index swap for 4.70 percent plus expenses (assuming 30 basis points for expenses), for a total of 5.00 percent. The fixed swap rate is the present value of expected SIFMA index over the life of the swap. The issuer expects to save 50 basis points (5.50 – 5.00) by issuing floating rate debt and executing the swap.

The issuer and the counterparty must have the legal authority to enter into a swap. After that, there are inherent risks in any swap. These include, but are not limited to, the following:

- *Counterparty credit risk.* The issuer and the counterparty have credit risk exposure to each other over the life of the swap. Each must feel confident that the other will be able to perform under the contract. Both issuers and counterparties may set minimum credit levels for each other. Collateral is sometimes posted by a bank or swap dealer to mitigate the municipal borrower's credit risk.
- *Interest rate risk.* The issuer and counterparty may enter into a swap under one set of interest rate expectations. If actual rates differ dramatically from expectations, one side or the other may end up paying a higher overall interest cost.
- *Basis risk.* The issuer may experience a mismatch between the floating index used to hedge its exposure, such as the SIFMA index, and the actual rate paid on its outstanding floating rate debt.

- *Event risk*. The issuer and counterparty may encounter an unexpected event, such as a change in tax law, which would make the economics of the swap less attractive.

Swap contracts have termination events delineated and agreed to by both parties. Termination events vary from issuer to issuer, and from counterparty to counterparty.

Interest rate swaps are by far the most commonly used financial products among municipal issuers. For several years prior to the 2008 financial crisis, many issuers were able to obtain a significantly lower nominal interest costs by issuing variable rate debt and simultaneously entering into floating to fixed interest rate swaps rather than issuing fixed rate bonds.

During and after the 2008 financial crisis, short-term interest rate indices fell to near zero and remained at that level for an extended period. At the same time, some underlying variable rate debt reset at higher rates, often because of downgrades of bond insurers or bank liquidity providers or because of failures of auction rate securities so the rates on some variable-rate bonds no longer matched the variable rates on the corresponding swaps. Long-term rates also fell, leaving issuers with significant mark-to-market losses on their swap positions. In some cases, issuers chose to refinance outstanding variable rate debt by issuing fixed rate bonds, typically at a lower rate than they would have been able to obtain when the original financing was done. Proceeds of the new bonds were used in part to unwind interest rate swaps that were no longer needed, which often required a cash payment to the counterparty, reflecting the market value of the swap on the date it was unwound. This termination payment was a mark to market adjustment, not a penalty, although for some borrowers, at the time these swaps were unwound the market price was affected by the preponderance of issuers seeking to exit their positions, resulting in higher than expected costs. Other issuers have been able to refinance out of their floating rate bonds using other financing options such as bank loans or floating rate notes based on the SIFMA index. For many issuers, their synthetic financings performed exactly as expected, resulting in significant savings relative to other financing options available at the time.

The use of floating to fixed rate swaps declined after 2008 because the risks associated with the transactions, such as exposure to bank credit quality, became more apparent. In addition, letters of credit became more expensive for a time, eliminating much of the benefit of the synthetic fixed rate structure.

Issuers may use fixed to floating rate swaps in combination with fixed rate debt as an alternative to issuing floating rate debt. Fixed to floating rate swaps may lower the cost of floating rate debt if the cost of bank letters of credit required to support the issuance of VRDOs exceeds the cost of a swap. A swap also removes the remarketing rate reset risk associated with VRDOs.

The Securities Industry and Financial Markets Association Municipal Swap Index

The SIFMA Municipal Swap Index, produced by Municipal Market Data, is a seven-day market index composed of tax-exempt VRDOs, calculated weekly. The Index, which is also known in the market as SIFMA, acts as a benchmark floating rate in a swap transaction.

In order for an issue to qualify for inclusion in the index, it must:

- Be a weekly reset, effective on Wednesday (no lag resets considered).
- Not be subject to alternative minimum tax.
- Have an outstanding amount of $10 million or more.
- Have the highest short-term rating (VMIG1 by Moody's or A-1+ by S&P).
- Pay interest on a monthly basis, calculated on an actual/actual basis.

In addition, only one quote per obligor per remarketing agent will be included in the Index. Issues from all states are eligible for inclusion.

The SIFMA Index is calculated on a weekly basis, and released to subscribers on Thursday. The weekly SIFMA Index calculation is based on the following:

- The standard deviation of the rates is calculated. Any issue falling outside ±1.0 standard deviations is dropped.
- Each participating remarketing agent is limited to no more than 15 percent of the Index by an averaging method.

The actual number of issues that make up the Index varies over time as issues are called, converted, mature, or are newly issued. In addition, if changes occur that violate the criteria or calculation methods, an issue is dropped. Typically, the SIFMA Index includes approximately 650 issues in any given week.

Table 10.1 shows the average SIFMA Index for each year from 2000 to 2010. The lowest value in this time period was 0.15 percent on January 6, 2010, and the highest value was a brief spike to 7.96 percent on October 1, 2008.

TABLE 10.1   SIFMA Municipal Swap Index: Average Annual Index, 2000 to 2010

Year	Average Index
2000	4.12
2001	3.62
2002	3.45
2003	2.61
2004	2.46
2005	2.24
2006	1.38
2007	1.23
2008	1.03
2009	0.40
2010	0.27

Source: Securities Industry and Financial Markets Association, Municipal Market Data.

INTEREST RATE CAPS, FLOORS, AND COLLARS

Issuers may use other derivative tools to manage interest rate risk preceding a bond offering or during a construction period. An *interest rate cap* is an agreement in which a party pays a premium up front or in installments to the counterparty. If the floating interest rate exceeds a stated fixed rate during the time of the cap agreement, the counterparty will pay the difference, based on the notional amount. The cap rate is also called the *strike rate*. Interest rate caps may be used to protect the issuer against rising interest rates above a threshold on its variable rate debt.

An *interest rate floor* is an agreement in which a party receives a premium up front or in installments from a counterparty. If the floating rate is lower than the stated fixed rate during the time of the floor agreement the party pays the difference based on the notional amount. The floor rate is also called the *strike rate*. An interest rate floor lets a party receive up-front payments in exchange for the risk of making payments if interest rates fall. Municipal issuers seldom use floors on their own, but may do so as part of an interest rate collar.

An *interest rate collar* is an agreement that combines an interest rate cap and an interest rate floor. The party pays if the floating rate exceeds the cap rate and the counterparty pays if the floating rate drops below the floor rate.

OTHER SWAP PRODUCTS

In addition to floating to fixed and fixed to floating interest rate swaps, municipal issuers sometimes swap two different streams of floating rate interest payments in a *basis swap*. Variable rate instruments are typically based on the SIFMA Municipal Swap Index, and issuers can use basis swaps to exchange the SIFMA Index rate for a rate equal to a percentage of LIBOR. A basis swap typically results in a lower expected interest cost, but issuers must assume a greater risk that their funding cost may differ from the benchmark rate. LIBOR reflects conditions in the wider taxable money markets, while the SIFMA Index is tied to the tax-exempt municipal money market. For example, the attraction of municipal bonds to individual investors may decrease if tax rates drop, which may cause percentage of LIBOR-based interest costs to increase relative to interest rates based on the SIFMA Index.

A *forward swap* is an agreement between the party and the counterparty to begin a swap at some future date. Issuers who plan to issue bonds and want to swap fixed for floating or vice versa can lock in the swap rate in advance through a forward swap.

A *rate lock* fixes the interest rate based on a benchmark index, insulating the issuer from the effect of market movements between the date it enters into the rate lock and the date bonds are sold. If the interest rate on the bonds is higher than the rate lock, the issuer receives a cash sum equal to the present value of the difference over the life of the bonds to offset the higher rate. If the bonds are sold at a lower interest rate, the issuer must pay the counterparty a corresponding amount in cash but will reap the benefit of lower rates over the life of the bonds.

A *swaption* is an agreement that gives a party the option to execute a swap at some future date.

MANAGING THE ASSET SIDE

Bond documents often require that the issuer maintain specific funds such as debt service reserve and project funds. Arbitrage regulations and indenture requirements limit the amount of yield that the issuer can earn on these funds and the types of investments that are allowed. Following is a summary of some financial products, some derivatives and some not, which issuers can use to maximize yield or minimize risk within the products' constraints.

- *Repurchase agreements.* A repurchase agreement, or *repo*, is the sale of U.S. Treasury or agency securities, with an agreement by the seller of these securities to repurchase all or a portion of them back at an agreed price at some future date. The seller of the securities usually over-collateralizes them, allowing the purchaser to have additional security and to have some protection from price fluctuations. Repos are effectively a form of secured borrowing. Repos are marked to market regularly and may be held by a third party.

- *Reverse repurchase agreements.* In a reverse repurchase agreement, or *reverse repo*, a party purchases U.S. Treasuries or agencies, while simultaneously agreeing to resell them at a given price at a given future date. Reverse repos are effectively a form of secured lending. Similar custody and valuation arrangements for repos apply to reverse repos.
- *Investment agreements.* Investment agreements, offered by financial institutions, offer a guaranteed interest rate for the life of the agreement. Issuers often use these for investing construction funds, especially if there is a draw schedule for the funds.
- *Other products.* Other products include *forward supply contracts* for escrows for refundings, and *constant maturity swaps* to manage mismatched maturities between assets and liabilities or to hedge against anticipated changes in the shape of the yield curve.

CREDIT DEFAULT SWAPS

A *credit default swap* is an agreement between two counterparties to exchange the credit exposure of a fixed income obligation. In a typical transaction, the buyer agrees to pay a fee each year for the duration of the swap and receives in return the right to sell the underlying bond or other obligation to the seller at par if certain events of default (including failure to pay interest and principal when due) specified in the contract occur. The practical effect is to shift the credit risk from the buyer to the seller of the swap.

Credit default swaps are generally used by investors to hedge their credit exposure. In addition, due to the large number of issues and lack of a repo market, it is not possible to sell municipal bonds short, so credit default swaps provide an alternative means of adopting short trading positions.

Significant demand for credit default swaps on municipal issuers emerged around the time of the financial crisis in late 2007 and 2008, which caused investors to refocus on the credit risk of municipal issuers rather than bond insurance companies, although the municipal CDS market remains small and thinly traded compared to other credit sectors.

In April 2008, Markit introduced the tradable MCDX municipal credit default swaps indices, based on 50 equally weighted reference credits intended to represent a broad profile of active municipal bond issuers. Available in 3-, 5-, and 10-year maturities, the index enables market participants to take long or short exposure in a diversified pool of municipal credits and to hedge their existing positions in the cash bond market.

Some municipal issuers have criticized the development of credit default swaps on municipal credits on the basis that they encourage market participants to "bet against" municipal credit performance. Proponents argue that the ability to hedge municipal bonds like other securities helps to expand the buyer base, increase liquidity, and ultimately narrow spreads, which benefits municipal issuers. At time of writing, the market is still relatively small, with approximately $50 billion gross notional outstanding as of May 2011 according to DTCC.[1]

This is a brief summary of financial products used in the municipal market, which are continuously evolving to meet the needs of issuers and investors in their goals of stable and responsible financial management.

---

[1] The Depository Trust & Clearing Corporation Trade Information Warehouse Reports, Open Positions Data.

Municipal Securities Rulemaking Board Rule G-33*

Calculations

Rule G-33.

(a) *Accrued Interest.* Accrued interest shall be computed in accordance with the following formula:

$$\text{Interest} = \text{Rate} \times \text{Par value of transaction} \times \frac{\text{Number of days}}{\text{Number of days in year}}$$

For purposes of this formula, the "Number of days" shall be deemed to be the number of days from the previous interest payment date (from the dated date, in the case of first coupons) up to, but not including, the settlement date. The "Number of days" and the "Number of days in year" shall be counted in accordance with the requirements of section (e) below.

(b) *Interest-Bearing Securities*

(i) Dollar Price. For transactions in interest-bearing securities effected on the basis of yield, the resulting dollar price shall be computed in accordance with the following provisions:

(A) *Securities Paying Interest Solely at Redemption.* Except as otherwise provided in this section (b), the dollar price for a

---

*Information published by the Municipal Securities Rulemaking Board (MSRB) is subject to change and revocation. Such information is included in this edition as it exists at a specific time. For additional and updated information, you should consult the Board's web site at www.msrb.org.

transaction in a security paying interest solely at redemption shall be computed in accordance with the following formula:

$$P = \left[\frac{RV + \left(\frac{DIR}{B} \cdot R \right)}{1 + \left(\frac{DIR - A}{B} \cdot Y \right)} \right] - \left[\frac{A}{B} \cdot R \right]$$

For purposes of this formula, the symbols shall be defined as follows:

"A" is the number of accrued days from the beginning of the interest payment period to the settlement date (computed in accordance with the provisions of section (e) below);

"B" is the number of days in the year (computed in accordance with the provisions of section (e) below);

"DIR" is the number of days from the issue date to the redemption date (computed in accordance with the provisions of section (e) below);

"P" is the dollar price of the security for each $100 par value (divided by 100);

"R" is the annual interest rate (expressed as a decimal);

"RV" is the redemption value of the security per $100 par value (divided by 100); and

"Y" is the yield price of the transaction (expressed as a decimal).

(B) *Securities with Periodic Interest Payments.* Except as otherwise provided in this section (b), the dollar price for a transaction in a security with periodic interest payments shall be computed as follows:

(1) for securities with six months or less to redemption, the following formula shall be used:

$$P = \left[\frac{\frac{RV}{100} + \frac{R}{M}}{1 + \left(\frac{E - A}{E} \cdot \frac{Y}{M} \right)} \right] - \left[\frac{A}{B} \cdot R \right]$$

For purposes of this formula, the symbols shall be defined as follows:

"A" is the number of accrued days from the beginning of the interest payment period to the settlement date (computed in accordance with the provisions of section (e) below);

"B" is the number of days in the year (computed in accordance with the provisions of section (e) below);

"E" is the number of days in the interest payment period in which the settlement date falls (computed in accordance with the provisions of section (e) below);

"M" is the number of interest payment periods per year standard for the security involved in the transaction;

"P" is the dollar price of the security for each $100 par value (divided by 100);

"R" is the annual interest rate (expressed as a decimal);

"RV" is the redemption value of the security per $100 par value; and

"Y" is the yield price of the transaction (expressed as a decimal).

> (2) for securities with more than six months to redemption, the following formula shall be used:

$$P = \left[\frac{RV}{\left(1 + \frac{Y}{2}\right)_{exp} N - 1 + \frac{E-A}{E}} \right] + \left[\sum_{K=1}^{N} \frac{100 \cdot \frac{R}{2}}{\left(1 + \frac{Y}{2}\right)_{exp} k - 1 + \frac{E-A}{E}} \right]$$
$$- \left[100 \cdot \frac{A}{B} \cdot R \right]$$

For purposes of this formula, the symbols shall be defined as follows:

"A" is the number of accrued days from beginning of the interest payment period to the settlement date (computed in accordance with the provisions of section (e) below);

"B" is the number of days in the year (computed in accordance with the provisions of section (e) below);

"E" is the number of days in the interest payment period in which the settlement date falls (computed in accordance with the provisions of section (e) below);

"N" is the number of interest payments (expressed as a whole number) occurring between the settlement date and the redemption date, including the payment on the redemption date;

"P" is the dollar price of the security for each $100 par value;

"R" is the annual interest rate (expressed as a decimal);

"RV" is the redemption value of the security per $100 par value; and

"Y" is the yield price of the transaction (expressed as a decimal).

For purposes of this formula the symbol "*exp*" shall signify that the preceding value shall be raised to the power indicated by the succeeding value; for purposes of this formula, the symbol "K" shall signify successively each whole number from "1" to "N" inclusive; for purposes of this formula, the symbol "sigma" shall signify that the succeeding term shall be computed for each value "K" and that the results of such computations shall be summed.

(ii) *Yield.* Yields on interest-bearing securities shall be computed in accordance with the following provisions:

> (A) *Securities Paying Interest Solely at Redemption.* The yield of a transaction in a security paying interest solely at

redemption shall be computed in accordance with the following formula:

$$Y = \left[\frac{(RV + (\frac{DIR}{B} \cdot R)) - (P + (\frac{A}{B} \cdot R))}{P + (\frac{A}{B} \cdot R)} \right] \cdot \left[\frac{B}{DIR - A} \right]$$

For purposes of this formula, the symbols shall be defined as follows:

"A" is the number of accrued days from the beginning of the interest payment period to the settlement date (computed in accordance with the provisions of section (e) below);

"B" is the number of days in the year (computed in accordance with the provisions of section (e) below);

"DIR" is the number of days from the issue date to the redemption date (computed in accordance with the provisions of section (e) below);

"P" is the dollar price of the security for each $100 par value (divided by 100);

"R" is the annual interest rate (expressed as a decimal);

"RV" is the redemption value of the security per $100 par value (divided by 100); and

"Y" is the yield on the investment if the security is held to redemption (expressed as a decimal).

(B) *Securities with Periodic Interest Payments.* The yield of a transaction in a security with periodic interest payments shall be computed as follows:

(1) for securities with six months or less to redemption, the following formula shall be used:

$$Y = \left[\frac{(\frac{RV}{100} + \frac{R}{M}) - (P + (\frac{A}{E} \cdot \frac{R}{M}))}{P + (\frac{A}{E} \cdot \frac{R}{M})} \right] \cdot \left[\frac{M \cdot E}{E - A} \right]$$

For purposes of this formula, the symbols shall be defined as follows:

"A" is the number of accrued days from the beginning of the interest payment period to the settlement date (computed in accordance with the provisions of section (e) below);

"E" is the number of days in the interest payment period in which the settlement date falls (computed in accordance with the provisions of section (e) below);

"M" is the number of interest payment periods per year standard for the security involved in the transaction;

"P" is the dollar price of the security for each $100 par value (divided by 100);

"R" is the annual interest rate (expressed as decimal);

"RV" is the redemption value of the security per $100 par value; and

"Y" is the yield on the investment if the security is held to redemption (expressed as a decimal).

      (2) for securities with more than six months to redemption, the formula set forth in item (2) of subparagraph (b)(i)(B) shall be used.

(c) *Discounted Securities.*

  (i) *Dollar Price.* For transactions in discounted securities, the dollar price shall be computed in accordance with the following provisions:

    (A) The dollar price of a discounted security, other than a discounted security traded on a yield-equivalent basis, shall be computed in accordance with the following formula:

$$P = [RV] - \left[DR \cdot RV \cdot \frac{DSM}{B} \right]$$

For purposes of this formula, the symbols shall be defined as follows:

"B" is the number of days in the year (computed in accordance with the provisions of section (e) below);

"DR" is the discount rate (expressed as a decimal);

"DSM" is the number of days from the settlement date of the transaction to the maturity date (computed in accordance with the provisions of section (e) below);

"P" is the dollar price of the security for each $100 par value; and

    "RV" is the redemption value of the security per $100 par value.

    (B) The dollar price of a discounted security traded on a yield-equivalent basis shall be computed in accordance with the formula set forth in subparagraph (b)(i)(A).

  (ii) *Return on Investment.* The return on investment for a discounted security shall be computed in accordance with the following provisions:

    (A) The return on investment for a discounted security, other than a discounted security traded on a yield-equivalent basis, shall be computed in accordance with the following formula:

$$IR = \left[\frac{RV - P}{P} \right] \cdot \left[\frac{B}{DSM} \right]$$

For purposes of this formula, the symbols shall be defined as follows:

"B" is the number of days in the year (computed in accordance with the provisions of section (e) below);

"DSM" is the number of days from the settlement date of the transaction to the maturity date (computed in accordance with the provisions of section (e) below);

"IR" is the annual return on investment if the security is held to maturity (expressed as a decimal);

"P" is the dollar price of the security for each $100 par value; and

"RV" is the redemption value of the security per $100 par value.

    (B) The yield of a discounted security traded on a yield-equivalent basis shall be computed in accordance with the formula set forth in subparagraph (b)(ii)(A).

(d) *Standards of Accuracy; Truncation.*

  (i) *Intermediate Values.* All values used in computations of accrued interest, yield, and dollar price shall be computed to not less than ten decimal places.

  (ii) *Results of Computations.* Results of computations shall be presented in accordance with the following:

    (A) Accrued interest shall be truncated to three decimal places, and rounded to two decimal places immediately prior to presentation of total accrued interest amount on the confirmation;

    (B) Dollar prices shall be truncated to three decimal places immediately prior to presentation of dollar price on the confirmation and computation of extended principal; and

    (C) Yields shall be truncated to four decimal places, and rounded to three decimal places, provided, however, that for purposes of confirmation display as required under rule G-15(a) yields accurate to the nearest .05 percentage points shall be deemed satisfactory.

Numbers shall be rounded, where required, in the following manner: if the last digit after truncation is five or above, the preceding digit shall be increased to the next highest number, and the last digit shall be discarded.

(e) *Day Counting.*

  (i) *Day Count Basis.* Computations under the requirements of this rule shall be made on the basis of a 30-day month and a 360-day year, or, in the case of computations on securities paying interest solely at redemption, on the day count basis selected by the issuer of the securities.

(ii) *Day Count Formula.* For purposes of this rule, computations of day counts on the basis of a 30-day month and a 360-day year shall be made in accordance with the following formula.

$$\text{Number of days} = (Y2 - Y1)\,360 + (M2 - M1)\,30 + (D2 - D1)$$

For purposes of this formula, the symbols shall be defined as follows:
"M1" is the month of the date on which the computation period begins;
"D1" is the day of the date on which the computation period begins;
"Y1" is the year of the date on which the computation period begins;
"M2" is the month of the date on which the computation period ends;
"D2" is the day of the date on which the computation period ends; and
"Y2" is the year of the date on which the computation period ends.
    For purposes of this formula, if the symbol "D2" has a value of "31," and the symbol "D1" has a value of "30" or "31," the value of the symbol "D2" shall be changed to "30." If the symbol "D1" has a value of "31," the value of the symbol "D1" shall be changed to "30." For purposes of this rule time periods shall be computed to include the day specified in the rule for the beginning of the period but not to include the day specified for the end of the period.

account. Also known as a *syndicate*. Can also refer to a customer account.

accrued interest. (1) The dollar amount of interest accrued on an issue, based on the stated interest rate on that issue, from its date to the date of delivery to the original purchaser. This is usually paid by the original purchaser to the issuer as part of the purchase price of the issue. (2) Interest deemed to be earned on a security but not yet paid to the investor calculated from settlement date to payment date.

ad valorem tax. [Latin: to the value added] A tax based on the value (or assessed value) of real property.

advance refunding. A financing structure under which new bonds are issued to repay an outstanding bond issue more than 90 days before its first call date. Generally, the proceeds of the new issue are invested in government securities, which are placed in escrow. The interest and principal repayments on these securities are then used to repay the old issue, usually on the first call date.

agency transaction. A sale and purchase of bonds when the dealer places bonds with the buyer on a commission basis rather than selling bonds that the dealer owns and acting as principal.

agreement among underwriters (AAU). Legal document used principally in negotiated sales by underwriters acting as a group, not individually. The document consists of the instructions, terms and acceptances, and standard terms and conditions.

all or none (AON). Where the offeror of a block of bonds will only sell all of the available bonds and not just a portion of them.

allotment. Distribution of bonds to syndicate members by the book-running manager.

alternative minimum tax (AMT). An alternative way of calculating income tax under the Internal Revenue Code. Interest on most private activity bonds (other than 501(c)(3) obligations) issued after August 7, 1986, is included in the calculation.

arbitrage. Arbitrage in the municipal market is the difference between the interest paid by issuers on tax-exempt bonds and the interest earned by issuers on normally higher-yielding taxable securities. Federal tax law restricts the yield that can be earned on the investment of tax-exempt bond proceeds.

arbitrage certificate. Transcript certificate evidencing compliance with the limitations on arbitrage imposed by the Internal Revenue Code and the applicable regulations.

ascending or positive yield curve. The interest rate structure that exists when long-term interest rates exceed short-term interest rates.

ask price. Price being sought for the security by the seller. Also called the offer.

assessed valuation. The value of property against which an ad valorem tax is levied, usually a percentage of true or market value.

auction rate bonds. Floating-rate bonds where the rate is periodically reset by a Dutch auction.

authority. A separate state or local governmental issuer expressly created to issue bonds or run an enterprise or both. Certain authorities issue bonds on their own behalf, such as a transportation or power authority. Authorities that issue bonds on the behalf of qualified nongovernmental issuers include health facility and industrial development authorities, among others.

authorizing resolution. Issuer document that states the legal basis for debt issuance and states the general terms of the financing.

basis point. One one-hundredth of one percent (.01 percent). Yield differences among fixed income securities are stated in basis points.

bearer security. A security that has no identification as to owner, that is, the bond is not registered. It is presumed to be owned by the bearer or the person who holds it. Bearer securities are freely and easily negotiable, as ownership can be quickly transferred from seller to buyer. Tax-exempt municipal bonds are no longer issued in bearer form.

bid. Price at which a buyer is willing to purchase a security.

bid list. Schedule of bonds distributed by an investor or broker to a dealer in order to get a bid or current price on the bonds.

bond. (1) The written evidence of debt, bearing a stated rate or rates of interest or a formula for determining that rate and maturing on a date certain, on which date and upon presentation a fixed sum of money plus interest is payable to the holder or owner. A municipal bond issue is usually comprised of a number of bonds that mature over a period of years; (2) for purposes of computations per bond, a $1,000 increment of an issue (no matter what the actual denominations are); (3) long-term debt securities with a maturity of greater than 13 months.

bond anticipation note (BAN). A note issued in anticipation of later issuance of bonds, usually payable from the proceeds of the sale of the bonds or of renewal notes. BANs can also be general obligations of the issuer.

bond bank. Agencies created by a few states to buy entire issues of bonds of municipalities. The purchases are financed by the issuance of bonds by the bond bank. The purpose is to provide better market access for small, lesser-known issuers.

The Bond Buyer. The daily newspaper of the municipal bond market. *The Bond Buyer* publishes news stories, new issue calendars, results of bond sales, notices of redemptions, and other items of interest to the market. *The Bond Buyer* also publishes weekly indices of bond yields that are widely followed by the market.

bond counsel. A lawyer or law firm that delivers a legal opinion to the bondholders that deals with the issuer's authorization to issue bonds and the tax characteristics of the bond. Bond counsel is retained by the issuer.

bond funds. Registered investment companies whose assets are comprised of portfolios of bonds.

bond insurance. Legal commitment by insurance company to make scheduled payment of interest and principal of a bond issue in the event that the issuer is unable to make those payments on time. The cost of insurance is usually paid by the issuer in case of a new issue of bonds, and the insurance is not purchased unless the cost is offset by the lower interest rate that can be achieved by the use of the insurance. Insurance can also be obtained for outstanding bonds in the secondary market.

bond purchase agreement (BPA). The contract between the issuer and the underwriter setting forth the terms of the negotiated sale, including the price of the bonds, the interest rate or rates that the bonds are to bear, and the conditions of closing. It is also called the purchase contract.

bond resolution. Issuer legal document that details the mechanics of the bond issue, security features, covenants, events of default, and other key features of the issue's legal structure. Indentures and trust agreements are functionally similar types of documents, and the use of each depends on the individual issue and issuer.

bond year. An element in calculating average life of an issue and in calculating net interest cost and net interest rate on an issue. A bond year is the number of 12-month intervals between the date of the bond and its maturity date, measured in $1,000 increments. For example, the number of bond years allocable to a $5,000 bond dated April 1, 2000, and maturing June 1, 2001, is 5.830 (1.166 [14 months divided by 12 months] × 5 [number of $1,000 increments in $5,000 bond]). Usual computations include bond years per maturity or per an interest rate and total bond years for the issue.

book-entry. A method of registering and transferring ownership of securities electronically that eliminates the need for physical certificates.

broker. A firm or person who acts as an intermediary by buying and selling securities to dealers on an agency basis rather than through its own account.

Build America Bonds. Municipal bonds authorized under the American Recovery and Reinvestment Act of 2009 on which the interest is taxable to investors and the issuers receive a subsidy from the federal government equal to 35 percent of the interest payments.

bullet. A security with a fixed maturity and no call feature.

call. Actions taken to pay the principal amount of a bond prior to the stated maturity date in accordance with the provisions for call stated in the bond documentation. Another term for call provisions is *redemption provisions*.

callable. Subject to payment of the principal amount (and accrued interest) prior to the stated maturity date, with or without payment of a call premium. Bonds can be callable under a number of different circumstances, including at the option of the issuer, or on a mandatory or extraordinary basis.

call premium. A dollar amount, usually stated as a percentage of the principal amount called, paid as a penalty or a premium for the exercise of a call provision.

call protection. Bonds that are not callable for a certain number of years before their call date.

carry. The cost of borrowing funds to finance an underwriting or trading position. A positive carry happens when the rate on the securities being financed is greater than the rate on the funds borrowed. A negative carry is when the rate on the funds borrowed is greater than the rate on the securities that are being financed.

certificates of participation (COP). A structure where investors buy certificates that entitle them to receive a participation, or share, in the lease payments from a particular project. The lease payments are passed through the lessor to the certificate holders with the tax advantages intact. The lessor typically assigns the lease and lease payments to a trustee, which then distributes the lease payments to the certificate holders.

closing date. The date for delivery of securities and payment of funds for a new issuance of bonds.

commission. The fee paid to a broker or dealer when the dealer acts as agent in a transaction, as opposed to when the dealer acts as a principal in a transaction. (See also *net price.*)

competitive underwriting or sale. An auction-type sale of municipal securities by an issuer in which underwriters or syndicates of underwriters submit sealed bids (or oral auction bids) to purchase the securities. The securities are won and purchased by the underwriter or syndicate of underwriters who submit the best bid according to guidelines in the notice of sale. This is contrasted with a negotiated underwriting.

concession. Fractional discount from the public offering of new securities at which the underwriter sells the bonds to dealers not in the syndicate.

confirmation. A document that states in writing the terms and execution of a verbal arrangement to buy or sell a security.

continuing disclosure agreement. Under amendments to Rule 15c2-12, the obligation from an issuer to an underwriter to provide annual financial information and operating data of the type included in the official statement for the primary bond offering. The issuer must also provide notice of specified material events.

convexity. A measure of the change in a security's duration with respect to changes in interest rates. The more convex a security is, the more its duration will change with interest rate changes.

counterparty. One of two entities in a swap or other agreement. In the municipal market a counterparty can be a state or local government, a broker-dealer, a corporation, or other party.

coupon. The nominal interest rate on a bond. Also, the detachable part of a bearer bond that denotes both the amount of interest due and on what date and where the payment is to be made. Coupons are generally payable semiannually.

covenant. The issuer's pledge, in the financing documents, to pursue or to avoid certain practices and actions.

cover bid. The second highest bidder in a competitive sale.

credit default swap. An agreement between two parties to exchange the credit exposure of a fixed income obligation. One party agrees to pay a sum of money each year for the duration of the swap and receives in return the right to sell the underlying bond or other obligation to the counterparty at par if certain events of default (including failure to pay interest and principal when due) specified in the contract occur.

credit enhancement. The use of the credit of a stronger entity to strengthen the credit of a lower-rated entity in bond or note financing. This term is used in the context of bond insurance, bank facilities, and government programs.

current yield. The ratio of interest to the actual market price of the bond, stated as a percentage. For example, a bond with a current market price of $1,000 that pays $60 per year in interest would have a current yield of 6 percent.

CUSIP. The Committee on Uniform Security Identification Procedures, which was established under the auspices of the American Bankers Association to develop a uniform method of identifying municipal, U.S. government, and corporate securities. CUSIP numbers are unique nine-digit numbers assigned to each security.

dated date (or issue date). The date of a bond issue from which the bondholder is entitled to receive interest, even though the bonds may actually be sold or delivered at some other date.

dealer. A securities firm or bank that engages in the underwriting, trading, and sales of municipal (or other) securities.

debt limit. Statutory or constitutional limit on the principal amount of debt that an issuer may incur (or that it may have outstanding at any one time).

debt service. Required principal and interest payments on a bond.

debt service coverage. The ratio of net revenues available to pay debt service to the debt service requirements.

debt service requirements. Amounts required to pay debt service, often expressed in the context of a time frame (such as annual debt service requirements).

debt service reserve fund. A fund maintained by a bond issuer that is required by the trust agreement or indenture as a reserve against a temporary interruption in the receipt of the revenues or other amounts that are pledged for the payment of the bonds. A common deposit requirement for a debt service reserve fund is six months' or one year's debt service on the bonds. The debt service reserve fund may be initially funded out of bond proceeds, over a period of time from revenues, or by a combination of the above.

deep discount. A price discount larger than traditional market discounts.

default. Failure to pay principal or interest when due. Defaults can also occur for failure to meet nonpayment obligations, such as reporting requirements, minimum coverage ratios, or when a material problem occurs for the issuer, such as a bankruptcy.

defeasance. Termination of the rights and interests of the trustee and bondholders under a trust agreement or indenture on final payment or provision for payment of all debt service and premiums and other costs, as specifically provided for in the trust instrument. The term is usually applied to bonds that are escrowed to maturity or prerefunded.

denomination. The face amount or par value of a bond or note that the issuer promises to pay on the maturity date. Most municipal bonds are issued in a minimum denomination of $5,000.

derivative. A derivative is a financial product that derives its value from an underlying security. In the tax-exempt market, there are primary and secondary derivative products.

discount. (1) Amount (stated in dollars or a percentage) by which the selling or purchase price of a security is less than its face amount. (2) Amount by which the amount bid for an issue is less than the aggregate principal amount of that issue.

discount bond. A bond sold at less than par.

discount rate. The rate the Federal Reserve charges on loans to member banks.

divided account. Syndicate account structure that is divided as to liability and not as to sales. Also called *Western account.*

dollar bond. A bond that is quoted and traded in dollar prices rather than by yield.

double-barreled bond. A bond secured by the pledge of two or more sources of payment. In some states, a bond secured in the first instance by a user charge for water or sewer, for example, may be additionally secured by ad valorem taxes.

double exemption. Securities that are exempt from state as well as federal income taxes. In states where this exemption occurs, the exemption is usually only for bonds issued by the state or its local governments. Debt of Puerto Rico and U.S. territories is also double tax exempt.

duration. The discounted, weighted average maturity of a fixed-income investment's cash flows, used in the estimation of the price sensitivity of fixed-income securities for a given small change in interest rates.

EMMA (Electronic Municipal Market Access). A comprehensive, centralized online source for free access to municipal issuers' disclosure information, real-time bond prices, market data, and educational materials about the municipal securities market.

exempt facilities bond. Bonds issued for privately owned or privately used facilities that are authorized to be issued on a tax-exempt basis under the Internal Revenue Code.

extraordinary redemption. A bond redemption that occurs under an unusual circumstance such as destruction of the facility financed.

face amount. The par value (i.e., principal or maturity value) of a security appearing on the face of the instrument.

federal funds rate. The interest rate charged by banks on overnight loans of their excess reserve funds to other banks.

financial advisor. A consultant to an issuer of municipal securities who provides the issuer with advice with respect to the structure, timing, terms, or other similar matters concerning a new issue of securities or certain other functions.

financial and operations principal. A municipal securities employee who is required to meet qualifications standards established by the MSRB. The individual is the person designated to be in charge of the preparation and filing of financial reports to the SEC and other regulatory bodies.

FINRA (Financial Industry Regulatory Authority). Securities industry self-regulatory organization in the United States.

firm. Free option to buy securities for a stated time at a stated price.

flow of funds. The structure established in the bond resolution or the trust documents that set forth the order in which funds generated by the enterprise will be allocated to various purposes.

forward cap. An agreement to enter into an interest rate cap at some date in the future.

forward floor. An agreement to enter into an interest rate floor at some date in the future.

forward swap. An agreement to enter a swap at some date in the future.

fully registered. A security that is registered as to principal and interest, payment of which is made only to or on the order of the registered owner.

general obligation bond (GO). A municipal bond secured by the pledge of the issuer's full faith, credit, and taxing power.

good faith requirement. Security deposit on new securities, ranging from 1 percent to 5 percent of the par amount, provided to the issuer at the time of a competitive bid by each underwriting syndicate, also called good faith deposit. A surety bond can be used as a good faith deposit.

high-yield bonds. Bonds where the rating is below investment grade. Also called noninvestment grade bonds.

indenture. Issuer legal document that details the mechanics of the bond issuer, security features, covenants, events of default, and other key features of the issue's legal structure. Bond resolutions and trust agreements are functionally similar types of documents, and the use of each depends on the individual issue and issuer.

indexed rate bonds. Tax-exempt bonds where the rate is periodically reset on a formula that incorporates an index, such as the SIFMA Swap Index.

initial delivery. The delivery of a new issue by the issuer to the original purchaser on payment of the purchase price. Also called *original delivery*.

initial offering price. The price (based on yield to maturity) stated as a percentage of par at which a syndicate account determines to market the issue during a set period of time, called the initial offering period. Members of the account may not offer any part of the issue at any other price during that period.

interest. Compensation paid or to be paid for the use of money, generally expressed as an annual percentage rate. (See also *coupon.*)

interest rate cap. An agreement where a party pays a premium up front or in installments to a counterparty. If the floating interest rate exceeds a stated fixed rate during the time of the cap agreement, the counterparty pays the difference, based on the notional amount. The cap rate is also called the *strike rate*. An interest rate cap can protect the purchaser against rising interest rates.

interest rate collar. An agreement that combines an interest rate cap and an interest rate floor. One party pays if the floating rate exceeds the cap rate or drops below the floor rate.

interest rate floor. An agreement where a party receives a premium up front or in installments from a counterparty. If the floating rate is lower than the stated fixed rate during the time of the floor agreement the party pays the difference based on the notional amount. The floor rate is also called the *strike rate*. An interest rate floor lets a party receive up-front payments in exchange for the risk of making payments if interest rates fall.

interest rate swap. A contract where two parties agree to make payments to each other. One party pays a fixed rate. The counterparty makes floating rate payments, generally based on an index such as the Securities Industry and Financial Markets Association Municipal Swap Index. The payments are based on the notional amount of the swap and are generally netted against each other, with the party owing the greater amount paying the other the net amount on a periodic basis.

inverse floater bonds. A floating rate bond where the interest payable is based on a formula that has a ceiling rate less a specified floating rate index. The floating rate on an inverse floater generally moves in the opposite direction to market interest rates.

inverted or negative yield curve. The interest rate structure that exists when short-term interest rates exceed long-term interest rates. (See also *ascending or positive yield curve.*)

investment grade. Bonds of lower credit risk considered suitable for preservation of invested capital; ordinarily, those rated Baa3 or better by Moody's Investors Service, BBB– or better by Standard & Poor's Corporation, or BBB– or better by Fitch.

issuer. A state, political subdivision, agency, or authority that borrows through the sale of bonds or notes. The public entity is the issuer even in those cases where the borrower or obligor is an entity other than the issuer.

joint managers. Multiple dealers who share management responsibilities in an underwriting account.

legal opinion. An opinion concerning the validity of a securities issue with respect to statutory authority, constitutionality, procedural conformity, and usually the exemption of interest from federal income taxes (or qualification for the federal interest rate subsidy on Build America Bonds). The legal opinion is usually rendered by a law firm recognized as specializing in public borrowings, often referred to as *bond counsel.* Other legal opinions in an issue may include tax opinions, defeasance opinions, underwriters' counsel opinions, and others.

letter of credit (LOC). A commitment, usually issued by a bank, used to guarantee the payment of principal and interest on debt issues. The LOC is drawn if the issuer is unable to make the principal and/or interest payments on a timely basis.

level debt service. A debt service schedule where total annual principal plus interest is approximately the same throughout the life of the bond. This entails a maturity schedule with increasing principal amounts each year.

level principal. A debt service schedule where total annual principal plus interest declines throughout the life of the bond. This entails a maturity schedule with the same amount of principal maturing each year, with a resulting smaller interest component each year. This is also called *declining debt service.*

limited tax bond. A bond secured by a pledge of a tax or category of taxes limited as to rate or amount.

line of credit. A commitment by a bank to provide funds to a borrower if certain conditions have been met or if certain conditions do not exist.

long. Securities or trading positions owned by a dealer or investor that gain if interest rates fall, prices rise, or credit spreads narrow.

manager (or senior manager). The underwriter who serves as the lead underwriter for an account. The manager generally negotiates the interest rate and purchase price in a negotiated transaction or serves as the generator of the consensus for the interest rate and purchase price to be bid in a competitive bidding situation. The manager signs the contracts on behalf of the account and generally receives either a fee or a larger spread for its services in this capacity. (See also *joint managers.*)

mandatory sinking fund redemption. A requirement to redeem a fixed portion of term bonds, which may make up the entire issue, in accordance with a predetermined schedule. Although the principal amount of the bonds to be redeemed is predetermined, the specific bonds that will be called to satisfy the requirement as to amount are selected by the trustee by lot.

marketability. A measure of the ease with which a security can be sold in the primary and secondary market without an extraordinary price concession.

material events. In the municipal market, with regards to Rule 15c2-12, one of 14 specified events that must be disclosed to the market if they occur.

maturity date. The date when the principal amount of a security becomes due and payable.

maturity schedule. The listing, by dates and amounts, of principal maturities of an issue.

modified duration. Duration adjusted to price and yield levels to represent the percentage change relationship of price and yield.

monetary default. Failure to pay principal or interest when due.

moral obligation bond. A municipal bond that, in addition to its primary source of security, possesses a structure whereby a state pledges to make up shortfalls in a debt service reserve fund, subject to legislative appropriation. There is no legal obligation for the state to make such a payment, but market participants recognize that failure to honor the moral pledge would have negative consequences for the state's own creditworthiness.

mortgage revenue bond. A security issued by a state, certain agencies or authorities, or a local government to make or purchase loans (including mortgages or other owner financing) with respect to single-family or multifamily residences.

municipal advisor. A person who provides advice to an issuer with respect to financial products, the issuance of municipal securities, or other functions or who solicits a municipal entity, including financial advisors, guaranteed investment contract brokers, third-party marketers, placement agents, solicitors, finders, and swap advisors. The definition does not include broker-dealers serving as underwriters, lawyers, investment advisors, and engineers providing technical advice. Municipal advisors must register with the SEC and MSRB.

municipal bond. A bond issued by a state or local governmental unit.

municipal over bond (MOB). Spread measures the relative difference between the yield on municipal bonds and U.S. Treasury bonds of the same maturity.

municipal securities principal. A municipal securities employee under MSRB rules who has supervisory responsibility for the municipal securities operations of the firm.

municipal securities representatives. The broadest class of municipal securities professionals who are required to pass a qualification examination under the rules of the MSRB. This group includes individuals who underwrite, trade, or sell municipal securities, do research or offer investment advice, provide financial advisory services, or communicate with investors in municipal securities.

Municipal Securities Rulemaking Board (MSRB). An independent, self-regulatory organization established by the Securities Acts Amendments of 1975 that is charged with primary rule-making authority over dealers, dealer banks, brokers, and municipal advisors active in the municipal securities market. Its current 21 members are divided into four categories—four securities firms representatives, three bank representatives, three municipal advisor representatives, and 11 public members, who constitute the majority of the board.

mutual fund. Mutual funds invest pooled cash of many investors to meet the fund's stated investment objective.

negative convexity. A characteristic of callable or prepayable securities that causes investors to have their principal returned sooner than expected in a declining interest rate environment or later than expected in a rising interest rate environment. In the former scenario, investors may have to reinvest their funds at lower rates (*call risk*); in the latter, they may miss an opportunity to earn higher rates (*extension risk*).

negotiated underwriting. A bond sale where the offering price and other terms are determined through a negotiation between an issuer and an underwriter or underwriting syndicate selected by the issuer before the moment of sale. This is in contrast to a competitive or an advertised sale.

net direct debt. Total direct debt of a municipality less all self-supporting debt, any sinking funds, and short-term debt such as tax anticipation notes and revenue anticipation notes.

net interest cost. An old method of calculating bids for new issues of municipal securities. The total dollar amount of interest over the life of the bonds is adjusted by the amount of premium or discount bid and then reduced to an average annual rate. The other, more widely used method is known as the true interest cost. (See also *true interest cost.*)

net order. Bond sold to investors at the price or yield shown in the reoffering scale. This is the price with no concessions.

net price. Price paid to a dealer for bonds when the dealer acts as principal in a transaction, that is, the dealer sells bonds that he owns, as opposed to an agency transaction. (See also *agency transaction.*)

noncallable bond. A bond that cannot be called for redemption at the option of the issuer before its specified maturity date or in extraordinary circumstances.

noninvestment grade bond. Bonds with higher credit risk considered unsuitable for preservation of invested capital; ordinarily, those rated Ba1 or below by Moody's Investors Service, BB+ or below by Standard & Poor's Corporation, or BB+ or below by Fitch. Bonds that are noninvestment grade are also called *high-yield bonds.*

notes. Promises to pay specified amounts of money, secured usually by specific sources of future revenues, such as taxes, federal and state aid payments, and bond proceeds (often mature within 13 months).

notice of sale. An official document disseminated by an issuer of municipal securities that gives pertinent information regarding an upcoming bond issue and invites bids from prospective underwriters.

notional amount. A stated principal amount in a swap on which the swap is based. Payment exchanges are based on the notional amount.

odd lot. Block of bonds of less than $250,000 or, sometimes, $100,000.

offer. The price at which a seller will sell a security. (See also *ask price*.)

offering price. The price at which members of an underwriting syndicate for a new issue offer securities to investors.

official statement (OS). The principal offering document for municipal securities that is prepared by or for the issuer. The OS discloses security features and economic, financial, and legal information about the issue. The final OS contains the pricing information on the issue that is not contained in the preliminary official statement.

option-adjusted duration (effective duration). A measure of a bond's price movement for a shift in the yield curve. For noncallable bonds, modified duration and effective duration are the same.

option-adjusted spread. The average spread over the AAA spot curve based on potential future expectations of interest rates. The potential paths of the cash flows are adjusted to reflect the options (puts/calls) embedded in the bond.

optional redemption. A right to retire all or part of a bond issue before the stated maturity during a specified period of years, also called a call option. The right can be exercised at the option of the issuer or, in pass-through issues, of the primary obligor. Exercising an optional redemption usually requires the payment of a premium with the amount of the premium decreasing the nearer the option exercise date is to the final maturity date of the issue.

order period. Specific length of time when orders for new issues are placed by investors.

original delivery. See *initial delivery*.

original issue discount bond (OID). A bond initially issued at a dollar price less than par that receives special treatment under federal tax law. The difference between the issue price and par value accrues as tax-exempt interest over the life of the bond rather than capital gain at maturity.

overlapping debt. On a municipal issuer's financial statement, the debt of other issuers that is payable in whole or in part by taxpayers of the subject issuer.

over-the-counter market (OTC). A securities market where transactions are executed through dealers, not through a centralized platform.

par. Price equal to the face amount of a security; 100 percent.

par amount. The principal amount of a bond or note due at maturity.

parity debt. Securities issued or to be issued with equal and ratable claim on the same underlying security and source of payment for debt service.

participation. Principal amount of bonds to be underwritten by each syndicate member.

party. One of two entities in a traditional interest rate swap. In the municipal market a party can be a state or local government, a broker-dealer, or a corporation.

paying agent. Entity through which principal and interest are paid. Usually a designated bank or the office of the treasurer of the issuer.

performance. An investment's return, usually total return.

point. Shorthand reference to 1 percent. In the context of a bond, a point means $10 as a bond with this reference means $1,000 (no matter what the actual denominations of the bonds of the issue). An issue or a security that is discounted two points is quoted at 98 percent of its par value.

primary tax-exempt derivative products. Swaps or other derivatives executed by municipal issuers.

private activity bonds. Municipal bonds where (1) more than 10 percent of the proceeds of the issue will finance property that will be used by a nongovernmental person in a trade or business, and (2) the payment of debt service on more than 10 percent of the proceeds of the issue will be (A) secured by property used in a private trade or business or payments in respect of such property, or (B) derived from payments in respect of property used in a private trade or business. Private activity bonds are defined in the Internal Revenue Code.

private placement. The negotiated offering of new securities directly to investors without a public underwriting.

preliminary official statement (POS). The offering document for municipal securities, in preliminary form, which does not contain pricing information. It is also called a POS, or a red herring.

premium. The amount by which the price of a security exceeds its principal amount.

premium bond. Bonds priced greater than par.

prepayment provision. Provision specifying at what time and on what terms repayment of the principal amount may be made by the issuer before the stated maturity. Includes calls, but prepayment usually connotes less formal procedures than a call.

price. The dollar amount to be paid for a security, stated as a percentage of its face value or par.

primary market (new-issue market). Market for new issues of municipal bonds and notes.

principal. The face amount of a bond, exclusive of accrued interest and payable at maturity.

principal transaction. A sale and purchase of bonds when the dealer commits its own capital in effecting the transaction.

put bond. A bond that gives the holder the right to require the issuer or the issuer's agent to purchase the bonds at a price, usually at par, at some date or dates before the final stated maturity.

put option. A put option allows the holder of a bond to put, or present, the bond to the issuer or third party and demand payment at a stated time before the final stated maturity of the bond.

rate covenant. A covenant in the financing proceedings requiring the charging of rates or fees for the use of specified facilities or operations at least sufficient to achieve a stated debt service coverage level.

ratings. Alphabetical or numeric symbols used to give indications of relative credit quality. In the municipal market these designations are published by rating services. Internal ratings are also used by other market participants to indicate relative credit quality.

redemption provisions. Another term for call provisions.

red herring. A preliminary official statement.

refunding. Sale of a new issue, the proceeds of which are to be used, immediately or in the future, to retire an outstanding issue by replacing the outstanding issue with the new issue. Refundings are undertaken to save interest cost, extend the maturity of the debt, or relax existing restrictive covenants.

registered bond. A bond whose owner is registered with the issuer or its agent. Transfer of ownership can only be accomplished when the securities are properly endorsed by the registered owner.

remarketing. A periodic process by which a remarketing agent, usually a dealer, accepts sell orders from holders of variable rate demand obligations and places the bonds with other investors. The remarketing agent determines a rate for the VRDOs at which all the sell orders can be matched with new buyers, and that becomes the rate paid by the issuer until the next reset date.

remarketing agent. A dealer responsible for the pricing and remarketing variable rate demand obligations.

request for proposals. A series of questions sent by a potential bond issuer to evaluate the qualification of potential underwriters of their negotiated issues, widely referred to as an RFP. Written and sometimes oral responses to questions may include a marketing plan for the bonds, the plan of finance, and estimated costs. Also referred to as *Request for Qualifications* or *RFQs*.

revenue anticipation note (RAN). RANs are issued in anticipation of future revenue other than taxes. This may include intergovernmental aid.

revenue bond. A bond on which the debt service is payable solely from the revenue generated from the operation of the project being financed or a category of facilities or from other nontax sources.

risk. A measure of the degree of uncertainty and potential financial loss of an investment or decision. There are many different risks including, among others:

Credit risk. The risk that the obligor on the bonds will be unable to make debt service payments because of a weakening of their credit.

Event risk. The risk that an issuer's ability to make debt service payments will change because of unanticipated changes, such as a corporate restructuring, a regulatory change, or an accident, in their environment.

Interest rate risk. Potential price fluctuations in a bond caused by changes in the general level of interest rates.

Underwriting risk. The risk of pricing and underwriting securities and then ultimately being able to sell them to the investor.

round lot. Block of bonds $100,000 or higher or $250,000 or higher depending on the market.

scale. Listing by maturity of the price or yields at which a new issue will be offered.

  ▪ Consensus scale. In a negotiated issue, the very early price indications.
  ▪ Preliminary scale. Initial prices and yields, before a bid is submitted.

- Final scale. Scale that is submitted to the issuer at the time of the sale.
- Reoffering scale. Scale offered to the investor by the underwriter who has purchased bonds. Also called the winning scale.

secondary market. Ongoing market for bonds previously offered or sold in the primary market.

Section 501(c)(3). The section of the Internal Revenue Code defining the status of charitable, nonprofit organizations.

security. Specific revenue sources or assets pledged by an issuer to the bondholder to secure repayment of the bond.

selling group. A selling group includes dealers or brokers who have been asked to join in the offering of a new issue of securities, but who are neither liable for any unsold syndicate balance nor entitled to share in the profits of the overall syndicate. They obtain securities for sale at prices net of the take-down.

senior manager. The underwriter who coordinates the sale of a bond or note issue and manages a syndicate or selling group. The senior manager runs the books. If other securities firms share in the management responsibilities, they may be called co–senior managers or comanagers.

serial bonds. A series of bonds comprising all or a portion of an issue with stated maturities in consecutive years. (As opposed to mandatory sinking fund redemption amounts.)

settlement date. The date for the delivery of securities and payment of funds.

short. Borrowing and then selling securities that one does not own in anticipation of a price decline. When prices fall, the short is covered by buying the securities back and returning them to the lender. Short can also refer to any trading position that benefits when interest rates rise, prices fall, or credit spreads widen.

short-term debt. Generally, debt that matures in one year or less. However, certain securities that mature in up to three years may be considered short-term debt.

sinking fund. Separate accumulation of cash or investments (including earnings on investments) in a fund in accordance with the terms of a trust agreement or indenture, funded by periodic deposits by the issuer (or other entity responsible for debt service), for the purpose of assuring timely availability of cash for payment of debt service. Usually used in connection with term bonds.

special tax bond. A bond secured by a special tax, such as a gasoline tax or a sales tax.

spread. (1) The difference between the price at which an issue is purchased from an issuer and that at which it is reoffered by the underwriters to the first holders, or the difference between the purchase price and sale price of a bond trading in the secondary market. (2) The difference in price or yield between two securities. The securities can be in different markets or within the same securities market between different credits, sectors, or other relevant factors.

swap. (1) A transaction in which an investor sells one security and simultaneously buys another with the proceeds, usually for about the same price and frequently for tax purposes. (2) A derivative instrument in which two parties agree to exchange future payment streams, such as an interest rate swap.

syndicate. A group of underwriters formed for the purpose of participating jointly in the initial sale of a new issue of municipal securities. The terms under which a syndicate is formed and operates are typically set forth in an agreement among underwriters. One or more underwriters act as manager of the syndicate and one of the managers acts as lead manager and runs the books. A syndicate is also often referred to as an account or underwriting account.

take-down. The discount from the list price provided to a member of an underwriting account on any bonds purchased from the account.

taxable municipal bond. A municipal bond where the interest on the bond is not excluded from the gross income of its owners for federal income tax purposes. Certain municipal bonds are taxable because they do not qualify for tax-exempt financing under the terms of the federal tax code. An important subset of taxable municipals includes Build America Bonds, which provide the issuer a federal subsidy on interest payments.

tax anticipation note (TAN). TANs are issued by states or local governmental units to finance current operations in anticipation of future tax receipts.

tax-backed bond. A broad category of bonds that are secured by taxes levied by the obligor. The taxes are not necessarily unlimited as to rate or amount, so while all GO bonds are tax-backed, not all tax-backed bonds are GOs. Examples of tax-backed bonds include moral obligations and appropriation-backed bonds. This category is also known as *tax supported.*

tax base. The total property and resources subject to taxation. (See also *assessed valuation.*)

tax-exempt bond. A common term for municipal bonds, excluding Build America Bonds. The interest on tax-exempt bonds is excluded from the gross income of its owners for federal income tax purposes under Section 103 of the Internal Revenue Code of 1986, as amended. Municipal bonds that are also exempt from state and local as well as federal income taxes are said to have double or triple tax exemption.

tax-exempt commercial paper (TECP or TXCP). A short-term promissory note issued for periods up to 270 days is often used in lieu of fixed-rate BANs, TANs, and RANs because of the greater flexibility offered in setting both maturities and determining rates. The purpose for issuing TECP or TXCP can be the same as BANs, TANs, and RANs.

tax-exempt/taxable-yield equivalent formula. A formula that equates the lower yield of a tax-exempt security with the higher yield of a taxable security. The tax-exempt yield is divided by 1 minus the investor's marginal tax rate (expressed as a fraction), and the resulting quotient is expressed as a percentage. This allows investors to compare equivalent yields on the two securities.

technical default. A default under the bond indenture terms, other than nonpayment of interest or principal. Examples of technical default are failure to maintain required reserves or failure to maintain adequate fees and charges for service.

term bonds. Bonds of an issue that have a single stated maturity date. Mandatory redemption provisions require the issuer to call or purchase a certain number of term bonds using money set aside in a sinking fund at regular intervals before the stated maturity date.

total bonded debt. Total GO bond debt outstanding of a municipality, regardless of the purpose.

total direct debt. The sum of the total bond debt and any unfunded debt (typically short-term notes) of a municipality.

total return. Investment performance measure over a stated time period that includes coupon interest, interest on interest, and any realized or unrealized gains or losses.

trade date. The date that a trade, or sale and purchase, is executed. (See also *settlement date.*)

transcript of proceedings. Final documents relating to a municipal bond issue.

transparency. The concept of disseminating to the public price, volume, and other information about transactions in the financial markets for securities or material information related to securities.

true interest cost. A method of calculating bids for new issues of municipal securities that takes into consideration the time value of money. (See also *net interest cost.*)

true yield. The rate of return to an investor taking into account the payment of capital gains at maturity on a bond bought at a discount.

trust agreement. Agreement between the issuer and the trustee (1) authorizing and securing the bonds; (2) containing the issuer's covenants and obligations with respect to the project and payment of debt service; (3) specifying the events of default; and (4) outlining the trustee's fiduciary responsibilities and bondholders' rights.

trustee. A bank designated by the issuer as the custodian of funds and official representative of bondholders. Trustees are appointed to ensure compliance with the bond documents and to represent bondholders in enforcing their contract with the issuer.

underwrite. The purchase of a bond or note issue from an issuer to resell it to investors.

underwriter. The securities dealer who purchases a bond or note issue from an issuer and resells it to investors. If a syndicate or selling group is formed, the underwriter who coordinates the financing and runs the group is called the senior or lead manager.

underwriting spread. The difference between the offering price to the public by the underwriter and the purchase price the underwriter pays to the issuer. The underwriter's expenses and selling costs are usually paid from this amount.

undivided account. Syndicate account structure that is undivided as to sales and liability. Also called an *Eastern account.*

unit investment trust (municipal). A fixed portfolio of tax-exempt bonds sold in fractional, undivided interests (usually $1,000).

unlimited tax bond. A bond secured by the pledge of taxes that are not limited as to rate or amount.

variable-rate demand obligation (VRDO). A bond that bears interest at a variable or floating rate established at specified intervals (e.g., flexible, daily, weekly, monthly, or annually). It contains a put option permitting the bondholder to tender the bond for purchase when a new interest rate is established. VRDOs are also referred to as VRDNs (Notes), VRDBs (Bonds), or low floaters.

volatility. A statistical measure of the variance of price or yield over time. Volatility is low if the price does not change very much over a short period of time and high if there is a greater change.

volume cap. Dollar limitation of private activity bonds allowed to be issued in a state each year. Legislation enacted by Congress sets the volume cap.

yield. The annual percentage rate of return earned on a security. Yield is a function of a security's purchase price and coupon interest rate.

yield curve. The graphic relationship between yield and maturity among bonds of different maturities and the same credit quality. This line shows the term structure of interest rates.

yield to call. A yield on a security calculated by assuming that interest payments will be paid until the call date, when the security will be redeemed at the call price.

yield to maturity. A yield on a security calculated by assuming that interest payments will be made until the final maturity date, at which point the principal will be repaid by the issuer. Yield to maturity is the discount rate at which the present value of future payments (investment income and return of principal) equals the price of the security.

yield to worst. This is the lowest yield generated given the potential stated calls before maturity.

zero-coupon bond. A bond where no periodic interest payments are made. The investor receives one payment at maturity equal to the principal invested plus interest earned compounded semiannually at the original interest rate to maturity.

Bibliography

WEB SITES

American Bankers Association	www.aba.com
Bloomberg	www.bloomberg.com
Board of Governors of the Federal Reserve System	www.federalreserve.gov
The Bond Buyer—The Daily Newspaper of Public Finance	www.bondbuyer.com
CFA Institute	www.cfainstitute.org/pages/ index.aspx
CNN Money	www.money.cnn.com
CUSIP	www.cusip.com
EDGAR SEC Filings	www.sec.gov/edgar.shtml
Electronic Municipal Market Access (EMMA)	www.emma.msrb.org
The Federal Judiciary Homepage: Publications and Directories	www.uscourts.gov/Federal Courts/PublicationsAndReports .aspx
Financial Industry Regulatory Authority	www.finra.org
Fitch Ratings	www.fitchratings.com/index_ fitchratings.cfm
Government Accounting Standards Board	www.gasb.org
Government Finance Officers Association	www.gfoa.org
Internal Revenue Service	www.irs.gov
International Swaps and Derivatives Association	www.isda.org
Investment Company Institute	www.ici.org
Library of Congress	www.lcweb.loc.gov
Lipper, Inc.	www.lipperweb.com
Moody's	www.moodys.com
Morningstar	www.morningstar.com
The Municipal Securities Rulemaking Board	www.msrb.org
National Association of Bond Lawyers	www.nabl.org
National Federation of Municipal Analysts	www.nfma.org
Securities Industry and Financial Markets Association	www.sifma.org www.investinginbonds.com
Standard & Poor's	www.standardandpoors.com
Thomson Municipal Market Monitor	www.tm3.com

U.S. Bureau of the Census   www.census.gov
U.S. Securities and Exchange Commission   www.sec.gov
U.S. Securities and Exchange Commission,   www.sec.gov/info/municipal
   Office of Municipal Securities   .shtml

BOOKS AND PUBLICATIONS

The Bond Buyer. Various years. New York.
The Bond Buyer's Municipal Marketplace. Various volumes. Skokie, IL: Accuity.
Civic Research Institute. *Municipal Finance Journal.* Published quarterly
   Kingston, NJ.
Fabozzi, Frank J. *Bond Markets, Analysis and Strategies* (7th ed.). Englewood Cliffs,
   NJ: Prentice-Hall, 2009.
———. *Fixed Income Mathematics* (4th ed.). New York: McGraw-Hill, 2005.
Fabozzi, Frank J., and Steven V. Mann. *Introduction to Fixed Income Analytics:*
   Relative Value Analysis, Risk Measures and Valuation (2nd ed.). Hoboken, NJ:
   John Wiley & Sons, 2010.
Federal Reserve Board. *Flow of Funds.* Washington, DC. Published annually.
Feldstein, Sylvan G., and Frank J. Fabozzi. *The Handbook of Municipal Bonds.*
   Hoboken, NJ: John Wiley & Sons, 2008.
Governmental Accounting Standards Board of the Financial Accounting Foundation.
   Governmental Accounting Standards series. Norwalk, CT.
Government Finance Officers Association. *Making Good Disclosure: The Role and*
   Responsibilities of State and Local Officials Under the Federal Securities Laws.
   Chicago, IL, 2001.
Investment Company Institute. *Fact Books.* Published annually. Washington, DC.
Kurish, J. B., and Patricia Tigue. *An Elected Official's Guide to Debt Issuance*
   (2nd ed.). Chicago: Government Finance Officers Association, 2005.
Larson, Corinne. *A Public Investor's Guide to Money Market Instruments* (2nd ed.).
   Chicago: Government Finance Officers Association, 1994.
Leonard, Paul A. "An Empirical Analysis of Competitive Bid and Negotiated Offer-
   ings of Municipal Bonds." *Municipal Finance Journal* 17 (1996).
Moody's Investors Services. *Moody's Ratings Reports.* Published daily.
Municipal Securities Rulemaking Board. *2011 MSRB Rule Book.*
———. *Glossary of Municipal Securities Terms* (2nd ed.). Washington, DC, 2004.
National Association of Bond Lawyers. *Fundamentals of Municipal Bond Law.*
   Wheaton, IL, 2011.
———. *The Function and Professional Responsibilities of Bond Counsel* (2nd ed.).
   Wheaton, IL, 1995.
National Federation of Municipal Analysts. Various years. *Recommended Best Prac-*
   tices in Disclosure series. Pittsburgh, PA.
The Securities Industry and Financial Markets Association. *Investor Guides.*
   New York.
Standard & Poor's. *Credit Week.* New York.
Stigum, Marcia, and Antony Crescenzi. *Stigum's Money Market* (4th ed.). New
   York: McGraw-Hill, 2007.

About the Writer

Neil A. O'Hara is a freelance financial writer with intimate knowledge of domestic and international markets. His articles, written primarily for magazines aimed at professionals in the financial services industry, cover a wide range of subjects from hedge funds, private equity, and corporate governance to market and industry reviews as well as more technical topics, including exchange traded funds, options, securitization, credit derivatives, securities lending, prime brokerage, risk management, and financial industry regulations.

Before he became a professional writer in 2002, O'Hara worked in the financial services industry for more than 28 years. He spent 15 years with the British merchant bank, Morgan Grenfell, where he was an investment analyst, an advisor on merger and corporate finance transactions, and head of a merger arbitrage-trading desk. From 1988 to 2000, O'Hara managed merger arbitrage portfolios at three hedge funds, including his own firm. He joined Deutsche Bank in 2001 to manage an international merger arbitrage fund, leaving at the end of that year to begin his writing career.

Born and raised in England, O'Hara moved to New York in 1980 and is a naturalized United States citizen. He has a Bachelor of Science degree in engineering and economics from the University of Warwick. He lives with his wife, Katherine, in Lincoln, Massachusetts.

Index

Accrual basis, 90
Ad valorem taxation, 35
Additional bonds, 201
Adjusted issue price, 156
Administrative rules, 241
Advanced refunding, 84
Advertised sales, 8
After the sale, 113–115
Agreement Among Underwriters (AAU),
    103
Airport bonds, 205
Alternative minimum tax (AMT), 30, 34,
    160
Anticipation notes, 36
AON offerings, 128
Appropriation bonds, 193
Arbitrage, 84
Arbitrage bonds, 229
Arbitrage rebate specialists, 12
Ascending debt service, 81
Auction-rate securities, 42
Authorities, 4, 56
Authorities and special districts, 56–57
Authorizing resolution, 72

Bank letters of credit, 14
*Bankruptcies, Defaults, and Other Local
    Government Financial Emergencies*
    (AICR), 173
Banks, 15–17
Banks' underwriting roles, 97
Barbell strategy, 150–151
Basis risk, 249
Basis swap, 253
Bearer bonds, 24
Bearer bonds versus registered bonds,
    52–53
Bid list, 124
Bid-and-ask procedures, 128
Bid-and-offer procedures, 128

Bid-wanted process, 13
Bona-fide business loans, 158
Bond anticipation notes (BANs), 38, 190
Bond brokers, 13
Bond Buyer, 104, 106, 111
Bond buyer indexes, 132–135
Bond buyer placement ratio and visible
    supply, 132–135
Bond Buyer Revenue Bond Index, 211
Bond Buyer's 40 Bond Index, 131, 132
Bond counsel, 10, 69–70
Bond counsel opinion, 75–78
Bond insurance, 86–87
Bond insurance policies, 208–209
Bond insurers, 14–15
Bond premium, 155
Bond purchase agreement/purchase contract,
    78
Bond purchase agreements (BPAs), 11, 78
Bond resolution, indenture, and trust
    agreement, 72
Bond resolution or indenture, 197–198
Bond swapping, 151–152
Bond years, 85
Bonds, 23
Bonds at the takedown, 111
Bonds for other not-for-profits, 204
Book-entry securities, 52
Borah, William E., 227
Borrowing to buy tax-exempt bonds,
    158–159
Brokers' brokers, 12, 123
Budgeting, 89
Build America Bonds, 18, 30, 130, 139, 229
Business cycle, 212–213

Call privilege, 82
Call protection, 82
Call provisions, 49–52
Capital appreciation, 147–148

Capital gains
alternative minimum tax (AMT), 160
bond swaps, 151–152
call provisions, 52
federal tax laws, 29
long-term, 152, 153, 156
and losses, 153
redemption provisions, 141
short-term, 152, 153
tax effects, 222
Capital improvement plan, 68–69
Capital markets, 9–10
Capital preservation, 147
Capital projects fund, 88
Cash versus accrual basis of accounting, 89
Certification of participation (COP), 64
Clean Renewable Energy bonds, 233
Closing documents, 80–81
Collecting the interest, 53
College and university bonds, 203–204
Commercial banks, 169–171
Committee on Uniform Security
Identification Procedures (CUSIP), 22
Competitive and negotiated underwriting,
97–100
Competitive bidding disadvantages,
100–101
Competitive underwriting, 105–111
credit and research, 108–109
delivery of the bid, 111
forming a syndicate for a competitive
sale, 106–107
informing the market, 105–106
preliminary scale, 109–110
pricing call on the day of the bid,
110–111
syndicate letters and account structures,
107–108
Comprehensive annual financial report, 90
Concession order, 111
Consensus scale, 104
Constant maturity swaps, 253
Constant yield to maturity (CYM) method,
154
Consumer Protection Act of 2010, 226
Continuing disclosure, 47
Continuing Disclosure Agreement (CDA),
47, 80
Continuing education, 21
Convention (interest payment), 24

Conversion to fixed rate, 41
Convertible-coupon bonds, 48
Cost of carry, 98, 124
Counsel, 11
Counterparty credit risk, 249
Coupon rates, 140–141
Coupons, 24
Covenants, 201–202
Coverage ratio, 206
Credit, other factors affecting
bond insurance policies, 208–209
letters of credit and lines of credit,
207–208
Credit analysis
municipal credit quality, 173–175
rating agencies, 175–176
rating process, 176–177
Credit and research, 103–104, 108–109
Credit default swaps (CDSs), 253, 254–255
Credit enhancement, 13–14
Credit enhancers, 13–17
banks, 15–17
bond insurers, 14–15
Credit risk, 122, 149
Credit spreads, 126
Credit-enhancement documents, 78
Crossover refunding, 84
Current income, 147
Current refunding, 84
Current statutory exemption
arbitrage restrictions and rebate, 231
other restrictions, 232
private activity bonds, 230–231
recent changes, 232–233
Current yield, 24, 26–27
CUSIP number, 22, 25, 128

Dated date, 24, 53
De minimis discount, 156
Debt, pro-rata basis, 192
Debt factors, 190–193
Debt repayment schedules, 81–82
Debt structuring, 81–87
Debt-service fund, 88, 200
Debt-service reserve fund, 200
Declining debt service, 81
Deemed final official statement, 73
Deficit Reduction Act, 230
Definitional rules, 242
Delivery of the bid, 111

Delivery vs. payment, 137
Depository Trust & Clearing Corporation, 17, 52–53
Derivative, 247
Disclosure and the antifraud laws and regulations, 235–239
Disclosure Guidelines for State and Local Government Securities, 234
Discount bonds, 82
Diversification, 151
Divided account, 108
Documents, 80–81
Dodd-Frank Act, 226, 245
Dollar bonds, 8
Doubled-barreled bonds, 36, 65
Due diligence, 11
Duration, 162

Eastern account, 108
E-commerce, information, and technology, 119–121
Economic analysis, 193–194
   health care, higher education, and other not-for-profits, 203–204
   housing bonds, 204–205
   industrial revenue and pollution control bonds, 206
   structured bonds, 206
   transportation, 205–206
   utilities, 202–203
Electric utility bonds, 202
Electronic Municipal Market Access (EMMA), 19, 234, 244
Electronic trading systems, 119–121
Enterprise fund, 88
Escrowed to maturity (ETM), 84
Evaluations for individual investors, 163
Evans v. Gore, 227
Event and political risk, 149
Exchange market, 117
Exchange versus over-the-counter market, 117–119
Exchange-traded funds (ETFs), 166
Exempt facilities, 68
Exemption amount, 160, 162
Expectations, 220
Extraordinary bond features, 142

Face value, 23
Factors affecting credit, 207–209

Federal Open Market Committee (FOMC), 213
Federal Register, 213–215, 241
Federal securities laws on municipal securities
   about, 233–235
   disclosure and the antifraud laws and regulations, 235–239
Federal tax exemption, 29–30
Federal tax exemption basis, 226–228
Fiduciary funds, 89
Final official statement, 106
Financial advisors, 70
Financial advisors, specialists, and other consultants, 11
Financial factors, 194–196, 206–207
Financial Industry Regulatory Authority (FINRA), 20–21, 241
Financial Modernization Act of 2000, 97
Financial products, 86–87
   credit default swaps, 254–255
   interest rate caps, floors, and collars, 252
   interest rate swaps, 247–252
   managing the asset side, 253–254
   other swap products, 253
Financial reporting, 89–91
Financing documents, 71–81
   authorizing resolution, 72
   bond purchase agreement/purchase contract, 78
   bond resolution, indenture, and trust agreement, 72
   continuing disclosure agreement, 80
   credit-enhancement documents, 78
   lease agreement, 72–73
   official statement, 73–75
   opinion of bond counsel, 75–78
   other documents, 80–81
   other legal opinions, 78
Financing process
   capital improvement plan, 68–69
   political factors, 69
   selecting the financing team, 69–71
Financing team selection
   bond counsel, 69–70
   financial advisor, 70
   negotiated versus competitive sales, 70–71
   underwriter, 70–71
First call, 142
Fitch Ratings, 175

Fitch Ratings definitions, 186–188
Floaters, 40
Flow of funds, 72, 198–200, 216
Forward supply contracts, 253
Forward swap, 253
Full cash refunding, 85
Full-faith and credit backing, 63
Fund accounting, 87
   budgeting, 89
   cash versus accrual basis of accounting, 89
   financial reporting, 89–91
   governmental funds, 88
   proprietary funds, 88–89

GASB Codification, 90
General fund, 88
General obligation bonds (GOs)
   debt factors, 190–193
   economic analysis, 193–194
   financial factors, 194–196
   management factors, 196–197
   political mood, 179, 188–190
   rating agencies definitions, 180–188
   revenue bonds, 198–199
   security for, 35, 63
   as security for municipal bonds, 61
General obligation notes, 38
General revenue bonds, 128
Generally accepted accounting principals
   (GAAP), 87, 90
General-purpose financial statements, 90
Government Accounting Standards Board
   (GASB), 87, 197
Government credit-enhancement bonds, 63
Government Finance Officer Association
   (GFOA), 73, 197, 234
Governmental funds, 88
Grant anticipation notes (GANs), 38
Gross lien bonds, 197
Gross refunding, 85
Gross spread, 97
Group net orders, 112
Gulf Opportunity Zone bonds, 233

Health care bonds, 128, 203
Health care, higher education, and other
   not-for-profits, 65, 66–67, 207–208
   bonds for other not-for-profits, 204
   college and university bonds, 203–204
   health-care bonds, 203

Health-care bonds, 203
Hedge bonds, 232
High-to-low refunding, 84
High-yield bonds, 130
History of federal tax legislation affecting
   municipal securities, 228–230
Hoot and holler, 123
Households, 165
Housing, 67
Housing bonds, 128
   multifamily housing revenue bonds, 204
   single-family housing revenue bonds,
   204–205

Industrial development, pollution control,
   and other exempt facility bonds, 68
Inflation, 215
Inflation premium, 215
Information and technology, 18–19
Information repositories, 21
Informing the market, 105–106
In-state tax exemption, 148
Interest, 1
Interest disallowance rule, 158
Interest rate cap, 252
Interest rate caps, floors, and collars, 252
Interest rate floor, 252
Interest rate risk, 249
Interest rate swaps, 247–252
Interest rates, 84
Interest rates, determinants of the overall
   level of, 212–216
Interest rates, overall level determinants
   business cycle, 212–213
   federal reserve, 213–215
   inflation, 215
   nation's flow of funds, 216
Interest rates, term structure, 216–221
Interest rates, understanding
   about, 211–212
   determinants of the overall level of interest
   rates, 212–216
   municipal bond rates, 221–224
   term structure of interest rates, 216–221
Intermarket yield percentage, 222–224
Internal rate of return, 144–145
Internal service fund, 88
Investing in bonds, 139–172
   basic principles of, 139–143
   general obligation bonds, 179–197

investment objectives, 147–148
investor categories, 163–172
investor strategies, 150–152
measures of yield and return, 143–145
other factors affecting credit, 207–209
other investment factors, 161–163
revenue bonds, 197–207
taxation of municipal bonds, 152–161
yield to maturity and price, 145–146
Investing in bonds, basic principles
coupon rates, 140–141
redemption provisions, 141–143
term to maturity, 140
Investment agreements, 253
Investment factors, other
evaluations for individual investors, 163
measuring performance, 162–163
spread relationships, 161–162
Investment objectives
capital appreciation, 147–148
capital preservation, 147
current income, 147
risk factors, 148–150
in-state tax exemption, 148
timing the maturity, 148
Investor categories, 163–172
commercial banks, 169–171
households, 165
mutual funds, 165
property/casualty insurance companies, 171–172
Investor letters, 71
Investor strategies
barbell, 150–151
bond swapping, 151–152
diversification, 151
laddering, 150
Investors, 17–18
Issuance trends in the primary market, 93–96
Issuer name, 24
Issuer number, 25
Issuers, 1, 4–7
about, 55–56
authorities and special districts, 56–57
financing documents, 71–81
financing process, 68–71
security for municipal bonds, 61–68
state and local government accounting, 87–91

structuring the debt, 81–87
theory of municipal debt, 57–58
uses of municipal debt, 58–61

Laddered portfolio, 150
Laddering, 148, 150
Lawyers, 10–11
bond counsel, 10
other counsel, 11
underwriter's counsel, 11
Lead underwriter, 8
Lease agreement, 72–73
Lease rental bonds, 193
Leases and appropriation-backed obligations, 64
Legal opinions, 46, 78
Letters of credit (LOCs), 40, 207
Level debts, 81–82
Level principal, 81
Liberty Zone bonds, 233
Lines of credit, 14, 208
Liquidity and/or credit support, 40
Liquidity preference, 220–221
Long-term financial instrument, 23
Lower floaters, 40
Low-to-high refunding, 84

Making Good Disclosure (GFOA), 73, 234
Managed funds, 166–169
Management factors, 196–197
Managing the asset side, 253–254
Mandatory calls, 49
Mandatory sinking fund bond features, 142
Market discount, 155–157
Market risk, 122, 149–150
Market segmentation, 221
Market spreads, 125
Market statistics and indexes
bond buyer indexes, 132–135
bond buyer placement ratio and visible supply, 132–135
Material events, 128
Mature, 1
Maturity date, 24
McCulloch v. Maryland, 226
Measures of yield and return, 143–145
Measuring performance, 162–163
Members orders, 112
Midwest Disaster Area bonds, 233
Modified accrual basis, 90

Modified duration, 162
Moody's Investors Service, 175
Moody's rating definitions, 177–179
Moral obligation bonds, 63
Mortgage pledge, 197
Mortgage Subsidy Bond Tax Act, 229
MSRB rules
  Rule G-1, 242
  Rule G-3, 242
  Rule G-8, 136, 243
  Rule G-9, 243
  Rule G-11, 243
  Rule G-12, 113, 114, 136, 137, 243
  Rule G-13, 243
  Rule G-15, 114, 136, 137, 243
  Rule G-16, 243
  Rule G-17, 243–244, 245
  Rule G-19, 244
  Rule G-27, 242, 243
  Rule G-29, 241
  Rule G-32, 46, 114, 136, 244
  Rule G-33, 29
  Rule G-35, 244
  Rule G-36, 47, 244
  Rule G-37, 244
  Rule G-38, 12, 244
  Rule G-39, 245
  Rule G-40, 245
  Rule G-41, 245
Multifamily housing revenue bonds, 204
Multiples of offerings, 128
Municipal bankruptcies, 174, 189
Municipal bond brokers, 12
Municipal bond dealers
  capital markets, 9–10
  operations, 10
  public finance, 7
  research and credit, 9
  sales, 8–9
  sales liaison, 9
  trading, 8
  underwriting, 7–8
Municipal bond market overview
  about, 1–4
  bond brokers, 13
  credit enhancers, 13–17
  financial advisors, specialists, and other
    consultants, 11
  information and technology, 18–19
  investors, 17–18

  issuers, 4–7
  lawyers, 10–11
  other participants, 21–22
  rating agencies, 12–13
  regulators, 19–21
  trustees and paying agents, 17
Municipal bond rates, 221–224
  capital gains tax effects, 222
  intermarket yield percentage, 222–224
  supply and demand, 222
  upward-sloping yield curves, 224
  volatility, 222
Municipal bond trading, 124–130
Municipal bond trading basics, 123–124
Municipal bonds, 23
  security for, 61–68
  selling, 121–123
  tax exemption of, 29–35
  taxation of, 152–161
  tax-exempt status of, 160
  types of, 35–36
Municipal bonds, characteristics of, 45–53
  bearer bonds versus registered bonds,
    52–53
  call provisions, 49–52
  collecting the interest, 53
  continuing disclosure, 47
  legal opinion, 46
  official statement, 46–47
  serial and term bonds, 47–48
  size of the primary and secondary markets,
    45–46
  trading plus accrued interest, 53
  zero-coupon bonds, 48–49
Municipal credit quality, 173–175
Municipal debt history, 55
Municipal debt theory, 57–58
Municipal debt uses, 58–61
Municipal derivative specialists, 12
Municipal futures, 130–131
Municipal market cheap to Treasuries, 125
Municipal market rich to Treasuries, 125
Municipal securities and federal securities
  laws, 233–239
Municipal securities basics
  description of municipal securities, 23–25
  other characteristics of municipal bonds,
    45–53
  short-term securities, 36–44
  tax exemption of municipal bonds, 29–35

types of municipal bonds, 35–36
types of yields, 28–29
yield and price, 26–28
Municipal Securities Rulemaking Board
 (MSRB). *See also* MSRB rules
about, 20
administrative rules, 241
definitional rules, 242
dollar price calculation rule, 52
Electronic Municipal Market Access
 (EMMA), 19
general rules, 242–245
record-keeping rules, 136–137
regulatory authority, 239–240
regulatory structure, 240–241
Tower Amendment, 234
uniform practices and confirmation of
 transactions, 136–137
Municipal swap index, 251–252
Mutual funds
managed funds, 166–169
unit investment trusts, 165

National Council on Government
 Accounting (NGCA), 87
Negative convexity, 162
Negotiated issues, 97
Negotiated sale advantages, 101
Negotiated sale disadvantages, 101
Negotiated underwriting, 101–105
agreement among underwriters, 103
credit and research, 103–104
forming a syndicate, 102
marketing the bonds, 104
pricing the bonds, 104–105
selection of managers, 102
selling, 102–103
Negotiated vs. competitive sales, 70–71
Net designated orders, 112
Net direct debt, 190, 192
Net order, 111
Net revenues, 197
No-loads, 166
Notes, 140
Notice of sale, 105–106

Odd lots, 130
Official statement, 46–47, 73–75
Operations, 10
Operations and maintenance expenses, 200

Opinion of bond counsel, 75–78
Option calls, 49
Optional bond features, 142
Option-free bonds, 140
Order period, 104
Orders, types of, 111–112
Orders and procedures
after the sale, 113–115
priority of orders, 112–113
retail order period, 113
types of orders, 111–112
Original issue discount (OID), 82, 153–155
Out firm, 128
Overall net debt, 192
Over-the-counter market, 117–119

Par value, 23, 24
Participants, 123–124
Committee on Uniform Security
 Identification Procedures (CUSIP), 22
information repositories, 21
Participations, 107–108
Pay-as-you go approach, 57
Placement ratio, 132
Plus accrued interest, 53
Political factors, 69
Political mood, 179, 188–190
*Pollock v. Farmer's Loan and Trust
 Company*, 226, 227
Positive convexity, 162
Prefunded bonds, 84
Preliminary official statement (POS), 73
Preliminary scale, 104, 109–110
Premium bonds, 82
Present value, 143–144
Price, 26
Price volatility, 140, 148, 150, 162
Pricing call on the day of the bid,
 110–111
Primary and secondary markets, size of,
 45–46
Primary market
basics of underwriting, 96–101
competitive underwriting, 105–111
issuance trends in the primary market,
 93–96
negotiated underwriting, 101–105
orders and procedures, 111–115
Principal, 1
Principal amount, 23

Priority of orders, 112–113
Private activity bonds (PABs), 160, 230
Private placements, 71
Project notes, 36
Property taxes, 35
Property/casualty insurance companies, 171–172
Proprietary funds, 88–89
Pro-rata basis, 143
Providers of data in the municipal market, 131
Public finance, 7
Public power, 65
Public representatives, 240
Put bonds, 40
Put/putting notes, 17

Qualified bonds, 230–231
Qualified tax-exempt obligations, 158
Qualified Zone Academy bonds (QZABs), 232
Quantitative easing (QE), 215

Rate lock, 253
Rating agencies, 12–13, 175–176
Rating process, 176–177
Ratings, 12
Ratings changes, 127–128
Ratings upgrade, 12
Receipt vs. payment, 137
Record-keeping rules, 136–137
Red herring, 73
Redemption, 50–51
Redemption of bonds at a premium, 158
Redemption provisions, 82, 141–143
Refundings, 82–85
Regulators, 19–21
    continuing education, 21
    Financial Industry Regulatory Authority (FINRA), 20–21
    Municipal Securities Rulemaking Board (MSRB), 20
    Securities and Exchange Commission (SEC), 19–20
Regulatory and disclosure requirements
    about, 225–226
    application of federal securities laws to municipal securities, 233–239
    basis of federal tax exemption, 226–228

current statutory exemption, 230–233
history of federal tax legislation affecting municipal securities, 228–230
Municipal Securities Rulemaking Board, 239–245
Regulatory Element, 21
Regulatory structure, 240–241
Reinvestment risk, 150
Remarketing agent, 40
Repo, 253
Reporting of tax-exempt interest, 159
Repurchase agreements, 253
Requests for proposals (RFPs), 7
Research and credit, 9
Research and credit analysts, 9
Restrictions on tax-exempt bond issuance, 32–34
Retail order period, 113
Revenue anticipation notes (RANs), 37, 190
Revenue bonds, 5, 36, 61, 65
    bond resolution or indenture, 197–198
    covenants, 201–202
    economic analysis, 202–206
    financial factors, 206–207
    flow of funds, 198–200
Revenue line, 197
Reverse repo, 253
Reverse repurchase agreements, 253
Revolving funds, 66
Risk factors, 148–150
    credit risk, 149
    event and political risk, 149
    market risk, 149–150
    reinvestment risk, 150
Road show, 104

Sales, 8–9
Sales liaison, 9
Secondary market
    about, 117
    basics of municipal bond trading, 123–124
    e-commerce, information, and technology, 119–121
    how a trade is done, 128–130
    market statistics and indexes, 132–135
    MSRB record-keeping rules, 136–137
    municipal bond trading, 124–130
    municipal futures, 130–131

over-the-counter market, 117–119
participants, 123–124
providers of data in the municipal market,
131
selling municipal bonds, 121–123
Sector spreads, 125–126
Securities Act of 1933, 19, 225, 233, 236,
239
Securities Acts Amendments of 1975, 233,
234, 240
Securities and Exchange Commission (SEC),
19–20, 103
Securities and Exchange Commission (SEC)
Rule 15c2-12, 103, 234–237
Securities Exchange Act of 1934, 19, 47,
225, 233, 236
Security for municipal bonds, 61–68
Self-liquidity, 41
Selling groups, 102
Senior manager, 8
Serial and term bonds, 47–48
Short-term instrument, 23
Short-term municipal (bonds or notes), 38
Short-term products, 130
Short-term securities
Dutch auction securities (Auction Rate
Securities), 42–43
notes, 36–38
tax-exempt commercial paper, 38
tender option bonds (TOBs), 43–44
variable-rate demand obligations
(VRDOs), 38–42
SIFMA Municipal Swap Index, 250, 251
Single-family housing revenue bonds,
204–205
Sinking funds, 49
Solid waste bonds, 202, 203
South Carolina v. Baker, 228
Special districts, 56
Special redemptions, 142
Special revenue fund, 88
Special-assessment bonds, 64
Special-purpose district bonds, 64
Special-tax bonds, 36, 65
Spread relationships, 161–162
Squawk hog, 123
Standard & Poor's ratings definitions,
180–185
Standard & Poor's ratings services, 175

State and local government accounting,
87–91
fiduciary funds, 89
fund accounting, 87–89
State and local government services (SGLSs),
83
State information depositories (SIDs), 21
State tax treatment of tax-exempt bonds,
161
State taxation of municipal bonds, 32
State-aid intercept mechanism, 63
State-specific names, 130
Strike rate, 252
Stripped bonds, 49
Structuring the debt
bond insurance, 86–87
debt repayment schedules, 81–82
financial products, 86–87
redemption provisions, 82
refundings, 82–85
true interest cost and net interest cost,
85–86
Student-loan bonds, 204
Subordinate-lien bonds, 197
Super sinkers (funds), 51, 143
Supply and demand, 222
Surplus monies, 200
Swap advisors, 12
Swap products, 253
Swaption, 253
Syndicate, 8
Syndicate forming for a competitive sale,
106–107
Syndicate letters and account structures,
107–108

Takedown order, 111
Tax anticipation notes (TANs), 37, 190
Tax Equity and Fiscal Responsibility Act,
230
Tax exemption of municipal bonds
federal tax exemption, 29–30
restrictions on tax-exempt bond issuance,
32–34
state taxation of municipal bonds, 32
taxable bonds and alternative minimum
tax bonds, 34–35
tax-exempt/taxable yield equivalent
formula, 30–32

Tax Reform Act of 1986, 230
Taxable bonds, 23
Taxable bonds and alternative minimum tax bonds, 34–35
Taxable municipal bonds, 130
Tax-allocation bonds, 65
Taxation of municipal bonds, 152–161
  alternative minimum tax, 160
  bond premium, 155
  borrowing to buy a tax-exempt bond, 158–159
  capital gains and losses, 153
  effect of tax-exempt interest in calculation of Social Security benefits subject to taxation, 160–161
  market discount, 155–157
  original issue discount, 153–155
  redemption of bonds at a premium, 158
  reporting of tax-exempt interest, 159
  state tax treatment of tax-exempt bonds, 161
Tax-backed bonds, 5
  general obligation bonds, 63
  health care, higher education, and other not-for-profit, 66–67
  housing, 67
  industrial development, pollution control, and other exempt facility bonds, 68
  other tax-backed bonds, 63–65
  revenue bonds, 65
  security for municipal bonds, 63–65
  transportation, 67–68
  utilities, 65–66
Tax-equivalent yield, 146
Tax-exempt bonds, 23, 29, 158–159
Tax-exempt interest effect in calculation of Social Security benefits subject to taxation, 160–161
Tax-exempt/taxable yield equivalent formula, 30–32
Tax-increment bonds, 65
Tax-supported bonds, 5, 63
10(b)(5) opinion, 78
Tender option bonds, 43–44
Term structure of interest rates, 215, 216–221
  expectations, 220
  liquidity preference, 220–221
  market segmentation, 221

Term to maturity, 140
Theory of municipal debt, 57–58
Timing the maturity, 148
Toll-road bonds, 205
Total direct debt, 189–190
Total return, 146
Trade, factors in
  credit spreads, 126
  market spreads, 125
  material events, 128
  ratings changes, 127–128
  sector spreads, 125–126
Trade specialists, 129–130
Trades, how they are done, 128–130
Trading, 8
Trading factors, 125–138
Trading plus accrued interest, 53
Transcript of proceedings, 10
Transit revenue bonds, 205
Transitional Finance Authority (TFA), 69
Transportation, 67–68
Transportation bonds, 205
Triple-B hospital bonds, 125
Triple-B revenue bonds, 125
True interest cost and net interest cost, 85–86
Trust and agency funds, 90
Trustees and paying agents, 17

Underwriter, 70–71
Underwriter's counsel, 11
Underwriter's discount, 97
Underwriting, 1–2, 7–8
Underwriting basics, 96–101
  advantages and disadvantages of competitive and negotiated underwriting, 100
  advantages of negotiated sale, 101
  competitive and negotiated underwriting, 97–100
  disadvantages of competitive bidding, 100–101
  disadvantages of negotiated sale, 101
  role of banks in underwriting, 97
Underwritten, 105
Undivided account, 108
Uniform practices and confirmation of transactions, 136–137
Unit investment trusts, 165

Unlimited tax bonds, 63
Upgrade of ratings, 12, 127, 176
Upward-sloping yield curves, 224
Utilities, 65–66
Utility bonds, 202

Variable-interest rates, 40
Variable-rate demand obligations (VRDOs), 23, 38–39
Visible supply, 132
Volatility, 222

Washington Public Power Supply System (WPPS), 173, 235
Water and sewer system bonds, 202
Western account, 108
Wilson-Gorman Tariff Act of 1894, 226

Yield, 24
Yield and price, 24, 26–28
    current yield, 26–27
    yield to maturity, 27–28
Yield and return measure
    internal rate of return, 144–145
    present value, 143–144
Yield curve, 215
Yield to call, 24, 29
Yield to maturity, 24, 27–28
Yield to maturity and price, 145–146
    tax-equivalent yield, 146
    total return, 146
Yield to worst, 29, 125, 128, 146
Yields, types of, 28–29

Zero-coupon bonds, 23, 48–49, 142